TO THE

Dianetics (from Greek *dia* "thro... fundamental principles of the ... application of these discoveries, it ... dealt with a beingness that defied tim... ...an spirit—originally denominated the "I" and subsequently the "thetan." From there, Mr. Hubbard continued his research, eventually mapping the path to full spiritual freedom for the individual.

Dianetics is a forerunner and substudy of Scientology which, as practiced by the Church, addresses only the "thetan" (spirit), which is senior to the body, and its relationship to and effects on the body.

This book is presented in its original form and is part of L. Ron Hubbard's religious literature and works and is not a statement of claims made by the author, publisher or any Church of Scientology. It is a record of Mr. Hubbard's observations and research into life and the nature of man.

Neither Dianetics nor Scientology is offered as, nor professes to be physical healing, nor is any claim made to that effect. The Church does not accept individuals who desire treatment of physical or mental illness but, instead, requires a competent medical examination for physical conditions, by qualified specialists, before addressing their spiritual cause.

The Hubbard® Electrometer, or E-Meter, is a religious artifact used in the Church. The E-Meter, by itself, does nothing and is only used by ministers and ministers-in-training, qualified in its use, to help parishioners locate the source of spiritual travail.

The attainment of the benefits and goals of Dianetics and Scientology requires each individual's dedicated participation, as only through one's own efforts can they be achieved.

We hope reading this book is the first step of a personal voyage of discovery into this new and vital world religion.

THIS BOOK BELONGS TO

_____

Handbook for Preclears

Handbook for Preclears

L. RON HUBBARD

Bridge
Publications, Inc.

A
HUBBARD®
PUBLICATION

BRIDGE PUBLICATIONS, INC.
4751 Fountain Avenue
Los Angeles, California 90029

ISBN 978-1-4031-4411-9

Printed in the United States of America

Important Note

In reading this book, be very certain you never go past a word you do not fully understand. The only reason a person gives up a study or becomes confused or unable to learn is because he or she has gone past a word that was not understood.

The confusion or inability to grasp or learn comes AFTER a word the person did not have defined and understood. It may not only be the new and unusual words you have to look up. Some commonly used words can often be misdefined and so cause confusion.

This datum about not going past an undefined word is the most important fact in the whole subject of study. Every subject you have taken up and abandoned had its words which you failed to get defined.

Therefore, in studying this book be very, very certain you never go past a word you do not fully understand. If the material becomes confusing or you can't seem to grasp it, there will be a word just earlier that you have not understood. Don't go any further, but go back to BEFORE you got into trouble, find the misunderstood word and get it defined.

GLOSSARIES

In writing *Handbook for Preclears,* L. Ron Hubbard provided a glossary of all technical terms, defined as they are used in this book and in the sequence they should be learned. As such, the *LRH Glossary* forms a vital component of this text to be studied in full for a thorough comprehension of the nomenclature and subject itself.

To further aid reader comprehension, LRH directed the editors to provide definitions for other words and phrases. These are included in the Appendix, *Editor's Glossary of Words, Terms and Phrases.* Words sometimes have several meanings. The *Editor's Glossary* only contains the definitions of words as they are used in this text. Other definitions can be found in standard language or Dianetics and Scientology dictionaries.

If you find any other words you do not know, look them up in a good dictionary.

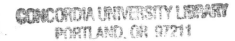

Contents

HOW TO USE THIS BOOK   1

CHAPTER ONE
ON THE STATE OF MAN   7

CHAPTER TWO
AN IDEAL STATE OF BEING   15

CHAPTER THREE
THE GOALS OF MAN   25

CHAPTER FOUR
THE HUMAN MIND   33

CHAPTER FIVE
THE CONTROL CENTER   43

CHAPTER SIX
EMOTION   53

CHAPTER SEVEN
PROCESSING   59

CHAPTER EIGHT

PROCESSING SECTION   65

    The First Act   71

    The Second Act   77

    The Third Act   91

    The Fourth Act   109

    The Fifth Act   129

    The Sixth Act   147

    The Seventh Act   163

    The Eighth Act   171

    The Ninth Act   187

    The Tenth Act   203

    The Eleventh Act   207

    The Twelfth Act   219

    The Thirteenth Act   231

    The Fourteenth Act   251

    The Fifteenth Act   257

DEFINITIONS, LOGICS AND AXIOMS   261

LRH GLOSSARY   299

APPENDIX

    Further Study   315

    Guide to the Materials   328

    Addresses   330

    Editor's Glossary of Words, Terms & Phrases   335

    Index   409

How to
Use this Book

THIS VOLUME OF SELF-PROCESSING is designed for use in any of four ways:

1. As a workbook to be used wholly by the auditor on the preclear; or

2. As a homework book to be given the preclear for use between sessions; or

3. As a process done by the preclear himself with only occasional auditor help; or

4. As a processing manual used wholly by the preclear without an auditor.

The last use is possible, particularly when the preclear knows considerable about this science from other sources. But it is possible by reading this book alone, and with considerable stamina, to carry straight on through.

If this book is given to you by an auditor, he expects to be consulted concerning any difficult points. And he expects to run out your SERVICE FACSIMILE, when the time comes, by Effort Processing.

The intention of this book is to decrease your reaction time, improve your health and efficiency, to extend your life and to immunize you against illnesses. This book is not intended for the people who would usually seek help by reason of severe aberration, neurosis or insanity: These should be worked upon by an auditor.

The optimum individual to which this book would be addressed for total self-use would be a person capable of considerable action such as a member of the armed services, a jet pilot, an artist, a musician desiring to speed his playing time and increase his ability. The address of this volume is to the person who, though normal enough, would like to excel physically and mentally. An engineer, for instance, using this volume could increase his ability to calculate and perform many times over.

DON'T CONFUSE THIS SCIENCE WITH PSYCHOTHERAPY, PSYCHOSIS OR NEUROSIS. JUST BECAUSE IT HANDLES THESE EASILY FOR THE FIRST TIME IN HISTORY IS NO REASON IT IS DEVOTED TO THE LAME, THE HALT AND THE ABERRATED. THIS SCIENCE HAS AS ONE OF ITS BRANCHES THE IMPROVEMENT OF HUMAN ABILITY ABOVE WHAT IT HAS BEEN. THIS BOOK WAS WRITTEN TO IMPROVE THE ABILITY OF THE ABLE.

Anyone using this volume, as written, can increase his skills, rehabilitate his goals and improve himself considerably above his fellows. We need people like that if we are going to have a better world.

Use this book as written. Don't try to combine it with old-time mumbo jumbo. Gasoline and alcohol—this book and psychotherapy mix similarly.

Use this book as written and no harm can come to you unless you are a case that badly needs an auditor.

Good luck in your voyage to YOU.

On the
St

ate of

man

On the State of Man

MAN STARTED HIS JOURNEY to present time some countless eons hence. Through blood and slaughter, earthquake and tidal wave, through muck and parching sand, through misery and strivings, grief and happiness, he has progressed, generation by generation, into the master of the world and the lord of all kingdoms.

What is the ideal state of this animal Man?

What are his goals?

What are his limitations?

What is there about him that is good and what is bad?

In the course of his adventures, Man made one very important discovery—and it has worried him ever since. He found that he had a mind. He found that he could think. Finally he understood that his mind was his best weapon. And he found that privation and injury or perhaps demons could deprive him of the full use of that weapon—his mind.

Through ages of philosophers, shamans and priests, he has attempted to resolve this primary worry and thus resolve a primary problem. Man wants to know what there is wrong with his mind, if anything, and he wants to know what might be the ideal state of his mind, if such a state exists.

He has wandered into countless strange bypaths in a quest for answers to these problems. He has seated himself on mountaintops and in caves for whole lifetimes just to ponder the riddle of himself. He has gone to war, he has starved, he has worked and reviled and written just to solve these two mysteries.

And now, as these words are written, his terribly perplexing mind has given birth to an idea and his hands have given form to a weapon which may resolve Man forever by destroying all civilization. Thus he *must* solve the two principal mysteries of his mind.

Can the nature of Man be changed before the works of Man vanish forever under the thud of Man's most powerful product, the atom bomb?

Can the nature of Man be changed at all?

Indeed, there is nothing more plastic than Man's ability to think and believe. At one time or another, in one part of the world or another, Man has accepted or believed things wilder than anything contained in philosophic books. His capacity for change is almost unlimited. It is no idle postulate, then, that Man's nature, across the whole world, might change entirely in a span of a few years. One has but to study his history to find such shifts of viewpoint and alterations of character. The "inertia of populaces" is a myth.

For instance, the coming of Saint Paul to Rome, almost two thousand years ago, changed the nature of all Roman slaves with a fire-like swiftness.

The appearance of a monk in England, at the beginning of the second millennium, altered the insularity of that island in a few months and sent hordes thundering off to the Crusades filled with a piety and zeal which, before his arrival, were markedly absent.

And in the last quarter of a century, the idea of collectivism has flooded out from a desperate band of revolutionaries to change the customs and methods of living of nearly a majority of the population of the world.

If Man can alter in such numbers, the alteration of an individual would seem to be relatively simple. And so it is. With new knowledge and with many of his past and present problems suddenly resolved, an individual in a few weeks can present a face to his fellows which has markedly changed.

Man is accustomed to change. The severity of his aberration is normally due to a feeling that he must protest against change. For his environment, all down through his evolutionary line, through any lifetime, has changed almost day by day.

Man is successful. That is evident because he is here today after eons of trial and error, good and bad planning. And he is successful because he can change.

The conquest of his environment has been his own engrossing purpose. Each time he has failed to conquer and control his environs, he has made wide changes in form and methods and has again returned into his kingship.

Man does *not* adapt to an environment. He adapts the environment to himself. And in that lies his success. When he fails to adapt the environment, when he lags in his complete control of that environment, he has altered himself or his ideas until he could again change the environment.

Amongst the many things Man has done, in his worries about his mind and his state of being, in his effort to control others, is the adoption of slave philosophies. Each person who invents or uses such a philosophy more or less tends to be, himself, exempt from the slavery thus imposed and to hold, by the invention, the force of others nullified. This is a trick of very limited workability, for it leads eventually into the entrapment of the user himself. It is a demonstrable law, not an opinion, that he who would enslave his fellows becomes himself enslaved. A "therapy" which teaches that Man should adapt himself to his environment, rather than adapt the environment to him, is such a slave philosophy and is not workable—only because it is quite the reverse from truth.

Each man of the species seeks, one way or another, to rise superior to all else. In that is his salvation and, in terms of his societies, his downfall.

Attempts at enslavement arise primarily from fear. Fear comes about with the loss of confidence in one's ability to make his way. Thus is posed a world where self-confidence is sought by robbing others of theirs. This cannot succeed in a complex society.

Man's problem today is not new. It is only more urgent of solution.

What is wrong, if anything, with his mind?

What is his ideal state?

an lc
Sta

eaL
te of
being

an Ideal
State of being

BEFORE ONE CAN DETERMINE what is wrong with a state of being, one should have some idea of what an IDEAL STATE OF BEING might be. In other words, before one can repair, for instance, a radio, one must have some knowledge of what the radio is supposed to do and how well it could play in a good state of repair.

What, it should have been asked a few millennia ago, is an ideal state of being for Man? In what state of mind does he best prosper? What is a well man? What is a happy man? What are the goals of Man? In what state of mind and body does Man live longest and fare best? What does Man want to do? What is he trying to do? What is he?

Before one could presume to advance "libido" theories and prefrontal lobotomies and magic healing crystals, one should have had some idea of the goal of his efforts.

The engineer, in repairing a bridge, has to have some idea of what a bridge is supposed to do, what loads it is supposed to carry, how strong it has to be and what might be expected to wreck it again. This is simple reasoning.

The engineer does not look at this bridge he is supposed to repair, sigh, say "the problem is too complicated," bicker with several other "authorities" on bridges, put some dynamite in the wrong place and blow it up and then wonder why there isn't any bridge left and begin to explain to passersby that "he was called too late, that was all," that "bridges aren't much good anyway."

Yet one fears this has been the method of address to the problem of the human mind and body.

To begin a rehabilitation of a human mind and body, one should know something about their optimum state. That would be the beginning of the answer as to how the mind and body could be rehabilitated. Further, it would be the beginning of an answer as to what environment and conditions best favor the human body and the human mind. After that, one could devise means of achieving an optimum condition.

In this new science, there are over two hundred Axioms which, one to the next, form a logical structure concerning the mind and body—which structure is demonstrated to be workable by the discovery of many new phenomena. This structure also predicts where phenomena might be found—and when one looks to see if the prediction was true, finds that it is. Accomplishments which people are calling miracles come about because of the logic and phenomena of these Axioms.

THE GOAL OF MAN HERE ON THIS EARTH IS APPARENTLY SURVIVAL.

And by SURVIVAL is meant everything necessary to survival, including honor and morals and idealism and other things which make life bearable.

A man survives as long as he can, in one lifetime, at the highest level he can attain in activity and happiness. When he can no longer attain to some hope of this ideal, he succumbs.

And although one is chary of exciting incredulity, the fact is so easily demonstrated in so many ways with such machine-like scientific consistency, it should be known that Man apparently dies in body only and gets born to live another day. The value of death is not small since without death Man would still be an alga in the sea, without death Man would be forced to live in a body which no longer fitted the environment. Your auditor can show you such an incident as an earlier death unless you are very occluded. Death has lost its sting in this new science and is seen to be rather practical after all.

Physically, on the evolution chain, Man is attempting a greater and greater control of his environment. The environment does not control a healthy man. He controls the environment. The surroundings of a sick man, a neurotic or insane man, have a tendency to control him. One sees this clearly as one advances, by this new science, into happier states of mind. One's health and ability rise directly as one asserts greater and surer control over his surroundings. Conversely, one asserts better and better control of his surroundings as he becomes healthier and happier.

Thus there is a second goal.

MAN IS EVIDENTLY SURVIVING TO ATTAIN A HIGHER AND STRONGER CONTROL OF THE PHYSICAL UNIVERSE.

The physical universe is composed of matter, energy, space and time. The coined word for the physical universe, in this new science, is "MEST." That is easy to remember, because it is composed of the first letter in each of the four words: "Matter," "Energy," "Space" and "Time."

Of course, Man may have other goals outside of the physical universe, but we note that he is most concerned here on Earth with a conquest of MEST. Naturally, he is concerned about his fellows and living organisms in general, for he is a sort of brotherhood with all life.

Life in general is engaged upon this conquest and Man is the highest form of life on Earth. Without this cooperative effort of all life, a conquest of the physical universe or even survival on a barest necessity basis would be impossible. Man is sufficiently complex as a mechanism that he must live upon lower orders of life which only, in their turn, can take sunlight and chemicals and evolve complex foods such as proteins.

Now one hopes that his reader is not engaging upon that trick common to many readers: People often search and recall only items which validate their old ideas. Pick up a book on philosophy which has been read by a reader who underscores with a pencil and one will find that the most utter banalities have been noticed. Only things which *agreed* with the old ideas of the reader were noted. One often wonders why such a fellow reads at all. The data in this new science aren't isolated opinions, but a structural whole. And with that whole, one can accomplish an occasional miracle and can almost always effect a marked improvement in an individual. This has never been done before with any consistency. And so one hopes that these data are being studied a little for themselves, not for how well they may agree with old ideas. For they don't agree with old ideas. And old ideas produced unhappiness, starvation, quick death, wars, insane asylums and much other unwanted bric-a-brac. This is not just a plea for understanding. If you want to get better than you ever could have been before, let's try these on for size and wear them until we clearly see their workability. If, after a thorough trial, you find they do not work, then you have every right to discount them. One can say this to you without any fear that you'll discover otherwise—too many miracles have been happening in this new science.

The list of Axioms in the back of this book will give you definitions for "pain," "pleasure," "anxiety" and other such things, in case you are curious.

Here, we are only treating the ideal state of being in the framework you will need to pursue the exercises in this volume.

The first item in the ideal state is I AM. Shakespeare was quite correct with his question, "To be or not to be?" When a man is trying to make a decision, that decision breaks down into a matter of choosing one of two courses: TO BE or NOT TO BE. The highest level of the desirable state is I AM. No doubts of the advisability of being, no qualms about the future. The lowest level on a survival course would be I AM NOT. In between we have the doubts and writhing and indecisions of the weary, the angry, the frightened. When a man has made up his mind as to a course, he is only then comfortable. So long as he hangs in a "maybe" on any decision, he is uncomfortable. In any course, there are just two decisions possible: To assume a STATE OF BEINGNESS or to assume a STATE OF NOT-BEINGNESS.

Included in these pages is a Tone Scale which is fronted with its own descriptive data. The ideal state of being is to be found across the top of that scale. The states of death, or not-beingness, are found across the bottom of the scale.

And here we have the matter of "gradient scales." Successes are little bits of living. Failures are little bits of death. Like the battle that was lost all for the loss of a horseshoe nail, a small failure can begin a series of failures which end in actual death. Not that death is very important, besides being painful, but that one tends, then, to give a very heavy weight to failures.

The ideal state of being could be said to be wholly successful in all things. This is opposed by being so unsuccessful that one is dead.

The next point in the ideal state of being is I KNOW, opposed by I KNOW NOT. Doubts, worries, grinding efforts at study—all these are simply gradients between I KNOW and I KNOW NOT.

What man does not quiver a trifle when confronted with the Unknown?

The next point in an ideal is SERENE. This drops away and at the bottom rung, having gone downwards through Exhilaration, Enthusiasm, Cheerfulness, Antagonism, Anger, Fear, Grief and Apathy, is DEAD.

TRUST is the ideal point on the scale of TRUST-DISTRUST. The most distrustful one can become is again DEAD.

The ideal point of longevity would be ALWAYS in a perfect body. The bottom of that scale would again be DEAD.

FULL RESPONSIBILITY would be an ideal, opposed by NO RESPONSIBILITY as an undesirable state.

And finally, but not least, there is CAUSE and EFFECT. The subject of CAUSE and EFFECT is so important that it will be mentioned several times in the exercises themselves. One's ideal state is to be the CAUSE. The least desirable state would be EFFECT. The ultimate in being EFFECT is DEATH.

Thus, we have a brief statement of what an ideal state might be. Only a few of the points have been given, but they will serve.

Ideally, one would be fully aware of being and would BE. That is I AM. One would be entirely SUCCESSFUL. One would KNOW. One would be SERENE. One would TRUST. One would be in perfect HEALTH physically. One could assume FULL RESPONSIBILITY. And one would be CAUSE without being unwilling to be CAUSE.

Of course, it would be not entirely desirable to attain these ultimates since one would then lack for action. But attaining them as nearly as possible would be a desirable condition.

The odd part of it is, when one drops on any one of these things, he drops on all the others—so interactive are these portions of life.

This volume and its exercises and auditing seek to assist the individual upwards toward this state of being which one could call IDEAL. How closely the individual may attain such a state depends largely upon his own willingness to work at the matter rather than the validity of the tenets themselves.

An ideal state of being, it goes without remark, would not include illnesses and inability to control oneself or his environment. Control of oneself and one's environment depend upon his attainment toward the ideal state of being.

the

goals
of Man

the goals
of man

THE GOAL OF LIFE in the finite universe may be easily and generally defined as:

AN EFFORT TO SURVIVE AS LONG AS POSSIBLE AND ATTAIN THE MOST DESIRABLE STATE POSSIBLE IN THAT SURVIVAL AND, IN ACCOMPLISHING THIS, TO CONQUER THE PHYSICAL UNIVERSE.

The cycle of survival is Conception, Growth, Attainment, Decay, Death, Conception, Growth, Attainment, Decay, Death, over and over again. This is the major cycle.

There is an inner cycle in a lifetime which has to do with emotion or action. This is Action, Attempt, Success, Attempt, Failure. Happiness down to Failure is the emotional cycle. But these are only part cycles. Just as every death begins new life, so does every failure eventually challenge forth new attempt until death itself is reached. Actually, both failure and death alike are transient. They are educational building blocks on a much longer road.

Occasionally, however, an individual becomes so overwhelmed that even successive attempts at life decline.

There is undoubtedly a much, much higher goal which prompts this effort to survive and to conquer. There is probably *reason* above that level. In this new science we are interested in *how* life is surviving, not *why*. Perhaps we know much of *why* right now. Perhaps we will know all of it someday. At the moment it is enough to know *how* life is surviving.

What is embraced in the survival and actions of one man? We see clearly that animal and vegetable efforts are necessary for Man's survival. We can see that living is teamwork on the part of all life. How much of this teamwork is included in the activities of one individual?

We have what we call DYNAMICS. Dynamics, in life, resemble somewhat effort in physics. A dynamic is the urge to survive along a certain course. A dynamic is the persistence in living. It is the effort to live.

Very low on the Tone Scale, in the psychotic or neurotic band, individuals think they survive for themselves alone. This, of course, would not be possible. As one rises up the Tone Scale into better states of being, he expands his sphere of interest and action. But no matter what he thinks in a low-tone state, he is still surviving on the many dynamics—even if in a limited state.

There are EIGHT DYNAMICS. These embrace all the goals of survival an individual has. They embrace all the things for which he survives.

None of these dynamics is more or less important than another. And, oddly enough, when one is blunted or shortened, so blunt or shorten all the rest. When one offends against one, he automatically offends against all the others. These dynamics are very easy to demonstrate.

The FIRST DYNAMIC is SELF. This is the effort to survive as an individual, to be an individual. It includes one's own body and one's own mind. It is the effort to attain the highest level of survival for the longest possible time for self.

The SECOND DYNAMIC is SEX. This dynamic has two sections, 2s and 2c. The first section is sex itself, the sexual act, anything relating to the physical action of sex. The second section is the urge for survival through children, the product of sex. This dynamic also includes a portion of family, since the family as a unit affects the rearing of children.

The THIRD DYNAMIC is GROUP. This is the effort to survive through a group, such as a community, a state, a nation, a social lodge, friends, companies or, in short, any group. One has a definite interest in the survival of a group.

The FOURTH DYNAMIC is MANKIND. This is the effort to survive as a species. It is the interest in the species as such.

The FIFTH DYNAMIC is LIFE FORMS. This is the effort to survive for any and every form of life. It is the interest in life as such.

The SIXTH DYNAMIC is MEST. This is the effort to survive as the physical universe and is the interest in the survival of the physical universe.

The SEVENTH DYNAMIC is LIFE SOURCE. This, in this new science, is separate from the physical universe and is the source of Life itself. Thus there is an effort for the survival of Life source.

The EIGHTH DYNAMIC is SUPREME BEING. This is written with the figure eight turned on its side (∞), meaning infinity. It is the postulated ultimate Creator of All and the effort to survive for the Supreme Being.

When one has a problem which embraces many of the subjects in these dynamics, the optimum solution of that problem lies in benefiting the largest possible number of dynamics. Solutions which injure one dynamic for the benefit of another dynamic result in eventual chaos. However, optimum solutions are almost possible to attain and human thinking seeks, at its highest level, only to bring the greatest order and the least chaos. At low levels on the Tone Scale, an individual will stress one or two dynamics to the expense of the rest and so lives a very disorderly existence and is productive of much chaos for those around him.

The soldier, flinging away his life in battle, is operating on the Third Dynamic (his company, his nation) at the expense of his First Dynamic, the Fourth and all the rest. The religionist may live on the Eighth, Seventh, Fifth and Fourth at the expense of the First and Sixth. The "selfish" person may be living only on the First Dynamic, a very chaotic effort.

There is nothing particularly wrong with bad emphasis on these dynamics until such emphasis begins to endanger them broadly, as in the case of a Hitler or a Genghis Khan or the use of atomic fission for destruction. Then all Man begins to turn on the destroyers.

The goal of an individual is to be, as much as possible, CAUSE or partner of CAUSE on all these dynamics at once, without becoming EFFECT or partner of EFFECT on any of them. He cannot do this completely. But the degree of his success depends upon how closely he can approximate CAUSE and how little he can be an EFFECT on each.

The whole of SURVIVAL is a dynamic, the only dynamic. But SURVIVE breaks down into these eight.

Philosophies in the past have laid emphasis on one or another of these dynamics to the exclusion of others and so such philosophies had but limited workability.

Psychotherapies have stressed this or that dynamic independent of the others and so did not achieve very great results. Freud, for instance, laid very heavy emphasis on the Second Dynamic, sex. There is some reason to give this a lion's share in therapy. But only because of the peculiarities of CAUSE and EFFECT and the sexual aberrations of the general culture, not because 2s is more important as an urge or drive than any of the others.

Not one of these dynamics will "drive one mad" when one fails more than another dynamic. But it is quite true that failure or impedance on any one of these dynamics causes impedance on all the rest. Fear on one becomes fear on all. Offense on one is offense on all. Success on one is success on all. Defense on one becomes defense on all.

The proofs of the existence of these dynamics are contained in the workability of the processes which develop from them. It happens that when one thinks of an individual as running wholly on the First Dynamic and tries to make a workable therapy on that supposition, the individual does not lose his psychosomatic ills and he does not improve. When one tries to treat the Second Dynamic exclusively as a therapy, the individual does not improve. When one uses all these dynamics in resolving his problems, one obtains marked and startling results. Perhaps the authoritarian will argue that just because a thing works is no reason one should use it. Authoritarians do not achieve any results beyond their own satisfaction—which is not reason enough for the student or technician who wishes to get things done.

The goals of Man, then, stem from the single goal of survival through a conquest of the material universe. The success of his survival is measured in terms of the broad survival of all. One man, working hard to save the First Dynamic, might shortsightedly destroy all the others. Where, then, would be the First Dynamic?

the

Human
Mind

the Human mind

IT IS COMMON to think of the human mind as something which just happened in the last generation or so. The mind itself is actually as old as the organism. And according to earlier guesses and proofs established by this new science, the organism—the body—is rather old. It goes back to the first moment of life's appearance on Earth.

First there was a physical universe, which happened we know not how.

And then with the cooling planets, there appeared in the seas a speck of living matter. That speck became, eventually, the complicated but still microscopic monocell.

And then as the eons passed, it became vegetable matter.

And then it became jellyfish.

And then it became a mollusk and made its transition into crustaceans.

And then as a land animal, this particular track of life which became Man evolved into more and more complex forms: the tarsus, the sloth, the anthropoid and finally Man. There were many intermediate steps.

A very materialistic man, seeing only the material universe, becomes confused and vague about all this. He tries to say that living organisms are simply so much clay, wholly a part of the material universe. He tries to say that, after all, it is only the "unending stream of protoplasm," generation to generation by sex, that is important. The very unthinking man is likely to make many mistakes not only about the human mind, but the human body.

We discover now that the science of Life, like physics, is a study of *statics* and *motion.* We find that Life itself, the living part of life, has no comparable entity in the physical universe. It isn't just another energy or just an accident. Life is a static which yet has the power of controlling, animating, mobilizing, organizing and destroying matter, energy, space and possibly even time.

Life is a CAUSE which acts upon the physical universe as an EFFECT. There is overwhelming evidence to support this now. In the physical universe there is no true static. Every apparent static has been discovered to contain motion. But the static of Life is evidently a true static. The basic text of Axioms of this new science demonstrates this conclusively.

Life began with pure CAUSE evidently. With the first photon it engaged in handling motion. And by handling motion, ever afterwards accumulated the experience and effort contained in a body. Life is a static, the physical universe is motion. The effect upon motion of CAUSE produced the combination which we see as the unity of a live organism. Thought is not motion in space and time. Thought is a static containing an image of motion. Thus one can say, with its first impingement upon motion, the first thought about the physical universe began. This static, without volume, wavelength, space or time, yet records motion and its effects in space and time.

This is, of course, analogy. But it is a peculiar analogy in that it sweepingly resolves the problems of mind and physical structure.

A mind, then, is not a brain. A brain and the nervous system are simply conduits for physical universe vibrations. The brain and nerve trunks are much like a switchboard system. And there is a point in the system where the vibrations change into records.

An organism is motivated by continuing, timeless, spaceless, motionless CAUSE. This CAUSE "mirrors" or takes impressions of motion. These impressions we call "memories" or, more accurately, FACSIMILES.

A facsimile, as you know, is a simple word meaning a picture of a thing, a copy of a thing, not the thing itself. Thus, to save confusion and keep this point before us in this new science, we say that the perceptions of the body are "stored" as facsimiles.

Sights, sounds, tastes and all the other perceptions of the body store as facsimiles of the moment the impression was received. The actual energy of the impression is not stored. It is not stored if only because there is insufficient molecular structure in the body to store these energies as such. Physical universe energy is evidently too gross for such storage. Further, although the cells perish, the memories go on existing, evidently, forever.

A facsimile of yesterday's hurt toe can be brought back today with the full force of the impact. Everything which occurs around the body, whether it is asleep or awake, is recorded as a facsimile and is stored.

There are facsimiles of anything and everything the body has ever perceived—seen, heard, felt, smelled, tasted, experienced—from the first moment of existence. There are pleasure facsimiles and bored facsimiles, facsimiles of sudden death and quick success, facsimiles of quiet decay and gradual struggle.

Memory usually means recalling data of recent times. Thus we use the word "facsimile." For while it is the whole of which memory is a part, the word "memory" does not embrace all that has been discovered.

One should have a very good idea of what a facsimile is. It is a recording of the motions and situations of the physical universe plus the conclusions of the mind based on earlier facsimiles. One sees a dog chase a cat. Long after dog and cat are gone, one can recall that a dog chased a cat. While the action was taking place, one saw the scene, one heard the sounds, one might even smell the dog or cat. As one watched, his own heart was beating, the saline content of his blood was at such and such a point, the weight of one's body and the position of one's joints, the feel of one's clothing, the touch of the air upon the skin—all these things were recorded in full as well. The total of all this would be a unit facsimile.

Now one could simply recall the fact that one had seen a dog chase a cat. That would be *remembering.* Or one could concentrate on the matter and, if he was in good mental condition, could again see the dog and the cat, could hear them, could feel the air on his skin, the position of his joints, the weight of his clothing. He could partially or wholly regain the *experience.* That is to say, he could partially or wholly bring to his consciousness the "memory"—the unit facsimile of a dog chasing a cat.

One does not have to be drugged or hypnotized or have faith in order to do this. People do variations of this recall without any knowledge of this science and suppose that "everybody does it." The person with a good memory is only a person who can regain his facsimiles easily. A little child in school learns today by repetition. It isn't necessary. If he gets good grades, it is usually because he simply brings back "to mind"—which is to say, to his awareness—the facsimile of the page of text on which he is being examined.

As one goes through life, he records twenty-four hours a day, asleep and awake, in pain, under anesthetic, happy or sad. These facsimiles are usually recorded with all perceptics—which is to say, with every sense channel. In the person who has a missing sense channel, such as deafness, that portion of the facsimile is missing.

A full facsimile is a sort of three-dimensional color picture with sound and smell and all other perceptions plus the conclusions or speculations of the individual.

It was once, many years ago, noticed by a student of the mind that children had this faculty of seeing and hearing in memory what they had actually seen and heard. And it was noted that the ability did not last. No further study was made of the matter and, indeed, so obscure were these studies that I did not know about them during the early stages of my own work.

We know a great deal about these facsimiles now—why they are not easily recovered by most people when they grow up, how they change, how the imagination can begin to remanufacture them as in hallucination or dreaming.

Briefly, a person is as aberrated as he is unable to handle his facsimiles. He is as sane as he can handle his facsimiles. He is as ill as he is unable to handle his facsimiles. He is as well as he can handle them.

That portion of this new science which is devoted to the rehabilitation of the mind and body deals with the phenomena of handling these facsimiles.

A person ought to be able to pick up and inspect and lay aside, at will, any facsimile he has. It is not a goal of this new science to restore full recall perception. It is the goal to rehabilitate the ability of a person to *handle* his facsimiles.

When a person *cannot* handle his facsimiles, he can pull them into present time and discover himself unable to get rid of them again.

What is "psychosomatic illness"? Demonstrably, it is the pain contained in a past experience or the physical malfunction of a past experience. The facsimile of that experience gets into present time and stays with the person until a shock drops it out of sight again or until it is processed out by this new science. A shock or necessity, however, permits it to come back.

Grief, sorrow, worry, anxiety and any other emotional condition is simply one or more of these facsimiles. A circumstance of death, let us say, causes one to grieve. Then one has a facsimile containing grief. Something causes the individual to bring that facsimile into present time. He is unaware of it, is not inspecting it, but it acts against him nevertheless. Thus he is grieving in present time and does not know why. The reason is the old facsimile. The proof that it *is* the reason lies in processing. The instant the facsimile is discharged of its painful emotion, the individual recovers. This is processing in one of its phases.

The human mind is only a phase of the continuing mind. The first spark of Life which began animating matter upon Earth began recording facsimiles. And it recorded from there on out. It is interesting that the entire file is available to any mind. In previous investigations, I occasionally found facsimiles—which were not hallucination or imagination—which seemed to go back much earlier than the present life of the preclear. Having by then the tool of Effort Processing, it was possible to "turn on" a facsimile with all perceptics at will and so it was possible to examine the earliest periods possible. The genetic blueprint was thus discovered and I was startled to have laid bare, accessible to any future investigator, the facsimiles of the evolutionary line. Many auditors have since accomplished the same results.

And thus, the biologist and anthropologist come into possession of a mine of fascinating data.

There are those who know nothing of the mind—and yet who get amply paid for it—who will talk wisely about "illusion" and "delusion." There happen to be exact and precise laws to delusion. An imaginary incident follows certain patterns. An actual incident is entirely unmistakable. There is a standard behavior in a facsimile of an *actual* experience, it behaves in a certain way: The individual gets the efforts and perceptions with clarity and the content of the incident expands and remains fairly constant on several recountings. An *imaginary* incident ordinarily contracts in content and the individual seeks to keep up his interest, then, by embroidering it. Further, it has no constant efforts in it. Those who cannot take time to establish the actuality of facsimiles before becoming wise about "delusion" are themselves possibly quite delusory people.

The human mind—as the present mind of Man—differs not at all from the most elementary of minds, that of the monocell, except in the complexity of brain appendage. The human being is using facsimiles to evaluate experience and form conclusions and future plans on how to survive in the best possible manner, or how to die and start over again.

The human mind is capable of very complex combinations of facsimiles. Further, it can originate facsimiles on the basis of old facsimiles. Nothing goes wrong with the mind except its abilities to handle facsimiles. Occasionally a mind becomes incapable of using a facsimile as past experience and begins to use it in present time, continually, as an apology for failure. Then we have aberration and psychosomatic illness. A memory of pain contains pain and can become present time pain. A memory of emotion contains emotion and can become present time emotion.

the
Cont

rol
Center

the
Control Center

EVERY MIND may be considered to have a CONTROL CENTER. This could be called the "awareness of awareness unit" of the mind, or it could be called simply "I".

The CONTROL CENTER is CAUSE. It directs, through emotional relay systems, the actions of the body and the environment. It is not a physical thing. Here is a diagram of the control center, "I", in relation to the emotions and the body and environment:

(over)

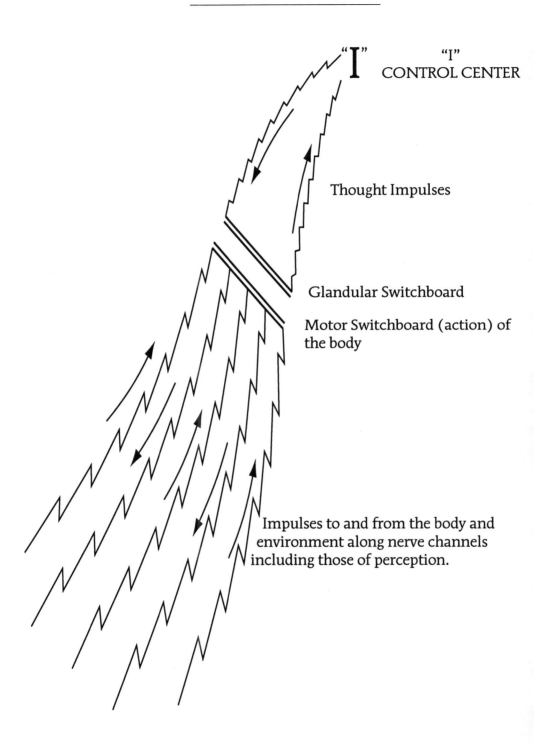

"I"   "I"
CONTROL CENTER

Thought Impulses

Glandular Switchboard

Motor Switchboard (action) of
the body

Impulses to and from the body and
environment along nerve channels
including those of perception.

The total function of "I" is the estimation of effort. It thinks and plans and resolves the problems of future effort.

When "I" has estimated a needful effort and puts it into action, its impulses impinge against the glandular system switchboard. The glandular system is a relay unit. It turns the emotional impulse into action.

The motor switchboard is a complex set of physical circuits and these go to various parts of the body and channels of perception in order to coordinate physical action at the direction of the glandular system.

On a return circuit, through the nerve channels of perception and the channels in the body itself, an impulse from the environment or the body goes into the switchboard and is directly recorded by "I" as a facsimile. The emotional system, in a mind in good condition, is bypassed on an incoming impulse unless "I" directs it expressly into the glandular system.

The physical body is a carbon-oxygen motor. It has been built out of the eons of experience, the summaries and conclusions of "I". Its internal motions and actions can be placed by "I" in the category of "automatic response." Thus the heartbeat and circulatory system are automatic in action. Thus many other motions of the body are automatic. But, as can be demonstrated, any of these motions can be altered by "I".

The glandular system is quite complex as such, but its function is simple. It is the translation medium, evidently, for thought. The system is partially physical and partially thought.

Thought is definitely comparable to "nothing" in the universe of matter, energy, space or time, having no wavelength, weight, mass or speed, and being therefore a zero which is an infinity or, in short, a true static.

Thought, thinking and Life itself are of the same order of being. Demonstrably they have no wavelength, therefore contain neither time nor space. Thought only appears to have time because in it is recorded physical universe time. There is obviously an "action" in thought. But, as obviously, it is not action in this universe. (To see the proofs of this character of thought, see the axiomatic text—Definitions, Logics and Axioms.)

Thoughts are these facsimiles which we have been discussing *plus* the Prime Thought, TO BE, which can occur at any time.

Now this subject can be made much more difficult than it is. Thought, or the Life static, acts upon the glandular system to produce physical actions. Physical actions act in the sensory channels (the nerves) to produce thought "recordings."

The environment does not control thought. Thought tries to be CAUSE. However, the body and the environment have certain needs in this action for the conquest of the physical universe and so thought, the "I", must give permission to be an EFFECT. When it gives permission to be affected, it can then be an EFFECT and only then can the environment control the body. Thought gives up a sphere of control and that control sphere can be affected thereafter. Here we have what has passed for the "stimulus-response mechanism," whereby the individual is restimulated or upset or stimulated by the environment.

Facsimiles are filed by TIME. A facsimile from an earlier time is more effective than a later facsimile. If one decides a thing today and decides the reverse tomorrow, today's decision remains active unless cancelled out by being recalled or processed. In the matter of a habit such as smoking, for instance, a young boy, to appear grown, decides to smoke. Twenty years later he decides not to smoke without doing anything about the original decision. Thus he "can't break the habit"—which is to say, he can't overcome an early decision with a later one.

He could stop smoking simply by recalling and knocking out the earlier facsimile *to* smoke.

Because of the stress of living, which was no less to the monocell than it is to the modern Man, the organism cannot help but become an EFFECT. It seeks to remain CAUSE as much as possible. But the mind is running a carbon-oxygen engine called the human body, an engine of narrow tolerance which operates between 95 degrees F and 106 degrees F and ordinarily at 98.6 degrees F, which cannot go two miles below the surface of the Earth or three miles above it, which has to be fed at least every twenty-four hours and which, because of its early training as a monocell dependent upon sunlight and minerals for its food, needs six to eight hours of sleep every night and which is capable of just so much physical stress before something breaks.

Further, the method of procreation used by the mammal requires another organism and thus one must admit to an EFFECT from another being. Further, Man developed into a pack hunter—which is to say, he was most successful as a group of men—and so had to submit to leadership or the onerous responsibilities of leadership in order to succeed and thus had to be a further EFFECT.

Fortunately, there is a working rule in the span of all lives that each new generation seems to begin with all old facsimiles submerged and inactive, except for "blueprinting" the new body, and with "I" ready to record experience freshly for this life. As soon as one begins to fail, "I" calls up old facsimiles and starts to use them. And we have trouble mentally and physically.

Without the vast background of past experience, the blueprint of the present body would not exist. A monocell cannot conquer very much physical universe—a man can. Thus, by these cycles of life and death, of starting as CAUSE and becoming EFFECT, the race develops.

The human mind is a natively self-determined computer which poses, observes and resolves problems to accomplish survival.

It does its thinking with facsimiles of experience or facsimiles of synthetic experience.

It is natively CAUSE. It seeks to be minimally an EFFECT.

It is in its best operating condition when it is most self-determined on all dynamics.

It becomes aberrated when it has desired to be an EFFECT and has lost track of when and why, thus losing control of the facsimiles.

Knowing these things about the human mind, we can resolve its aberrations and its psychosomatic illnesses.

e m

otion

CHAPTER SIX

Emotion

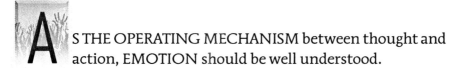S THE OPERATING MECHANISM between thought and action, EMOTION should be well understood.

Emotion exists to monitor motion. Thought itself seems to have an emotional impulse which is free of physical universe waves. This is studied in various ways, but it is only important to us in the resolution of the problems of the human mind.

Various emotions produce various actions:

Anger, for instance, is the catalyst for attack.

Fear is the signal to withdraw.

Grief is the signal to be quiet and initiate nothing.

Apathy is the signal to be dead or to feign death so that a marauder will go away.

Various glandular compounds are injected into the system to produce these results. Fear and grief, for instance, have an added compound to make the flesh taste bad—for Man is but recently a food animal.

There is an entire scale of emotions to produce certain motions. And there is a herd reaction, as witnessed in mass hysteria, whereby emotion acts upon others—a mechanism developed in the control of hunting packs, whereby the entire pack could feel afraid and run or feel angry and attack without any other command. This shows up additionally in any modern leadership. The leader is that one who emotionally affects others most strongly toward positive action.

In interpersonal relations, emotion plays an enormous role.

In this new science, we have what is called COUNTER-EMOTION. Incidents quite often will not reduce until the preclear is made to feel the emotion of others toward him. But quite aside from this manifestation as an ethereal something, there is the real mechanism of sympathy. One person shows grief in order to get support from the other. The other shows sympathy and gives the support. Man is so interdependent and the physical universe so occasionally rigorous that all interpersonal relations are built upon this dependency or its denial.

The broad field of the dynamics indicates the generalized character of emotion.

The test of these conclusions is their workability. You will discover, in processing, the enormous importance of emotion. The emotion of an individual can be "frozen" by some facsimile he once wanted, but now does not want, and he thereafter handles motion according to that emotion. Thus a person can be chronically angry or chronically in apathy and his behavior on all dynamics is the behavior of that emotion. By knowing this and the activities of *any* level on a Tone Scale of emotion, one can predict completely the actions of any given individual or handle him with ease.*

---

*See the *Hubbard Chart of Human Evaluation* in the book *Science of Survival*.

The ideal state is fully self-determined emotion. Only then can one be happy and successful.

proce

ssing

CHAPTER SEVEN

Processing

THE EFFORT IN PROCESSING is devoted to the goal of raising the individual on the Tone Scale. This involves rehabilitating his ability to handle his own facsimiles.

Processing may necessitate the reduction of a number of facsimiles by Thought, Emotion or Effort Processing.

It is a peculiarity of a facsimile that no matter how violent may be the efforts and counter-efforts of its content, no matter how sad or terrible may be the situation it involves, once that facsimile is processed by impressing it against reality several times, it no longer has any power, force, effort or thought content. There are many ways of accomplishing this. In earlier works, cruder and longer methods were used, but they accomplished the same purpose.

A memory, a facsimile, contains a record of everything that happened in the actual incident—sight, sound, taste, pain, emotion, efforts of the individual, efforts of the environment against the individual. The individual moves it into present time and keeps it for various reasons and then believes he is unable to rid himself of it. It produces strange compulsions or obsessions or aberrations in general. And it can produce, with its efforts, its original physical pain.

A facsimile so held by the individual can make him ill. It can even kill him. Such facsimiles produce over 70 percent of the illness of Man and make him weak enough to fall prey to the diseases and accidents which account for the other 30. Sinusitis, arthritis, eye trouble, liver difficulties, ulcers, migraine headaches, polio aftereffects and so on down the long, long list surrender if one reduces the facsimile causing the trouble.

Whether or not the facsimile is reduced depends to some degree upon the skill of the auditor. For instance, in my first book on this new science, I was guilty of overestimating the ability of my fellow man and have had to work hard since to simplify the techniques and theory so as to make the success of processing much more certain. It is now in the miracle-class, so they say. But, even now and then someone is too old or too inaccessible for the skill of the auditor working upon him and so only an alleviation occurs rather than an eradication of the trouble.

The end goal of processing has no finite end. The auditor simply tries to raise his preclear up the scale as far as possible in the time allowed and to eradicate the most evident psychosomatic. There are levels of the Tone Scale which have not been attained but which seem attainable. These unattainable levels—at this time—are so far above anything ever attained by any man before this that the preclear need not worry about being lifted only a little way.

The preclear generally starts with the environment in rather heavy control of him. The modern educational system, various laws and parental authority all seek to cause the preclear to be an EFFECT of the environment rather than a CAUSE of environmental effects.

When he has come to a level where he can be self-determined on the majority of the dynamics, his case is considered closed.

This book assists him to attain the goal.

proces
s

ssing
ection

Processing
Section

THE PROCESSING SECTION of this volume is divided into FIFTEEN ACTS.

Each one of these covers a certain phase of a case. If the individual is working with an auditor, then he will find that the auditor is piloting him through these same fifteen Acts and that this book is being used supplementarily to auditor checking. If the individual has given himself the task of going through this volume by himself, he follows the same procedure and each section is, of necessity, to be taken up in turn.

Each Act is begun by a description of what the process means and how it is applied and the end it is intended to accomplish.

It is not necessary to *believe* what you find in this volume for the material to work. If you begin processing as in the doubtful-class, you will find your doubts resolving as you proceed.

Another can read these processes to you. You can read them yourself. You can do them between sessions with an auditor. You can get an auditor to do all the work for you.

You will find included a Chart of Attitudes toward life.*

This might be called a "button chart," for it contains the major difficulties people have. It is also a self-evaluation chart. You can find a level on it where you agree and that is your level of reaction toward life. This chart complements the Hubbard Chart of Human Evaluation** but is specially prepared for this volume and for this type of processing. Your use of the chart in your processing is described later.

You will also find a disk included with this book. The disk is employed whenever there is a long list of questions. Its use is described where it is first used in the section.

You may find these processes too difficult for you and would therefore desire some assistance. There are many professional people qualified in the application of the processes of this new science. By writing to the publisher of this book, you may obtain the name and address of the professional auditor nearest you.***

This new science has moved very rapidly and new developments have cut down the number of hours required in processing to below one hundred with the new techniques. You should count on spending at least a hundred hours with this present book including any Effort Processing you may receive from an auditor.

This book, by itself, will do more for you than professional processing could have done in June of 1951, much less June of 1950. Into it has gone an additional two years of intensive work and investigation. Anywhere that this text or these processes disagree with books or data earlier than December of 1951, this book—not the earlier work—is correct. The line of advance has been very consistent, but sometimes a superficial student cannot follow the logical advance line.

*A foldout version of this chart is contained at the back of this book.
**See the book *Science of Survival.*
***See *Addresses* in the Appendix.

While an individual does not have to understand this new science if he is being audited, one who is working this volume by himself should have a fairly good understanding of basic theory.

the
first
act

the First act

IT WILL SAVE TIME if you will review the text of this volume up to this point and understand it. Then answer the following questions. Write in the book with a pencil.

WHAT IS THE GOAL OF LIFE?

WHAT IS LIFE TRYING TO ACCOMPLISH?

HOW MANY FIELDS IS THE LIFE ORGANISM INTERESTED IN?

WHAT IS A FACSIMILE?

WHAT IS THE PURPOSE OF THE HUMAN MIND?

WHAT IS MEANT BY CAUSE AND EFFECT?

IS A FACSIMILE PERMANENT?

HOW DOES "MEMORY" OR "REMEMBERING" DIFFER FROM RE-EXPERIENCING FACSIMILES?

The
Second
Act

The Second Act

THE ANATOMY of the static of Life demonstrates it to have three interdependent characteristics. Each one of these three is as important as the other two.

They are REALITY, AFFINITY and COMMUNICATION.

Reality itself could be considered that on which Man agrees to be real. There is an old, moth-chewed philosophic concern about perception. Are things real only when we see them? Or are things real? In other words, is there *any* reality? Well, desks and chairs seem very real to me. And they seem very real to you. Thus we agree that there are desks and chairs and people and cars and a world and the stars. Sane men have a very solid agreement on reality. They agree that things are real. Insane people have hallucinations. Hallucinations are imagined realities with which nobody else agrees. When an individual does not agree with the rest of the race upon the reality of matter, energy, space and time, the rest of the race locks him up. Ideas are not matter, energy, space or time and so there can be disagreement on ideas and agreement upon the reality of matter, energy, space and time. This agreement upon MEST, then, is reality. Reality could be said to be agreement above 2.0 on the Tone Scale—agreement not so much with people, but with MEST's actuality. This is one corner of our triangle.

The next corner is affinity. The physical universe has what is known as cohesion. Matter stays together. This is, in the Life static as it operates on matter, affinity. Affinity is love above 2.0. "Love," as a word, has too many meanings and so we use an old, old word, "affinity," as meaning the feeling of love or brotherhood from one dynamic to another.

The third corner of the triangle is communication. Communication is actually done via the sense channels. One sees a rock. By sight he is communicating with the rock. He feels a blade of grass. He is then communicating, via a sense channel, with the blade of grass. When one talks to another person, he is sending an impulse from "I" to the vocal cords, which set up physical universe sound waves, which reach the ears of the other person, are translated into nerve impulses and so convert into an impingement upon "I" of the other person. Communication by talk, then, goes from life to life via the physical universe. It is the same with touch. One person touches another. This is communication via the physical universe persons. There may be direct, nonphysical universe communication channels from "I" to "I". The most tangible of these is emotional impact.

One cannot have affinity without agreement. One cannot have agreement without some form of communication. One cannot have communication without agreement. One cannot have agreement without affinity. One cannot have communication without affinity. This inevitable triangle may be at any level on the Tone Scale, high or low. If communication is destructive, the affinity drops to anger and agreement is violent disagreement.

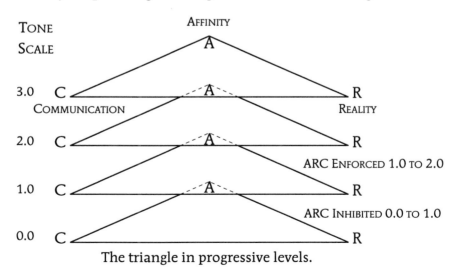

The triangle in progressive levels.

At 0.0, which is DEATH, affinity, communication and reality are wholly physical universe for the body and are the cohesions, the connections and the aspects of the physical universe.

At 1.0, which is FEAR, the affinity is poor, being fearful, the communication is twisted and consists of lies, the reality is poor and is agreed upon for covert purposes.

At 2.0, which is ANTAGONISM, the affinity is broken into hostility, the communication is nagging or disagreeable, the reality is contradictory to others just to contradict and is therefore poor.

At 3.0, which is ABOVE THE NORMAL person, affinity is love, it is present but reserved, the communication is conservative, the reality is cautious but is agreed upon after being proven.

At 4.0, which is CHEERFULNESS, affinity is affectionate, communication is free and constructive, reality is good and agreement is general.

Above 4.0 we have many levels, but ARC (Affinity, Reality and Communication) are getting above a physical universe aspect. Out of ARC, we can derive any UNDERSTANDING. In fact, logic evolves out of ARC. At 4.0 we have lower-level understanding. And understanding increases to complete knowledge when a very high band is reached—above 20.0.

ARC are actually the interplays of Life active in the physical universe.

When you communicate with an antagonistic person, you have to enter into an "affinity" and a reality of 2.0. When you show affinity for 1.0, which is FEAR, you inherit the communication and agreement level of the 1.0. An individual, to escape this inevitable transaction, has to be above 4.0 on the Tone Scale.

In order to have an understanding of yourself, you must have good ARC with yourself.

It is *not* evil to like yourself or love yourself. It is very low toned not to be fond of yourself.

All the dynamics are interactive. If you love others, you will love yourself. If you hate others, you will hate yourself. If you hate men, you will hate along the other dynamics even when you cover it with "sympathy" as you will discover in a later Act.

A healthy state of being is to be a friend to yourself. If you have few friends, if you don't like friends, you won't like yourself either.

If you are afraid of people, you won't trust yourself and will be afraid of what you might do.

If you are afraid of animals, you will also be afraid of possessions and sex and people and anything else.

Occasionally people have special fears. These are only concentrations upon one thing. A person, without admitting it, will also be afraid on the other dynamics, but will not have recognized it.

It is not enough to suddenly determine to *love* everybody. That is forcing affinity on yourself.

Affinity is enforced from 2.0 down to near 1.0. Around 1.0 we have "propitiation"—buying people off, pretending affection. From here on down, affinity is inhibited.

Thus, we see that enforced, demanded ARC is aberrative. And we see that inhibited ARC is also aberrative.

Let's put this to test. Do you recall a person you had to kiss? Well, did you feel agreeable toward this person? Did you want to touch (communicate with) or talk to this person?

And another test. Do you recall a person who pushed you away when you felt affectionate? What was your immediate communication reaction? What was your agreement?

And another one. Do you recall a person who demanded that you talk to them? What was your level of affinity? What degree of agreeableness did you feel?

And yet another. Do you recall a person who demanded that you agree with him against your wishes? What was your level of affinity? What was your level of communication?

And still another. Do you recall a person who continually corrected you? This is inhibited agreement. What was your reaction level on affinity? What was your reaction as to communication?

Do you recall a person who was afraid of anything and everything? What was your affinity? What was your agreement?

A person high on the Tone Scale reacts down toward, but does not necessarily reach the level of the person he addresses. However, he tends to reach toward that level. And if he stays in the proximity of a lower-toned person long enough, he will eventually become chronically in that tone.

Do you know somebody who affects you badly after you have been in his company for a while? Does this person like people? Does he tell the truth? Does he communicate easily? Do you agree with his views? Here is ARC in action in present time.

After you have been in the vicinity of somebody who insists you talk, insists you agree, insists you feel as he feels, what is your own tone level toward him?

After you have associated with a person who won't let you talk, won't agree with you, won't let you feel as you want to feel, what is your reaction? Where is this person on the Tone Scale? This is an inhibited ARC person, or below 1.0. This person is afraid or apathetic. This person has endocrine ills. This person lies. This person hides things. This person is physically and mentally maladjusted.

It happens that anyone on a given level of the Tone Scale seeks to pull everyone else to that level of the Tone Scale. A low-level individual is pulled up a bit by a high-level individual and then the high-level individual comes down a bit.

Low-toned people work toward succumb. Below 2.0, the effort is toward death, one way or another, covertly or overtly, toward succumb. The angry person, failing to destroy others, will destroy himself. The apathetic person is almost dead. The activity of persons below 2.0 is directed toward the gaining of sympathy. They try to make higher-toned people sympathetic and thus destroy them. Sympathy for low-toned cases is a social aberration. It is deadly.

No low-toned person can be "helped." Try to help a person below 2.0 and the result is ingratitude plus in the end. For the goal of that person is to succumb. Higher-toned individuals don't need help.

Low-toned persons can be audited to above 2.0, however, after which they will seek to survive along all dynamics. If you suppose you lie below 2.0 and have persevered this far, you don't.

There is, by the way, very practical present time use of this data about ARC. If you want a person to agree with you, address him at his obvious tone level and you will go into communication with him and he will feel affinity for you. If you want affinity from a person, use his methods of communication to others *with* him and go into agreement with him on his concept of the other dynamics. A salesman can sell a 1.5 (anger case) anything if that thing is shown to be destructive to other dynamics.

This is why the government, a rather 1.5 affair, buys atomic fission as a weapon rather than a means to send Man to the stars.

Here, then, is the Second Act. First achieve an understanding of the factors in UNDERSTANDING—ARC—contained in this section. Then answer these questions.

LIST THE PERSONS IN YOUR PRESENT TIME ENVIRONMENT WHO ENFORCE AFFINITY ON YOU.

LIST THE PERSONS IN YOUR PRESENT TIME ENVIRONMENT WHO ENFORCE AGREEMENT UPON YOU.

LIST THE PERSONS IN YOUR PRESENT TIME ENVIRONMENT WHO DEMAND THAT YOU COMMUNICATE WITH THEM.

LIST THE PERSONS IN YOUR PRESENT TIME ENVIRONMENT WHO REFUSE YOUR AFFECTION.

LIST THE PERSONS IN YOUR PRESENT TIME ENVIRONMENT WHO WON'T LET YOU COMMUNICATE WITH THEM.

LIST THE PERSONS IN YOUR PRESENT TIME ENVIRONMENT WHO REFUSE TO LET YOU AGREE WITH THEM.

NOW GO BACK AND PUT A TONE SCALE NUMBER AFTER EACH NAME AS AN ESTIMATE. WHERE IS EACH ONE ON THE CHART OF TRIANGLES EARLIER IN THIS SECTION?

Don't worry about your accuracy. This is only to give you an estimate of the kind of reaction your environment might have on you and to promote your understanding of these people.

NOW TAKE THE FIRST PERSON YOU LISTED AND GO TO THE CHART OF ATTITUDES WHICH ACCOMPANIES THIS VOLUME. FROM THE NUMBER YOU ASSIGNED THE PERSON, GO ACROSS THE BIG CHART AT THAT LEVEL. IF YOU ASSIGNED SOMEBODY TO 2.0, FOLLOW 2.0 ACROSS THE BIG CHART. READ EACH ATTITUDE ON THE 2.0 LINE HORIZONTALLY ACROSS THE CHART. THIS SHOULD GIVE YOU SOME UNDERSTANDING OF THAT PERSON. AND IT SHOULD TELL YOU WHAT HIS EFFECT MIGHT BE ON ANOTHER.

TAKE THE NEXT PERSON WITH YOUR ASSIGNED NUMBER ACROSS THE CHART. FOLLOW ON THROUGH WITH EACH PERSON YOU LISTED.

You probably duplicated several listings with the same number.

With this exercise complete, let us delve a little into the past.

LIST PERSONS IN THE PAST WHO INSISTED THEY WERE YOUR FRIENDS. THIS IS A VARIETY OF ENFORCED AFFECTION.

LIST PERSONS IN THE PAST WHO INSISTED YOU AGREE WITH THEM.

List persons in the past who insisted you communicate with them.

List persons in the past who would not show you affection.

List persons in the past who refused to communicate with you.

List persons in the past who would not let you agree on things.

(Include all your parents and relatives here and as they come into these classifications.)

ASSIGN A TONE SCALE NUMBER TO EACH ONE.

CHECK EACH ONE FOR ATTITUDES ACROSS THE BIG CHART.

WHAT EFFECT DO YOU SUPPOSE ALL THESE ATTITUDES, PAST AND PRESENT, HAVE ON YOU?

the
third
act

The Third Act

WITH THE HELP of the CHART OF ATTITUDES let us take a look at your present-day environment.

You may have realized, while inspecting this chart, that you yourself were not quite at the top. You need not worry particularly if you discovered this. Unlike some witch doctors in modern dress, this book is making no effort to condemn you. There were various reasons why you permitted yourself to be lowered on this Tone Scale—for you had to give your permission to have anything serious happen to you (a matter which we will cover under SELF-DETERMINISM in a later section of this volume).

Let us make an assessment of how you regard things in your today. Write the answers. (See the chart for the data in each column given.)

USE PHRASES AND WORDS OF CHART IN YOUR ANSWERS. WRITE TONE SCALE NUMBER OF PHRASE.

WHAT IS YOUR MOST COMMON EMOTION?

How do you feel about survival?

How right are you about what you do?

What responsibilities are you willing to shoulder?

How do you feel about possessions?

DO YOU FEEL YOU ARE ANYBODY?

DO YOU THINK MOST ABOUT THE PAST, THE PRESENT OR THE FUTURE?

HOW DOES MOTION AFFECT YOU?

HOW DO YOU HANDLE TRUTH?

DO YOU TRUST OR DISTRUST?

DO YOU KNOW OR ARE YOU DOUBTFUL?

DO YOU WANT TO CAUSE THINGS OR BE AN EFFECT?

WHAT IS YOUR "STATE OF BEINGNESS"? (NEXT TO LAST COLUMN)

TURN BACK TO THE SECOND ACT AND LOOK OVER THE PEOPLE YOU HAVE LISTED. DO ANY OF YOUR REACTIONS MATCH THEIRS? IN OTHER WORDS, ARE YOU COMPARABLE TO ANY OF THOSE PERSONS LISTED?

You should be able to discover that you are carrying, in present time, the past attitudes of others. In present time you should be YOU. The phrases you listed in this Third Act actually don't describe YOU. They describe those parts of YOU which you have turned over to other people in the past. You are carrying on attitudes of people who are probably departed long since. They are not very survival.

A little bit or a great deal of YOU is described up along the 16.0 to 40.0 band of the chart. Our job is to get all of YOU as high as possible on the chart and leave the parts of "you" which rightly belonged to others behind us.

Human beings operating along all the dynamics are actually rather heroic and noble characters. They see cruelty or suffering and they, particularly in their youth and strength, take it on to spare the world. They see someone, even themselves, perform a cruel act or have an unhappy experience and they regret it. Then they discover that they themselves can fail. They then blame others for their plight. It is a cycle of nobly accepting something and then, to save one's own being, trying to get rid of it in time. Youth is so high on the chart, innately, that it accepts the evil of the world with open arms in an effort to make it a better world. Then, staggering under the burden, finding none to share it, they fight to give it away either by being evil or being sick.

This will become much clearer before we have finished here. And you will be a lot higher on the chart.

Let's assess your present time now.

WHAT PHRASE ON THE WHOLE CHART BEST DESCRIBES YOUR ATTITUDE TOWARD LIFE IN GENERAL RIGHT NOW?

CAN YOU RECALL A SPECIFIC INSTANT WHEN SOMEBODY ELSE UTTERED THAT PHRASE?

WHERE WERE YOU AT THE TIME?

OUTDOORS OR INDOORS?

STANDING OR SITTING?

CAN YOU RECALL AN EARLIER TIME YOU HEARD IT?

WHEN DID YOU FIRST TELL YOURSELF THAT PHRASE? AND DON'T TELL IT TO YOURSELF AGAIN, BECAUSE YOU ARE THE FIRMEST INFLUENCE UPON YOU. WHAT YOU SAY TO YOU STICKS.

GO STRAIGHT ACROSS THE LIST AND, COLUMN BY COLUMN, PICK OUT YOUR ATTITUDE TOWARD THE WORLD IN WHICH YOU ARE NOW LIVING. WRITE THESE DOWN IN THE SPACE BELOW.

1.

2.

3.

4.

5.

6.

7.

8.

9.

10.

11.

12.

NOW TRACE EACH ONE OF THESE PHRASES BACK TO THE EARLIEST TIME YOU HEARD SOMEBODY ELSE USE IT. GET THE EXACT MOMENT IF POSSIBLE. GET A VISIO (A VIEW IN MEMORY) OF THE PERSON SAYING IT. GET AS MANY AS YOU CAN OF EACH PHRASE AND THE EARLIEST TIME IT WAS UTTERED. FOR THIS, USE YOUR DISK. PUT THE DISK OVER THE PHRASE YOU WROTE AND RECALL THE INCIDENT WITH THE PERCEPTION OF IT CALLED FOR ON THE DISK OR THE EMOTION AS REQUESTED BY THE DISK.

You can see now that your present time concerns are to some degree the worries and concerns of somebody else in the past.

The value of past experiences lies in the estimation of the future. Past experiences are not nearly as valuable as one might suppose. There is an enormous emphasis on the value of experience. Go to make out an application form for a job and you will find that they are mostly concerned with experience. It is a sort of trap to enslave people, giving their experiences such value.

Actually, a snapping bright mind and an alert body are worth a hundred thousand years of "experience" behind some dusty desk or counter. And an ability to do a "quick study" of a subject is so much more valuable than an education—complete with a hundred As in that subject—that one might be led to suppose that maybe "education," as it is laughingly called, might possibly be overstressed. Check your history and you will discover that the men whose marble busts adorn the modern halls of learning did not, themselves, have a formal education: Bacon, Spencer, Voltaire, etc., etc., etc., down the whole list, two or three exceptions prove the rule. Not even long study has as much value as people might have wanted you to believe.

Your life, from any instant in it, can be free of all past experience. And your carbon-oxygen motor would continue to run and you could pick up what you needed to know in a couple of months—even change your name—and yet survive handsomely. If you won a Nobel prize last year, that's tough. You will try madly to keep the experience and be a Nobel prize winner instead of trying to be enthusiastic enough in the tomorrows to win another prize. The getting is the sport, the having is a defensive action and makes you a platoon pinned down by enemy fire. Thus with experience as with MEST.

So let's look at present time.

And let's be blunt.

What are you trying to hide in present time?

What would happen to you if it were discovered?

How many things like this are there in present time?

Don't bother to list them. If other people found these things out they would probably blink, maybe they'd "chatter over fences." You might get fired or divorced.

But I'll tell you a secret about secrets: No single person to whom you uttered the confidence would *not* have a similar list to hide. They've all masturbated and had clandestine affairs and a lot of them venereal diseases. They've stolen money and maybe some have even left a cold dead body in a culvert. They've lied and cheated and done blackmail. And the funny part of it is, only those who have a long, long list of things to hide would even begin to reprimand you.

And another thing: Anyone who punished you would someday regret it. A dean in college who threatened to flunk me for writing a bit of truth in what was the longest sentence in the English language (five hundred words without colons or semicolons) had it weigh upon his mind to such an extent that he wrote me, years afterwards when he had retired and was nearly dead, the most astonishing apology.

You are treating yourself in present time much as you were treated by others in the past. And you punish yourself far more than anyone would ever punish you. The suicide is simply self-executioner, having been found guilty by his own court.

NEXT, HOW HARD AND TO WHOM ARE YOU TRYING TO BE RIGHT IN THE FACE OF ANYTHING AND EVERYTHING, INCLUDING FACTS?

WHAT RESPONSIBILITIES ARE YOU SHIRKING? WHY?

WHAT ARE YOU DOING WITH YOUR POSSESSIONS? WHY?

WHAT DO YOU THINK OF YOURSELF? WHY?

IS THE FUTURE OR THE PAST RECEIVING YOUR MOST INTENSE THOUGHT? WHY?

DO YOU FLINCH AT MOTIONS? WHY?

HOW CLOSELY DO YOU STAY TO TRUTH IN PRESENT TIME?
WHY NOT?

DO YOU TRUST YOUR ENVIRONMENT? WHY NOT?

WHAT DON'T YOU KNOW? WHY NOT?

WHAT ARE YOU TRYING TO CAUSE? WHY?

WHAT ARE YOU TRYING TO MAKE EFFECT YOU? WHY?

WHO ARE YOU TRYING TO BLAME IN PRESENT TIME? WHY?

WHAT ARE YOU BLAMING YOURSELF FOR IN PRESENT TIME? WHY?

DO YOU LIKE YOUR WORK? WHY?

IS YOUR SEX LIFE SATISFACTORY? WHY?

WHAT THREATENS YOUR PRESENT SECURITY? WHY?

Self-confidence alone is security. Your ability is your security. There is no security but you. Let's make the best possible YOU we know how. Almost all the things you thought of in the above list can be remedied by your own action without consulting for a moment the permission of anything or anyone. Innately, deep down, you know this. Actually you are a giant tied down with cotton lint. You tied the knots and furnished the string and said where you'd lie. The only trouble you might have in processing is refusing—for some strange but discoverable reason, having to do with concern for others—to burst these light strands and stand up. Fortunately this volume offers more than such inspiration. But the cold, basic truth is that you are a vital and necessary part of this world and anything that is wrong with you, you have assumed in an effort to be what has passed for "human."

the
Fourth
act

the Fourth act

YOU WILL NOTE on the edge of the CHART OF ATTITUDES that from 0.0 to 1.5 is considered to be severely aberrated, that from 1.5 to 2.8 is considered to be neurotic, that from 2.8 to 10.0 is considered acceptable.

When these figures were first calculated, it was thought that normal was about 2.8. It isn't. That is generous beyond generosity. Normal is well below that according to amassed data since the first computations. The reason for this seems to be in two distinct fields: The first is the environment. The second is education.

Education, continued long enough in the usual school and college, depresses the individual toward 0.3 or apathy. The person being "educated" is, day after day, immobilized, made into an EFFECT by instructors and denied original thought. He becomes a habitual EFFECT and ceases to CAUSE. He begins to respond automatically according to a pattern of manners given him by the home and the school system.

This is the primary reason why the modern college has yet to turn out an artist from an arts major. An artist must be a CAUSE and continue to be CAUSE. Majoring in writing, for instance, is a sure route to being an editor or, worse, a critic rather than a writer. All the editors and critics, according to writers, are failed writers. They are also arts majors, for the most part, with wonderful grades. The writers revolted early. This is no criticism of modern education or educators; it is a small signpost pointing toward the source of low tone.

Education is also done in the home. The level of that education is the level of the home. The goal of most parents is obedience. Obedience is apathy. Most "bad" children become good the moment you let them up the Tone Scale.

The general society today may be commented upon by a review of the front pages of the newspapers. The "public" buys the news it wants. The newspapers, being an expanded version today of the old house-to-house advertising handout, print news to sell papers. The tone range of the usual front page today is from 1.5 down to 0.1. A man could invent something that would feed all the starving people in the world with ease and get a news notice one inch high near the obituary column. The blood-soaked and sordid front pages of the world's newspapers tell you that Man has sunk pretty far down. His newspaper is the modern American's Roman Circus, his government is becoming his "corn." Bluntly, the normal is a very sick man.

There are three valid therapies: The first is processing. The second is education. The third is environment. We find the first two in this new science. The third must sometimes be changed, for a preclear may be in such a vigorously painful environment that his gains in processing are lost in his struggle against his surroundings. Very fast processing is one answer to the environmental problem. Wives have been known to practically murder husbands who dared try to get up out of apathy via processing.

Apathy is a very docile and obedient, if sick, state of not-beingness. Husbands have been known to react similarly when their wives tried to get well. And, in the past, some mental practitioners have gone raving insane when one of their patients started to climb into well-being via processing.

The chief difference between the severely aberrated, the neurotic and the acceptable bands is concerned with TIME.

The severely aberrated gives his attention mainly to the past. The neurotic is giving his attention mainly to the immediate present. The acceptable is giving his attention to the future.

By forcing attention into the present (raising necessity level) one can raise a severely aberrated person into a neurotic level. The AAs (Alcoholics Anonymous) do this with alcoholics, persuading them to live for the present only. Your alcoholic, of course, is still trying to untangle the past with a forgetter known as alcohol, just as your drug addict is shutting off the agony of yesterday with an anesthetic.

However, almost anyone is giving more attention than necessary to the past, reserves his living in the present and restrains his planning for the future. Your 1.5, for instance, considers it bad taste to be enthusiastic about the future: "Don't hope too much." For the 0.5, both present and future are unthinkables.

ATTENTION is a remarkable thing in that it must be at optimum sweep for a person to be happy. When attention is too fixed on one thing, if that thing is a survival threat, it tends to remain fixed. If a threat to survival is understood to be present and yet cannot be located, attention swings endlessly without fixing. This is "fear of the unknown." Fixed and unfixed attention, when given to dangerous problems, tend to remain that way unless the problem is solved.

THE HUMAN MIND'S BASIC PURPOSE IN OPERATION IS THE POSING AND RESOLVING OF PROBLEMS IT OBSERVES AS RELATED TO SURVIVAL ALONG ANY OF THE DYNAMICS.

A problem is resolved when it is answered "Yes" or "No." A problem such as "Should I go?" must be answered "Yes" or "No" if the mind is to file it as a conclusion. If it continues as "Maybe," the problem stays in the computer and influences the next solutions. Did you ever know a person who had a lot of trouble reaching decisions? Recall a specific time? Well, somewhere in that person's past was a problem which was not answered "Yes" or "No," but only "Maybe." A very "serious" sort of a problem comes up with "Was it my fault?" When that one lands on "Maybe," the computer tends to jam. (The answer, by the way, is that nothing is anybody's fault.)

Problems do not solve for two reasons: The first is lack of data. The second is an earlier unsolved problem on the same subject.

One has to evaluate data in order to resolve problems. When one fixes his attention on something dangerous, he is probably overevaluating the data. When one is unable to fix his attention, it is because he cannot find data to evaluate.

This will become clearer to you when you have completed the following exercise. Do it with your pencil.

LIST FIVE PROBLEMS WITH PEOPLE OR OBJECTS OR CIRCUMSTANCES WHICH YOU ARE NOT SOLVING IN THE PRESENT.

1.

2.

3.

4.

5.

NOW LIST WHAT YOU WISH YOU KNEW ABOUT EACH ONE OF THE PROBLEMS ABOVE. (THE MISSING DATA YOU WISH YOU HAD.)

1.

2.

3.

4.

5.

NOW LIST HOW IMPORTANT YOU NOW FEEL THESE PROBLEMS ACTUALLY ARE OR WHETHER OR NOT THEY ARE NOW SOLVED.

1.

2.

3.

4.

5.

IF ANY OF THE FIVE PROBLEMS REMAIN UNSOLVED, LIST WHAT YOU WOULD HAVE TO DO TO SOLVE THEM.

1.

2.

3.

4.

5.

Now let us take a glance at the past. There are several problems, undoubtedly, which you feel you did not solve.

LIST FIVE PROBLEMS WITH PEOPLE OR OBJECTS OR CIRCUMSTANCES WHICH YOU FEEL YOU DID NOT SOLVE IN THE PAST.

1.

2.

3.

4.

5.

NOW LIST WHAT YOU WISH YOU HAD KNOWN ABOUT EACH ONE OF THE PROBLEMS ABOVE.

1.

2.

3.

4.

5.

NOW LIST HOW IMPORTANT THESE PROBLEMS ACTUALLY ARE TO YOUR PRESENT CIRCUMSTANCES.

1.

2.

3.

4.

5.

IF ANY OF THE ABOVE PROBLEMS STILL BOTHER YOU, WHAT WOULD YOU HAVE TO DO OR KNOW IN ORDER TO RESOLVE THEM?

1.

2.

3.

4.

5.

Let us now take a look at the problems of the future.

LIST FIVE PROBLEMS WITH PEOPLE OR OBJECTS OR CIRCUMSTANCES
WHICH YOU THINK YOU WILL HAVE TO SOLVE IN THE FUTURE.

1.

2.

3.

4.

5.

NOW LIST WHAT YOU WILL HAVE TO DO NOW TO SOLVE THESE
PROBLEMS IN THE FUTURE.

1.

2.

3.

4.

5.

NOW LIST HOW VITAL THESE PROBLEMS MAY BECOME TO YOUR EXISTENCE.

1.

2.

3.

4.

5.

IF ANY OF THE ABOVE PROBLEMS WORRY YOU, IT IS BECAUSE YOU HAVE NOT DECIDED UPON YOUR COURSE OF ACTION. TRY TO LIST YOUR COURSE AS IT WILL PROBABLY BE TAKEN.

1.

2.

3.

4.

5.

In this same Act, we should take up GOALS. Some poet once said that a man's dreams were important and that when the last of a man's dreams were dead, dead was the man. He didn't know about this new science.

Dreams, goals, ambitions—these are the stuff Man uses for fuel. SURVIVAL is nothing but the effort to accomplish action. There is the broad goal of "all survival." There is the small goal of "a good action." Survival, action and goals are inseparable.

Happiness could be defined as the emotion of progress toward desirable goals. There is an instant of contemplation of the last goal in which one is content. But contentment becomes boredom immediately that new goals do not come to view. There is no more unhappy thing than a man who has accomplished all his ends in life. Gibbon, for instance, died immediately after finishing his great work. It is doubtful if men die when they have great goals ahead of them, save perhaps in the violent action of some attempted attainments. It is doubtful if it would take more than a flick with a feather to kill somebody who has no goals. The Filipino irregular of 1901, battling for an independent state, would charge seventy-five yards and kill his man *after* that man had put a Krag-Jørgensen bullet through the heart of the Filipino. A neurotic without goals catches a harmless bug, sneezes and dies. Or sneezes and dies without a bug getting near him.

People always begin with goals. They often fail. When they have failed often enough, they stop thinking about the future and start worrying over the present. When the present hands them a few failures, they start worrying about the past. They go "out of present time." If you were simply to walk through an insane asylum and tell each inmate, "Come up to present time," a small percentage would immediately become sane and stay sane. The order would unfix their attention from a past "maybe" or fix their attention on the present. It has been tried and has succeeded.

More happily, let's examine your goals and fears.

IN THIS COLUMN LIST FIVE GOALS YOU HAD IN THE PAST.	IN THIS COLUMN LIST FIVE FEARS YOU HAD IN THE PAST.
1.	1.
2.	2.
3.	3.
4.	4.
5.	5.

IN THIS COLUMN LIST WHAT HAPPENED TO THE FIVE GOALS IN THE PAST.	IN THIS COLUMN LIST WHAT HAPPENED TO THE FIVE FEARS IN THE PAST.
1.	1.
2.	2.
3.	3.
4.	4.
5.	5.

IN THIS COLUMN
LIST FIVE GOALS
WHICH SHOULD HAVE
BEEN ACCOMPLISHED IN
YOUR PRESENT, NOW.

1.

2.

3.

4.

5.

IN THIS COLUMN
LIST FIVE FEARS
WHICH YOU HAVE
IN YOUR PRESENT.

1.

2.

3.

4.

5.

IN THIS COLUMN LIST
FIVE GOALS WHICH YOU
WOULD LIKE TO SET INTO THE
FUTURE.

1.

2.

3.

4.

5.

IN THIS COLUMN LIST FIVE
FEARS WHICH YOU MIGHT
EXPECT TO ENCOUNTER IN
THE FUTURE.

1.

2.

3.

4.

5.

NOW GO BACK OVER YOUR LISTS AND FOR EACH ITEM IN THE GOALS COLUMNS, SEE IF YOU CAN FIND SOME PERSON IN YOUR PAST OR PRESENT WHO MIGHT HAVE THESE GOALS OR WHO MIGHT HAVE HAD THEM—SOME PERSON OTHER THAN YOURSELF.

NOW GO DOWN THE PAST AND PRESENT AND FUTURE FEARS COLUMN AND SEE IF YOU CAN FIND SOME PERSON IN YOUR PAST WHO MIGHT HAVE HAD THESE FEARS, OTHER THAN YOURSELF.

When you have noted down these people or one person, answer the following:

IS THAT PERSON DEAD? ARE THOSE PEOPLE DEAD? DID THEY FAIL?

You should be able to sort out your own goals from "dead men's goals." And you should be able to sort out your own fears from "dead men's fears."

It's a very peculiar thing that you may be seeking a life continuation and life realization from people no longer amongst us in that precise identity.

Out of nobility and grief, so does one take on the burdens of those who have laid down their burdens. This includes pets.

THERE MAY BE ONE DEAD PERSON OR HALF A DOZEN. ONE DEAD PET OR TWO OR THREE. LIST BRIEFLY THE GOALS OF EACH DEAD PERSON YOU HAVE LOVED. THEN BRIEFLY LIST THE GOALS OF EACH PET.

YOU MAY HAVE WEPT DOING THIS. IF SO, COME UP TO PRESENT TIME. NOW RECALL THE LAST GOOD TIME YOU HAD IN THE FULLEST DETAIL. BE VERY PRECISE IN TRYING TO RE-EXPERIENCE THIS GOOD TIME.

Better?

Let's see now if you can recall the following for each person and pet you may have listed.

1. ANY MOMENT YOU DECIDED YOU HAD AFFECTION FOR THEM. THE PRECISE MOMENT YOU FIRST DECIDED YOU HAD AFFECTION FOR THEM.

2. ANY MOMENT YOU DECIDED YOU WERE LIKE THEM. THE FIRST MOMENT YOU DECIDED YOU WERE LIKE THEM.

3. ANY TIME YOU REGRETTED SOMETHING YOU HAD DONE TO THEM. THE FIRST TIME YOU REGRETTED SOMETHING YOU HAD DONE TO THEM.

4. ANY TIME YOU FELT SYMPATHY FOR THEM. THE FIRST TIME YOU FELT SYMPATHY FOR THEM.

DO THIS FOR EACH PERSON YOU LISTED, EACH PET YOU LISTED.

Now go over the same process again, even if you hit the same incidents.

Go over the same process a third time for each person and pet.

Go over the process a fourth time for each person and pet.

Go over the process a fifth time for each person and pet.

Go over the process a sixth time for each person and pet.

Go over the process a seventh time for each person and pet.

Now take a sweep through all the work you have been doing in this Act. Do that again. Call it concluded.

the
Fifth
act

ᕐᑕᕼᕮ ᖴᓯᖴᕼ ᗩᑕᕼ
ᑌᓍᑌᖇ ᑭᕼᒍᔑᔑᑕᗩᒪ ᗩᓍᒪᗰᕮᑎᕼᔑ

(If you have found that this processing is a trifle strenuous for you up to this point, it is advised that you give yourself some Validation Mᴇsᴛ Processing. This is contained in another volume.* But if you are only mildly in a state of collapse, continue. It gets easier from here on.)

S O FAR we have been dealing mainly with the processes of thought.

It is time we took up PHYSICAL FUNCTION and MALFUNCTION.

Once upon a time this was a rather serious subject. Two hundred years ago a medical doctor had to be able to sort the bones of the human body by touch only, blindfolded. Less ancient than that, the most fascinating theories existed concerning physical function. A doctor let out a pint or a quart of blood and that "cured" everything, even life. Recently, endocrinologists had to study for years to discover an occasionally effective method of handling glands. But in all this time, no effective method of treating physical function existed. A rare remission of symptoms kept medicine at work and eating. Surgery began to be resorted to in a vigorous but unsuccessful revenge for being unable to resolve physical ills.

*See the book *Self Analysis*.

The main reason this new science had such a dreadful time proceeding into the medical realm with its effectiveness was a tradition, built out of thousands of years of experience, that exactly nothing could be done for the human body except perhaps taking foreign matter out of it and sewing it up when it was gashed and strapping a bone when it was broken. The resilience of the body itself was responsible for the recoveries. "Magic drugs," such as penicillin, depend upon the ability of the body, not the drug.

With this much background failure, the world has been in apathy about the body. It was born, it grew, it died. Surgery and drugs could stem the tide of time a brief moment. But that was all. This dramatic struggle for knowledge of the human body was a struggle against time. Time's scythe in the hands of that grim gentleman, Death, won every contest.

Now and then a mystic would rise in the world and, with a few passes of the hand, cause the crippled, the sightless, the faltering to bloom with life once more. Then the mystic, the adept, the master would vanish and Man would struggle on with attention to their relics, but without many repetitions of the miracles.

That faith or thought could do such astonishing things in the hands of a master or adept brought men like Freud into heavy ambition to resolve the human body's ills by resolving the ills of the mind. The medical profession of his day ostracized Freud. Today, psychoanalysis and psychologists speak with contempt of Freud—perhaps they owe him too much. But Freud is the grand old man of psychosomatic healing. He popularized the idea that something could be done about human unhappiness via treatment of the mind and that human ills might be handled by handling the "ego," the "id" and other mental entities Freud thought he had discovered. Freud had many pupils—Jung, Adler and others—who decided only they themselves could "see the light" and so went sailing off into further and further incredibles.

Of all these, it now seems evident that Freud himself was the only one of them who had even started toward the straight and narrow road to complete physical rehabilitation of the body via the human mind.

In my boyhood, I studied Freud second-hand. His brilliant student, the late Commander Thompson of the US Navy, had just left Freud and Vienna when he saw fit to dazzle a young mind with the idea that perhaps the riddle of thought could be resolved. Studying Freud tenth-hand, through his books and what people thought people had said about what Freud said, the psychoanalysis and psychiatric world had broken cleanly with Freud years before I even came to a university. There was no studying Freud in any college. They did not teach Freud. He had been abandoned by the professional cliques.

In the meanwhile, a new subject had risen in the world. Nuclear physics they call it now, "atomic and molecular phenomena" they called it then. No atoms had been split effectively but, from Newton to Halley to Einstein, men had been studying the physical universe and had now encoded the subjects of matter, energy, space and time. Here was a new field of knowledge. It was so new that those of us who studied in it were known as the "Buck Rogers boys" (after a comic strip character of the day who sailed off to Mars or Venus and had incredible adventures). We experimented with rockets and the Doppler effect and later found employment difficult to achieve except as orthodox engineers. Although it was my father's ambition that I become one of these orthodox engineers, bless him, I found that with all this new knowledge, transits were dull. In order to pursue studies in this field, I had to write for any magazine that would buy. Many of us, in the decade of the thirties, were Buck Rogers boys in earnest, writing "science fiction" for a growing audience of fans. Then came Hiroshima and Buck Rogers boys started to have such importance to the governments of the world that they were almost prisoners.

Having escaped offered employment by Russia and the United States, I continued my work in the field where I had started—the human mind—from the viewpoint of mathematics and nuclear physics. As late as 1950, I was still acting fast to keep out of US Government research laboratories.

Culmination of research in this new science—what is popularly known as Dianetics and more correctly known as Scientology—had yet to occur. But in 1948 a thesis was written and submitted to the medical professions which demonstrated the workability of alleviating physical ills by an address to mental problems. Much as in the case of the grand old man of mental technology, Freud, the medical profession at first went all out in ignoring the work and then flew into print to blast it. But the new science had taken root. Tens of thousands of people were working in it. Millions knew about it.

Based on the background of thousands of years of mystic accumulation concerning the mind, Freud's effort to apply his knowledge to the medical concepts of the human body had not resulted in very startling results. But this same background knowledge filtered through what was now known about the physical universe, as in nuclear physics, did produce a uniformity of result comparable to engineering.

The occasional and spectacular effects of the masters in performing miracles could be repeated at will. For where there is occasional effect, according to engineering theory, natural laws exist which can make the occasionalness into predictable results.

New principles in mathematics had to be discovered to make it possible for one to address the mind and rid the body of physical ills. One such principle is that zero and infinity are equal. The qualities of a true static had to be delineated for the first time. Mathematics itself had to be defined. The quality and character of time had to be examined and the definitions improved.

All this has taken me about twenty years.

The current ability of the result makes it possible for mental aberration and psychosomatic ills to be treated with greater invariability in each passing year. It is doubtful at this time if cases exist—which yet retain sufficient life and physical completeness to be gotten into communication by an auditor—which will not resolve by the processes of this new science.

One of the most respected commentators on world affairs has paid me the compliment of saying that these developments would probably be regarded in the future as the most significant progress of this century. Another has said that they rank with the three most important discoveries of Man. However this may be, a good auditor can now do miracles with the workmanlike precision of an engineer building bridges. There are scores of people alive today who would not be alive except for this new science. There are children and old people who would not be walking except for this new science. Polio ravages, arthritis and scores of other ills are handled daily by this new science with success.

If the grand old man, Freud, were alive today, he would probably be cracking his heels in glee. He was amongst the first who supposed that it could be done with complete precision.

I have given you this short history so that you will have a background on what may happen to you.

You are not the first. You are about a hundred thousand cases from the first. For although it made its public debut less than two years ago, more people are in process in this new science than are being worked by psychology, psychoanalysis and psychiatry combined. It even works on me. It cost me my retirement from the Navy, as a disabled officer of World War II, because I was no longer disabled after processing.

Further responsibility is mine in the unthinking attitude toward this new science, for I did not properly estimate, a couple of years back, the ability of the average auditor. Thus I oversold the subject in my first book, for I based it only on my own ability to handle the techniques. It required a year and a half to refine these techniques to a point where the average auditor could handle them. This present volume, by the way, is a guarantee that he does.

Your body has a dual composition which is yet a unity. You, without Life animation, are only so much physical universe—atoms, molecules in space and time, complex compounds and so forth. That part of you is MEST. The other part of you is what we call the LIFE STATIC—the thought, soul, vital part of you which animates this MEST, the body. Disconnect the static and you are no longer an animated organism. Funeral processions are given these bits of MEST which are no longer animated by the static. This MEST portion of you is a carbon-oxygen motor. It ceases to be a motor when it can no longer function as a motor, when it is damaged or decayed. When this happens, the animating force, the static, could be said to withdraw support. Then the body becomes so much physical universe—97 cents worth, by old-time chemical costs.

You, as a personal identity, are the composite of all your experience *plus* an initial decision TO BE and occasional decisions NOT TO BE. YOU do not die as an identity or a personality or an individual. YOU and the MEST body "separate" and the MEST body gets a funeral. YOU then link into the protoplasm line with your genetic blueprint (the plans of construction of a new body) in the orthodox manner of conception, birth and growth. You depend upon some inherent abilities of protoplasm. But you, as experience and identity, monitor that protoplasm's ability and modify it. There is a family line, then, from generation to generation, modified by YOU as experience. YOU are not necessarily part of that family line.

Every child, for instance, distrusts his identity as a family member. And there are numerous cases of record wherein a child, up to the age of three or five, recalled entirely who he had been—but forgot it under the pummeling of his "imagination" by adults.

Perhaps you take off after some lifetime and go to heaven. Nobody can argue successfully about that.

But YOU are the source of yourself with regard to various generations. Now this, by Effort Processing, becomes so irrefutable, so clear and unmistakable, that if it can be disproven, then the laws of heat and fission can be disproven as well. We are on solid ground about immortality and all the rest of it for the first time in history.

YOU are evidently quite eternal as a personal identity. You get snarled up in the modern social aberrations about only living once and play the game as though you would never get another chance—which you will get as certainly as the sun will rise tomorrow.

Now if you can handle a body in construction, you can certainly modify one in growth and form. And so you do. You can modify it to the degree of going blind or getting arthritis and being bedridden or having migraines or putting any other imperfection on yourself. You, as CAUSE, are continually shouldering the ills of the world and modifying yourself accordingly.

Once having taken on such an ill to "help" another, you may be very reluctant to give up the infirmity. Evidently it doesn't help the other very much. But you, with your social aberration that a person lives only once and never again, take the illness or demise of another very seriously. Much too seriously. And so there you are with somebody's arthritis. Of course, it isn't his. It's an old injury of your own—your own facsimile—which you are holding in place for him. People will give up any illness or infirmity which is theirs—their very own—with immediate ease and no qualms.

But they are quite tenacious of the ills they have shouldered for others. This caused old workers in the field of the mind to suppose that people simply refused to get well. No, people simply refuse to give up the illness of others, for whom they have made themselves responsible, until they clearly see that holding the illness will not bring back or restore the health of that other.

It's a wonderful world. Man has condemned Man for selfishness for eons and here we find Man only gets lastingly crippled or lame to "help" another.

Once it was said that if people knew the world was going to end tomorrow, the communication lines of the world would be jammed with calls from people seeking to say they loved one another. It is probably quite true.

In the field of illness, however, once one realizes how little it helps, one can give up another's aches and pains and resume his own health. It is quite a decision, but one which processing itself assists. You may find that you will be trying to make that decision.

The other day, a totally blind man under processing stopped the session on the abrupt realization that he would see wholly and clearly for the first time in years. Just an instant before his sight turned on, he balked. Why? His trouble with sight had to do with the death of his brother. His brother had been injured and was blinded in an automobile accident. The moment the brother died, this preclear had taken on the burdens of his brother. And he held to them to the degree of total blindness for years. The auditor had processed the case a little too swiftly. All the emotion of love for his brother was still on the case. Although it obviously would not help the brother—who is probably somebody else now, some happy kid in school—this blind man yet carried that blindness. He is now, at this writing, struggling with his conscience about regaining his sight.

He will decide in favor of it. They always do, eventually. And it will not hurt or assist the MEST body of his brother, buried these many years. But the action of this blind man, snatching at his brother's life, trying to get his brother to live when death itself was graying the flesh, remains today as a facsimile containing such a powerful impulse—an impulse great enough to deny sight—that the blind man has to consult long with it before he will give it up.

Your most serious troubles, then, from a physical standpoint, apparently stem from moments when you tried to help and failed. What was done wholly to you, you will be able to bear and discard without hesitation. You might have to consult with yourself a little while to decide to give up your effort to shoulder the burdens of the world. You will give them up, but you'll think about it.

First you had to agree to be so disabled, mentally or physically. Then you had to shoulder another's travail to really get yourself into a second-hand condition. Apparently the very insane, themselves, to say nothing of the neurotic, are the very noble characters. They'll stand up to electric shock, prefrontal lobotomies, psychiatry and any brand of torture before they will surrender the facsimiles they are holding for others—and even then they don't give them up! Processed by this new science, the ties which bound them into this self-sacrificing difficulty surrender rather easily.

In view of the fact that you have a lot of margin, physically and mentally, we should be able to do the job rather quickly and easily. And you can go out with a clean slate and shoulder some more burdens, which you will. But you'll be in much better condition to do it even if you are what passes for "normal" now.

Thus, let us take an assay of the MEST you are using just now for a body.

First, answer this question honestly: Would you like to be in better physical condition than at present?

If the answer is "no," you are still trying to help. Even if the answer is "yes," you are still trying to help, but you probably don't realize it.

People usually fail when they try to help. Check over the number of people you have tried to assist in your lifetime. What is the level of gratitude on a long-term basis?

The times you aided somebody successfully, aided you. But when you tried to help and failed, the repercussion was bad on you. Thus we want the moments you tried to help and failed. The most flagrant of these, of course, is the case of people who died. You tried to bring them back to life. They died and you supposed you had failed. And later on you failed some more and then you found yourself with an imperfect physique and calmness a stranger to you.

A little child will try to keep a pet from dying or a grandfather from dying and "blame" himself ever after with the psychosomatic illness of that death.

Who have you tried to help? They're elsewhere now and doing fine. You didn't fail. So let's get you straightened out.

You've made an effort along every single dynamic and every part of every dynamic, including your own body and its parts. And you may have been very successful a lot of the time. The failures are what kicked back at you. Well, you can have a clean slate and go out and fight again and be successful again. More people need help than those you have helped. We can have a pretty fine world here if we clean up the slate of yesterday and use that slate to write all over tomorrow. We're in a rut of yesterday when all around us is the suffering of others in today and tomorrow. So let's go.

Let's make a summary of your present body.

LIST TEN THINGS WHICH YOU WOULD LIKE TO HAVE HAPPEN TO YOUR PRESENT BODY: TEN SPECIFIC CONDITIONS OF PHYSICAL BEING WHICH YOU WISH YOU COULD ATTAIN IN THE TOMORROWS, SUCH AS PHYSICAL BEAUTY OR STRENGTH, WHETHER YOU THINK YOU CAN ATTAIN THEM OR NOT. GET AS WILD AS YOU LIKE.

1.

2.

3.

4.

5.

6.

7.

8.

9.

10.

NOW LET'S BE CRITICAL. LIST FIVE THINGS WHICH YOU THINK MAY BE WRONG WITH YOUR PRESENT PHYSICAL BEING. LIST THEM WITH THE THOUGHT THAT THEY MIGHT BE REMEDIED. SUCH THINGS AS FREQUENT COLDS, ETC.

1.

2.

3.

4.

5.

NOW LIST THE PERSONS OR PETS WHO HAVE FAILED OR ARE DEAD WHO HAD THINGS WRONG WITH THEM. THERE MAY BE MORE THAN ONE WITH EACH. TAKE THE FIRST ERROR YOU LISTED ABOVE AS NUMBER ONE AND WRITE THE NAME OF THE PERSON WHO MIGHT HAVE HAD THAT ILL AFTER NUMBER ONE BELOW, AND SO ON. YOU MAY NOT BE ABLE TO ACCOUNT FOR SOME OF THE CONDITIONS. THAT IS ALL RIGHT.

1.

2.

3.

4.

5.

Now take the illnesses you have attributed to others and, by just memory, try to find a time when that person who had the illness before you demonstrated it or said he had it.

Recall when illness number one was seen or heard by you to be the possession of person number one or the persons you listed under number one.

Take the second ill or malfunction. Recall when person number two was seen to have it or was heard by you to have it.

Continue this process.

Now go all through the list again and recall all the incidents again and see if you can find new moments on the same subject.

NOW RECALL WHEN YOU FIRST DECIDED YOU LIKED PERSON NUMBER ONE. GO ON THROUGH THE LIST, RECALLING DECISIONS TO LIKE OR BE LIKE THE PEOPLE YOU LISTED.

RECALL NOW A TIME WHEN YOU WANTED TO BE LIKE EACH PERSON YOU LISTED.

NOW RECALL TIMES WHEN YOU DECIDED TO HELP THE PEOPLE YOU LISTED.

RECALL MANY INCIDENTS WHERE YOU TRIED TO HELP THESE LISTED PEOPLE OR PETS.

RECALL TIMES NOW WHEN YOU REALIZED YOU HAD FAILED TO HELP THESE PEOPLE. FOR IN THIS LAST EXTREMITY, YOU MIGHT HAVE TAKEN ON THEIR ILLS FOR THEM.

RECALL ANY TIME WHEN YOU FELT YOU WERE POWERLESS TO HELP ANYONE. WHY DID YOU ARRIVE AT SUCH A DECISION? WHAT WERE THE CIRCUMSTANCES OF IT?

GO OVER THE ENTIRE LIST ABOVE STEP BY STEP AGAIN, BUT NOW TRY TO GET AN ACTUAL SIGHT OR SOUND OF THE MOMENT YOU ARE RECALLING.

WITH THIS COMPLETED, RECALL DOING THIS PARTICULAR ACT IN DETAIL TWO OR THREE TIMES.

Do not count on your illnesses being gone with this Act. They might have vanished and, if so, they will stay that way. But if they are, any of them, still with you, there are many more Acts in this book.

The
Sixth
Act

The Sixth Act

THE SUBJECTS of EFFORT and COUNTER-EFFORT, EMOTION and COUNTER-EMOTION are very new in the knowledge of Man.

In continuous investigation of mental and physical phenomena, I chanced upon these manifestations and put them to work immediately. Such was their reach and significance that auditors from coast to coast, within sixty days, were "cracking cases" which they had found hitherto "uncrackable." Thus you can see that it is well to know something about them.

Let us take EFFORT. Your mind is continuously at work estimating efforts. When you go to open a door, your mind estimates the effort necessary to turn the knob and, via emotion, puts that effort into action. It estimates the effort necessary to pull the door back and puts that into action. If the door handle turned as desired and the door opened as desired, your estimation of effort was correct.

Your mind calculates efforts for the present and for the future. It puts efforts into action now or in the future. Or it simply estimates them and holds them back and never applies them. Your mind estimates the efforts of the environment—how fast cars go, how hard teacups have to fall to break. And it even estimates efforts when it "daydreams"—which is to say that it thinks of the efforts involved in that and, without even desiring to, puts them into action. Thinking of a goal is putting something into the future to which one can build by effort. An attained goal is a summation of efforts.

If you calculated the door properly, you opened it smoothly. If you calculated wrong and the door stuck, you were wrong. Did you ever have a door or a drawer stick on you consistently? After a while you became angry with it. Then you began to avoid it. For the mind which survives well, estimates efforts well. It is *right*—which is to say, it estimates efforts rightly.

The author writing a story estimates many, many efforts. If he is right, it is an interesting story and sells. If he is wrong, it is not an interesting story and it doesn't sell.

The mind, all through evolution, was subjected to COUNTER-EFFORTS on the part of the environment. The wind, sea, sun and other organisms all had efforts to throw at the organism. The organism that handled these counter-efforts well, survived well. It came to use these very counter-efforts as its own efforts. The evolution of efforts is from counter-effort to employed effort.

Effort means force and direction. Your life is a contest between your own efforts and environmental efforts.

Any psychosomatic illness you have is some counter-effort, some past effort of the environment you aren't handling or using right. The facsimile of the effort itself is in the facsimile. Facsimiles are recordings of effort. Perception is the recording of physical universe efforts and your thoughts, conclusions and efforts about them as well as your emotion.

Effort Processing is easily done. One finds where the facsimile of an effort is against the preclear and gets the preclear's effort against it. A pain or pressure turns on and, by constant re-experiencing, turns off. But Effort Processing is something which should be done by an auditor and although it can be done by a preclear on himself, must be thoroughly understood by that preclear. There is not enough data in this volume to permit a preclear to Effort Process himself.

To do that, he would have to study the main body of this science, preferably at the Foundation Auditor's School* or at least through the basic texts.

EMOTION and COUNTER-EMOTION are something else. The preclear should be able to handle these.

You know what your own emotion is—anger, fear, grief, apathy. You have experienced these things. They are part of facsimiles now. Grief is very important as a blocker in one's life. Grief takes place where one recognizes his loss and failure, as in the death of somebody he loved and tried to help.

A facsimile which contains chiefly emotion is called, in this science, a SECONDARY ENGRAM. This would be a unit of time (ten minutes, a day, a week) wherein one was under heavy stress of mis-emotion—anger, fear, grief.

The way one runs out such a secondary is simple. It is easier to have an auditor do it for you, because you are likely to bolt from it. If you start a secondary, you ought to finish it all the way.

No single act of processing is more beneficial to a case than running out a grief secondary.

If you have nerve enough, this is the way you can do it: You begin with the first moment of news of loss or failure and you run it through again and again, releasing its mis-emotion simply by re-experiencing it. You do this until long after you think it is gone.

You re-experience a facsimile by seeing it, hearing it, feeling everything in it including, especially, your own thoughts and conclusions. Just as though you were there again.

A death is done this way: You pick up the instant, the very first instant, you heard or knew anything bad about that event.

*See *Addresses* in the Appendix for current locations.

You "contact" who gave you the news or how you got it. You go through the whole thing, over and over and over, reliving every portion of it. You re-experience the mis-emotion. You finally get that facsimile to a point where it no longer has any "charge" in it. Then you run it until it is practically erased. You will find, as you run it, that more and more detail appears in it.

The danger of running it is that you may lose your nerve and leave it half finished. Don't. Take yourself in hand and run it until it is fully knocked out, so that you could even laugh about it. Don't fake it. Do it.

YOU CAN BEST GET STARTED ON ONE BY RECALLING AND RE-FEELING EARLIER TIMES WHEN YOU LOVED THE PERSON OR ANIMAL OR POSSESSION AND DWELL ON THIS EMOTION UNTIL THE LOSS OR DEATH FACSIMILE TURNS UP. IF THE FACSIMILE ELUDES YOU, THEN GET MORE TIMES WHEN YOU LOVED OR FELT SYMPATHY FOR THE PERSON, ANIMAL OR OBJECT. IF IT STILL ELUDES YOU, JUST RECALL THE MEAN THINGS YOU DID TO IT, YOUR NEGLECT FOR IT AND THE THOUGHT THAT IF YOU HAD BEEN BETTER AND HADN'T BEEN SO MEAN, IT WOULD BE WELL NOW. THINK OF THE WAY YOU TRIED TO HELP THE PERSON, ANIMAL OR THING. THINK OF HOW YOU FAILED. THINK OF YOUR LOVE. AND RUN THE FACSIMILE.

Better be in a quiet place where you won't be interrupted when you do this.

You may be an emotional wreck for days. But you'll come out of it when you've run it all and your level of recovery will be, even to you, fantastic. Your very physical appearance can change for the better on the running of such secondaries.

IF YOU FIND THE WHOLE PERIOD IS BLANK AND BLACK, RECALL THE TIMES WHEN YOU PROMISED YOURSELF YOU WOULD NOT GRIEVE ABOUT IT ANYMORE, OR THE TIMES WHEN YOU WOULD NOT GIVE IT UP.

THEN RUN THE TIMES YOU BLAMED YOURSELF OR OTHERS FOR
THE INCIDENT. AND RECALL THE TIMES YOU REGRETTED THINGS
ABOUT IT.

A man, almost dying, ran two secondaries by himself, with
this technique, and recovered. A woman, who had been branded
psychotic, ran a number of secondaries on herself, knowing this
technique, and became a lot saner than her family. A woman,
whose husband had been dead for ten days, had assumed the
character of an old woman and her entire glandular system
was interrupted. She ran out the secondary of his death in nine
exhausting hours and twenty-four hours later, although she
had built her whole life around this man, looked young and was
happy again. It not only can be done, but it is being done. Simply
crying about the matter in present time—without re-experiencing
it—serves no purpose. The grief has to come by re-experiencing
every moment of the secondary facsimile itself. It's rough, but it
can be done!

A secondary may be a little more difficult, because to fear is to
flee. So when you get the facsimile around you to run it, part of it
says to flee and you may obey it. The way to get around this is to
run the times when people wouldn't let you get away when you
wanted to run.

You can not only bring a secondary or any facsimile up around
you, you can also put them aside, throw them back into time.
Halfway through running one, this may seem difficult. The thing
to do is to "flatten" it. Then you can throw it away with ease. They
are flattened simply by re-experiencing them and getting your
old conclusions out of them.

A word of caution: Don't try to run yourself around somebody
who may be even faintly critical. And don't argue with
somebody about it. The wife, mother, father, the husband may
get into a terrible dither about your effort to feel stronger.

They may even have an interest in keeping you down so they can "take better care of you." Run one of these secondaries around such a person and you'll really fix yourself up.

And by the way, be very suspicious of somebody who doesn't think you ought to indulge in this new science. Auditors are always running into situations where they have a son or a daughter in good condition and well on the road to recovery when the parents step in and, with every argument in the book, with every "good intention," knock the poor preclear into limbo again. Such people want the preclear under control and instinctively realize that the preclear is getting very independent. The preclear who argues back simply gets himself snarled up again. Best to be calm and do your work in private. Then, when you are nine feet tall, do your arguing.

And don't plead with a wife or a husband or a friend to study this new science against his or her will and use it on you. They will manage, one way or another, to turn the processes around and wreck you. You may have an impulse to use your facsimiles to get sympathy from such a person. It is quicker and easier just to blow out your brains. The result will be the same. For when you force somebody to "help you" and "be sympathetic," who has an interest in keeping you sick, they will manage to make you sick in earnest. Out of their "good knowledge and intentions," of course. There is, for instance, a very sick woman who could be straightened out by an auditor in about fifteen hours. Yet her husband, hovering like a mother hen, is violent about letting her be helped. He knows nothing of this new science except that it is successful. She has had three unsuccessful operations for her condition. He is seeing to it that she is going to get a fourth, which will probably kill her. These are desires to help—out of a frame of reference which doesn't work. "Keep him calm," "Operate on him," "Control him," "Mama knows best" are the sources of the attitude.

Further, you have always had and use what is known as a SERVICE FACSIMILE.

Every time you fail, you pick up this facsimile and become sick or sadly noble. It's your explanation to yourself and the world as to how and why you failed. It once got you sympathy. Sympathy will turn it on again. It may contain the basic condition of being which is now passing for a common cold or sinusitis or a game leg. You fail at something, then you use the facsimile and you get sympathy from somebody. Well, heaven help you if you are around somebody who doesn't get the line signals. You use the facsimile and then they don't sympathize. You use the facsimile harder. And they are still stone cold. Then you really turn it on. Maybe it was measles that founded this facsimile. Maybe it was when you broke your leg. Well, you'll use it to a point where you'll get all the symptoms again if you don't get sympathy for it. You have two choices: Run out this service facsimile and the reasons for its use, as per the remainder of these Acts, or get yourself a new associate or partner. For that service facsimile will get you by and by. You didn't believe it yourself the first time you decided to use it. Then the use of it became automatic. And now you "wonder what caused it." You did.

We remark on the service facsimile at this place not to have it run in this Act, but to acquaint you with its existence. For you may hit it in running a secondary and be very loath to part with it. It is simply a time when you tried to do something and were hurt or failed and got sympathy for it. Then, afterwards, when you were hurt or failed and wanted an explanation, you used it. And if you didn't succeed in getting sympathy for it, you used it so hard it became a psychosomatic illness.

Let's take a summary of your body. Maybe we can discover what you are using for a SERVICE FACSIMILE. Everybody has one or more than one.

LIST ANYTHING WHICH GETS WRONG OR IS WRONG WITH THE FOLLOWING NAMED PORTION OF THE BODY, AS A REPEATED INFIRMITY OR PAIN OR MALFUNCTION.

THE HEAD:

THE EYES:

THE EARS:

THE NOSE:

THE NECK:

THE TEETH:

THE CHEST:

THE LUNGS:

THE HANDS:

THE SKIN:

THE ARMS:

THE SHOULDERS:

THE SPINE:

THE RECTUM:

THE GENITALS:

THE ABDOMEN:

THE LEGS:

THE FEET:

THE NAILS:

THE INTERNAL ORGANS:

Now do you recognize any one particular illness out of these symptoms. Measles? Whooping cough? Getting born? An accident?

WRITE WHAT YOU THINK IT MIGHT BE:

WHAT AGE DID THIS OCCUR?

WHO WAS PRESENT?

WHAT HAD YOU FAILED ABOUT?

WHAT FAILURES SINCE HAVE TURNED THESE ON?

WHO DOESN'T SYMPATHIZE WITH THEM?

WHO DID?

WHAT IS THE SIMILARITY BETWEEN THE PERSON WHO DID AND THE PERSON WHO DIDN'T OR DOESN'T?

WHAT ARE THE DIFFERENCES BETWEEN THE PERSON WHO DID SYMPATHIZE AND THE PERSONS WHO DIDN'T OR DON'T?

WHO DID YOU BLAME?

WHO DO YOU BLAME?

Having and using a service facsimile does not make you a hypochondriac. It simply makes you human.

The facsimile might release right here. If it doesn't, there's a lot of book left.

ONE WORD OF CAUTION ABOUT ALL THIS: PROCESS YOURSELF AT SPECIFIC TIMES, NOT ALL THE TIME. CHOOSE A PROCESSING TIME AND USE IT. THEN, WHEN IT IS OVER, WAIT UNTIL THE NEXT TIME. DON'T GO AROUND SELF-AUDITING.

In the pictures you get of old incidents, you may be seeing yourself "outside of yourself," not seeing the scene as you saw it then. This is being "out of valence." Simply move "in valence" to run the incident. Running it outside yourself won't do very much for you. But if you run it very many times, you'll be inside yourself in the scene.

Being outside oneself is the cause of "self-auditing." In an operation or somewhere, you slid out. When you self-audit, you may be in the role of somebody who hurt you (a counter-effort) and you'll just keep on hurting yourself. The section on counter-emotion, later, clears up this condition if it begins.

the
Seventh
act

The Seventh Act

AVE YOU BEEN a left-hander who is now a right-hander?

About 50 percent of the human race is natively southpaw, but have been "educated" to be right-handers.

As you know, the CONTROL CENTER of the left side of the mind-brain system runs the right side of the body. And the right side of the mind-brain system runs the left side of the body. This is a perfect governmental system. It ought to be employed in this atomic age. You take the government of Russia and put it in the United States and you take the government of the United States and put it in Russia. And then you'd have no war.

Thus the mind solved the difficulties of the double control center condition which began about the time Man's forebears—you, too—began to emerge from the sea, or shortly before.

One of these control centers is the "genetic" boss. It is stronger than the other control center. A natural right-hander is running on his left control center and it is natively the most powerful control center of the body. In such a case, the opposite control center is obedient to the chief control center and all is well, coordination is good and no confusions result.

Take a natural left-hander, however, who is running on his right control center and insist that he change to his right hand and you force him to become controlled by his sub-control center.

You invalidate his more powerful control center. This causes him to go down the Tone Scale and it causes poor physical coordination between left and right hands.

Did anyone in your family complain that this had happened to him or her? Do you recall that it happened to you?

It has been known for a long while that forcing a left-hander to be right-handed was bad, but none knew why and there was no remedy for it.

Further, a control center confronted with a major failure in life will abdicate, so to speak, and let the sub-control center take over. Then perhaps it fails markedly and the old failed center takes over. This switching centers can continue and repeat, each time with less power and security of control.

You see evidences of this in strokes and migraines where half the body gets ill. The control center, having failed often already, takes over again. It takes over suddenly. If it is already rather disorganized with past failures, its reign is marked with physical failures—particularly for that side of the body.

Thus, this Act is addressed not simply to left-handers who became right-handers by education, but to anyone. For the shifting of alternate centers can happen to anybody and usually does.

The way the old center is rehabilitated, or the way both centers are rehabilitated, is rather simple: One picks up the times of shift. These are marked by moments of major failure or the sudden recollection of a past situation, the recollection being strong enough to cause the shift. Center A is in control. Something in living suddenly recalls to Center B that it was once successful and a shift will occur. Or Center A will have a failure and Center B is left holding control. Or a charge is run off the case and an old center is relieved of its burden of failure and takes over.

In processing, you may run into these shifts. A shift may be followed by intense exhilaration. This, however, may fade out in a day or two. That doesn't mean that it will never come back. It means a temporary shift of centers took place.

The ideal condition is to relieve both centers.

The childhood is normally occluded in people before mis-emotion or physical pain incidents are discharged. This occurs by a shift of centers. The child starts out in good condition, but in childhood is handled so heroically that he fails on his native center. The other center then takes over. This shifting occludes the experience, to some degree, of the old center. Thus, early education, parents, pets may be occluded. As you pry them into view, you are actually rehabilitating an old center.

You should know this so that you will not be alarmed on several counts. The first is temporary "euphoria," where you stay happy for two or three days and then get sad again. That's a temporary shift, evidently. The second is physical unbalance which can occur as a temporary affair, where you get a toothache or a headache on one side and the other side seems numb. Another is a shift of interests.

You won't contract amnesia, but this shift of centers may be responsible for amnesia. A sudden shift of centers occludes present time experience and then may shift back. It doesn't happen in processing.

There is also a whole set of "pseudo-centers," the personalities of people whom you've tried to help and have failed. These are VALENCES. A person can have two or ten dozen of these valences, can be one personality to Joe and another to Agnes, can change at a certain period of life into an "entirely new person." This is simply a manifestation of the life continuation manifestation discussed earlier. All these are relieved by getting rid of mis-emotion.

The ideal state of affairs is the attainment of a SUPER-CENTER. Right and left centers are always sub-centers. A super-center is acquired on discharging all the sympathy and regret on a case or, in short, the mis-emotion.

Think this over carefully. The incidents are marked by sudden changes in physical health, old illnesses disappearing, new illnesses appearing. Falling in love may shift centers. A bump on the head may shift them. Any emotional shock might do it. In particular, incidents which diminish one's concept of his ability to handle his surroundings and people may shift centers. A sudden drop, because of an experience, of one's importance may shift centers. A death, a severe loss, a realization of one's unimportance may shift these centers.

Each incident listed should be run. If it is difficult to run as a facsimile, wait until later in the volume when you have learned how to "Lock Scan" yourself and then refer back to this list. If possible, use the technique for secondaries, as of the Sixth Act, to accomplish the purpose.

WRITE DOWN THE NUMBER OF TIMES, WITH APPROXIMATE DATES, WHEN YOU MIGHT HAVE SHIFTED CENTERS.

WRITE DOWN, BRIEFLY, THE SHOCK OR LOSS WHICH MIGHT HAVE OCCASIONED THESE SHIFTS.

The
Eighth
Act

the Eighth Act

DONE BY YOURSELF, without an auditor's assistance, you may find this processing rather heavy for you and again you may not, depending on how much Life endowment you have.

But here is a technique which is relatively simple. It does things for you quickly. This is LOCK SCANNING.

TAKE YOUR PENCIL AND DRAW A LINE, A VERTICAL LINE, ON THE SPACE TO THE RIGHT. MAKE THE LINE ABOUT FIVE INCHES HIGH.

NOW, AT THE BOTTOM OF THIS LINE, MARK IT CONCEPTION.

AN INCH ABOVE THE BOTTOM, DRAW A HORIZONTAL LINE AND MARK IT BIRTH.

AT THE TOP OF THE LINE, MARK IT PRESENT TIME.

NOW JUST ABOVE BIRTH, DRAW A VERY HEAVY HORIZONTAL BAR ABOUT AN INCH LONG.

AT INTERVALS OF EVERY QUARTER OR HALF AN INCH, IRREGULARLY, ABOVE THE HEAVY BAR, DRAW A LIGHT LINE HORIZONTALLY, HALF AN INCH LONG. THERE SHOULD BE A DOZEN OR TWO OF THESE LIGHT LINES.

NOW MARK THE HEAVY HORIZONTAL BAR PAINFUL INCIDENT.

NOW MARK THE LIGHT BARS ABOVE IT, EACH ONE, LOCK.

Here is a picture of a TIME TRACK. That is the long vertical line. It is a way to plot your facsimiles, experiences in life, against time. Actually, these facsimiles can be sorted around at will by you. But stretching them all out this way, they can be conceived as a track of time through which you have lived.

Now during this lifetime, on this time track, various things happened to you. Some were good and some were bad. Up to your teens you had the big goal of growth and after that you had other goals.

This track is a continuous facsimile. But it is made up of a lot of facsimiles, particular experiences which either stand out or remain hidden.

PAINFUL INCIDENT is any incident which was painful: A death, an operation, a big failure—big enough to render you unconscious, such as an accident. You've had many of these, but we are graphing just one to show you what happens to any of them.

LOCKS occur when you decide that the environment is similar to the painful incident. Locks occur when an individual is tired or has had a minor failure in life which reminds him, perhaps, of the major failure.

The technique known as Lock Scanning starts off from an early lock of the painful incident, but not the painful incident itself. One doesn't pay any attention to that. It is more or less inflated by the locks and can be handled as an incident just like any other facsimile—which is to say, put aside at will. But sometimes the locks have to be cared for before the painful incident slips away. Of course, the painful incident itself can be run by Effort Processing. But that's pretty heavy to do by yourself. Further, these locks have to be scanned anyway.

A lock, then, can be treated by LOCK SCANNING.

To Lock Scan, one contacts an early lock on the track and goes, rapidly or slowly, through all such similar incidents straight to present time. One does this many times and the whole chain of locks becomes ineffective in influencing one.

Now more work with the pencil. Number the LOCKS. Mark the first one above PAINFUL INCIDENT, 1, the next, 2, and so on.

When you start to Lock Scan, you will find an incident of the type required. You will scan yourself through all such similar incidents to present time. Maybe the earliest one you found on this scan was lock 8 and you scanned from there through the remaining locks to present time.

On your next scan, try to find an earlier lock. The first scan made an earlier one accessible to you. This new start may be lock 5. Scan from lock 5 to present time through all similar incidents.

On your next scan you may find an even earlier lock. Scan from there to present time through all similar incidents.

You do this scanning on any one chain until you are "extroverted" about it—which is to say, until you find yourself in present time thinking about something else, your tone probably up.

If you continue to Lock Scan after you have extroverted, you will "drop through" into another chain on some other subject. This isn't bad, but you want to stop scanning when you are extroverted. One more scan will find you scanning another chain.

It can happen that during scanning you hit what is known as a "boil-off." This means that you become groggy and seem to go to sleep. This is evidently caused by old "unconsciousness" coming off. It hasn't much benefit and apparently occurs when two facsimiles conflict with each other.

Actually, you could Lock Scan yourself into a great deal of boil-off. You could probably spend five hundred hours Lock Scanning this and that and boiling-off. That's the slow road.

THE OBJECT OF LOCK SCANNING IS NOT BOIL-OFF. BOIL-OFF MEANS TOO MANY SECONDARIES, TOO MUCH GRIEF AND TOO MUCH REGRET. IF YOU FIND YOURSELF BOILING-OFF TOO MUCH (A LITTLE IS QUITE IN ORDER) RUN REGRET AND BLAME AS IN A LATER SECTION.

This technique has to be known and understood if your processing is to go swiftly.

To show you what happens, here's some work with an eraser. Take the graph you made. Run your eraser from LOCK 7 to PRESENT TIME. Some of the lines lightened. Now run the eraser from LOCK 5 to PRESENT TIME. Now from LOCK 1 to PRESENT TIME. Now pass the eraser from 1 up many times until the lines are almost erased. That is what happens to the facsimiles you Lock Scan.

It is possible for you to "hang up" in Lock Scanning. You start to run a chain of incidents and find yourself "stuck" halfway to present time. Don't flounder around or get alarmed. You've hit a POSTULATE—a decision you have made—not to get rid of something or never to get over that incident. You've hit something you yourself *thought* which keeps you from going on by the incident. Possibly it is regret. Feel the feeling of regret and you may become unstuck. Or feel the feeling of blaming you or somebody else for the incident. Or simply feel the counter-emotion, which will be covered in a moment and is a ripe subject for scanning. It's expected you'll finish reading all this before you try it.

You can Lock Scan at various speeds. You can scan so fast you don't even know what the incidents are. That's MAXIMUM. Or you can scan so slowly that you know every word said.

That's VERBAL. Or you can scan speeds in between. You may have been living with somebody who insisted you hear every word they said and you may find yourself scanning at a speed which might, facetiously, be called "turtle." That is too slow. Most scanning is done at ACCELERATED, which simply gives one a glimpse and concept of each successive incident.

Light emotion, counter-emotion, blame, phrases, people, anything can be scanned.

One of the most important things to scan is COUNTER-EMOTION which was mentioned, but not explained in Act Six.

Have you ever walked into a room and known that people had been talking about you, or fighting, just before your entrance? The "atmosphere" seems charged. When somebody stands and bawls you out, do you feel the anger?

You have emotion which you discharge at people. You try to make them enthusiastic or make them see the seriousness of something or you show them your contempt. Well, they sense it not so much as words, but as emotion.

A good orator is one who can throw out a great deal of emotion and so thrill or energize an audience. The same thing could be done with mis-emotion, anger, grief, etc.

Mass hysteria is a well-known phenomenon. One person in a crowd is panicky. The whole crowd becomes panicky without even knowing what is wrong. This is a built-up manifestation of "herd instinct." Man traveled in packs. It was safer to run or to charge instantly than it was to dawdle around for verbal orders. Thus, mass emotion. This is a survival instinct.

More than that, emotion is the relay between thought and action. Emotion is the "glue" in facsimiles.

There is THOUGHT, EMOTION and EFFORT. Thought is one fringe of emotion. Effort, or physical action, is the other fringe of emotion.

EFFORTS and COUNTER-EFFORTS have been mentioned. Somebody hits you. That is a counter-effort. You resist the blow. That is the effort. You use two kinds of effort: The effort to remain at rest and the effort to remain in motion. There are two counter-efforts which you can experience: One which moves against you and one which refuses to move. You can see this very easily. Right now you are making a tiny effort to hold up this book while the counter-effort of gravity is pulling it down. Every day the counter-effort of gravity makes a person shrink, during his waking hours, about three-quarters of an inch. At night, he gains it back.

EMOTION and COUNTER-EMOTION are similar to effort and counter-effort. You have two goals with emotion: Thought, via emotion, seeks to *stop* action, self or exterior. Thought, via emotion, seeks to *start* action, self or exterior. Anger, for instance, seeks to stop exterior-action. Fear seeks to start self-action to get away.

Now emotion is emotion, whether it is yours or another's. Live around a person who is continually angry and you will begin to emotionally react toward that anger, for the anger seeks to stop you whatever you do. Live around a person who is afraid and you will pick up their fear and try to counteract it with emotion of your own, usually seeking to stop their flight. Or you can get into the unhappy state of duplicating their counter-emotion with your emotion. You do this whenever you agree with somebody. (The chief hole in light books which seek to "win friends and influence people"—they also make people ill, eventually, because of agreement on emotion.) Agree with an angry man and you'll get angry too. Agree with an afraid man and you'll get afraid.

Agree with a man in grief and you'll feel your own grief. And so on, as covered in ARC in an earlier Act.

You can feel your own emotion and the counter-emotion when examining a facsimile. Or you can feel simply your own emotion. Or you can feel the counter-emotion only. You can take what you want out of a facsimile. The trick is to take what is essentially aberrative out of it.

Now let's see what happens to a counter-effort. This, let us say, is that pressure you sometimes feel in your stomach. That's just a facsimile of an old blow, but it is sometimes very uncomfortable. How do we get rid of that facsimile? Well, we can Lock Scan all the times it ever bothered you. And we can Lock Scan it until it won't bother you again. That's one way. It's around a lot, so we can run it as a service facsimile by Effort (or an auditor can run it, which is best when effort is in question). Or we can run a "grief charge" off grandfather's death, grandfather having had a stomach that bothered him. Or we can run off the counter-emotion. We have a dozen dozen ways to handle that stomach trouble.

Let's see how the *fastest* way.

That may be COUNTER-EMOTION SCANNING.

If it's a pressure or a pain, it is a facsimile of some pain that happened before and which still exists "in memory" as a facsimile. Obviously, it eludes our control of it or it wouldn't hurt. What makes it elude our own control of it? Well, after the blow was struck, or whatever the counter-effort was, somebody in the environment began to throw emotion at that very spot. That is counter-emotion to you. The counter-emotion took over that facsimile of the counter-effort and it is being held there by somebody else's counter-emotion. That's the way the pressure or pain in the stomach may add up.

Don't let's try to get complicated about this. It's simple. George has been hit in the stomach by a baseball. Later his mother is sympathetic. That makes it a "good facsimile," so George holds on to it. Then one day he gets married. His wife, a 1.5, begins to nag him about eating. She gets angry at him. He wants sympathy instead. So he holds up this facsimile for sympathy and it doesn't work. Her counter-emotion, anger, alters the baseball-in-the-stomach "somatic" and puts anger on it. Now George doesn't control it anymore. It is controlled by his wife and her counter-emotion of anger. In processing, George starts to run his wife's anger. This old baseball facsimile turns on strongly and then goes away, never to return.

Where the emotion of others is concerned, an ache or a pain is fair game. But oddly enough, one has to have loved or felt sympathy for another in order for that person's counter-emotion to have much effect.

The cycle is then as follows: Blow or a pain becomes a facsimile. Facsimile is used by individual. Or isn't handled well by him. Somebody close to him gets angry at him or fearful or sad. That emotion (counter-emotion) turns on the old blow or pain.

If the counter-emotion is heavy, not even Effort Processing can touch that old facsimile until the counter-emotion is removed from it.

The process is this: You have an ache or a pain. You can't get rid of it simply by identifying its source or other light means. You locate a time when somebody you loved threw counter-emotion at that particular spot. You scan, by Lock Scanning, all the counter-emotion thrown at that spot, whether it was sympathy or anger or fear. It doesn't matter what you do about your own emotion.

One of two things will happen: You will find the old facsimile and throw it away. Or you will find counter-emotion from a great many people, run that off by scanning, and then discover a big secondary which will have to be run or a PAINFUL INCIDENT which has to be run by Effort Processing and is the service facsimile.

Whatever happens, you won't go wrong by running any and all counter-emotion you can find.

Every atmosphere in which you have lived has an "emotional quality." You will find that emotion doesn't come from humans only. You will find times in your life when you ran away from an atmosphere alone, not for any other reason than that you did not like the "feel" of it. You will find you have avoided people, certain persons, certain groups because you did not like the counter-emotion. You may discover that that vague blur which you recalled as your "education" was thrust out of sight just because you hated the school atmosphere, its counter-emotion.

Primarily and foremost, you will find counter-emotion sitting around by tar-bucketsful whenever you failed. This is a mixture of counter-emotion and your own emotion or regret and blame.

Counter-emotion has been thrown at you, your thoughts, specific parts of your body and, in particular, that great or slight infirmity which you carry around.

Don't be alarmed if, in scanning counter-emotion, some chronic pain begins to turn up like a five-alarm fire. Don't run for a water bucket. Just run more counter-emotion. It's doubtful if it will kill you for, you see, you didn't die before when you actually experienced it.

These are just facsimiles. If the real thing didn't ruin you, the facsimile probably can't.

If you have a very weak heart, however, or some such infirmity which means razor-edge between life and death, USE MEMORY ONLY FROM PRESENT TIME, DON'T LOCK SCAN, ON COUNTER-EMOTION.

In two years, these processes in the hands of the public, an often careless public, have never lost a preclear by reason of a weak heart or some such hair-trigger infirmity. But I must state that that doesn't mean it can't occur. See a doctor *and* an auditor, but don't let the doctor talk you out of the auditor. Doctors always tell people with weak hearts to slow down. That's what's wrong with the individual—he's too slow already.

The assignment of the Eighth Act is, first, a thorough study of Lock Scanning. Then, a thorough study of counter-emotion. Then, finally, testing out Lock Scanning and Counter-Emotion Scanning separately and then as one process. Do the following practice exercises:

LOCK SCAN EVERYTHING YOU HAVE EVER THOUGHT ABOUT THIS SCIENCE, GOOD AND BAD, UNTIL YOU EXTROVERT ON THE SUBJECT.

LOCK SCAN EVERYTHING YOU HAVE EVER HEARD OR READ ABOUT L. RON HUBBARD, GOOD OR BAD, UNTIL YOU EXTROVERT ON THE SUBJECT. IF YOU HAVEN'T HEARD ANYTHING—FINE.

LOCK SCAN EVERY CONCLUSION OR POSTULATE YOU MAY HAVE MADE ABOUT THE SCIENCE AND EVERY DECISION ABOUT IT.

IF YOU HAVE EVER BEEN AUDITED BEFORE BY OLD STANDARD PROCEDURE, LOCK SCAN ALL SESSIONS OF THAT AUDITING.

IF YOU HAVE EVER BEEN AUDITED BEFORE, PICK UP EVERY TIME YOU AGREED TO CONTACT AN INCIDENT.

IF YOU HAVE EVER ASKED TO BE AUDITED, LOCK SCAN EVERY TIME YOU ASKED SOMEBODY TO AUDIT YOU.

When you have completed this, do this further exercise:

IF YOU HAVE EVER BEEN AUDITED, LOCK SCAN THE
COUNTER-EMOTION OF YOUR AUDITOR AND THE ENVIRONMENT.
Get the way his emotion might have felt to you. If you haven't
any contact on it, don't worry—you didn't like him.

PICK UP SOMEBODY IN YOUR LIFE OF WHOM YOU WERE FOND.
LOCK SCAN ALL THE TIMES WHEN YOU WERE SYMPATHETIC TO HIM OR
HER. BUT CONCENTRATE WITH YOUR SCANNING ON THE EMOTION
FROM THAT PERSON WHEN HE WAS IN TROUBLE OR IN PAIN. SCAN
UNTIL YOU EXTROVERT ON THE SUBJECT.

LOCK SCAN THROUGH ALL THE TIMES YOU HAVE TRIED TO
HELP PEOPLE IN MINOR WAYS. DO IT IN GENERAL WITHOUT ANY
ATTENTION TO COUNTER-EMOTION.

NOW LOCK SCAN THROUGH ALL THE COUNTER-EMOTION OF
PEOPLE YOU HAVE TRIED TO HELP. THEIR EMOTION TOWARD YOU
BEFORE AND AFTER THE AID OR OFFER WAS EXTENDED.

These are exercises. The last action, however, is a very effective
process. Now follow with these effective processes:

GO TO THE SECOND ACT (ARC) WHERE YOU MADE A LIST OF
PEOPLE WHO ENFORCED AND INHIBITED AFFINITY, COMMUNICATION
AND REALITY ON YOU. LOCK SCAN THE COUNTER-EMOTION OF THESE
PEOPLE OF THE PRESENT AND OF THE PAST IN EVERY INCIDENT OF
ENFORCED AND INHIBITED ARC. CHECK OFF EACH NAME WRITTEN
IN THE SECOND ACT. SCAN UNTIL YOU EXTROVERT ON EACH ONE.

When you have completed everything to this point and, in particular, the scanning of all people mentioned in the Second Act, continue with the following:

IN THE THIRD ACT YOU LISTED YOUR ATTITUDES TOWARD THE WORLD IN WHICH YOU ARE LIVING. LOCK SCAN EACH AND EVERY TIME YOU MADE A DECISION OR FELT THE ATTITUDE LISTED. TAKE EACH PHRASE YOU WROTE AND SCAN EVERY TIME YOU FELT THAT WAY. THEN GO TO THE NEXT PHRASE.

WHEN YOU HAVE FINISHED THIS SCANNING, SCAN OFF THE COUNTER-EMOTION IN ALL SUCH INCIDENTS.

WHEN YOU HAVE COMPLETED COUNTER-EMOTION IN EVERY INCIDENT RECALLED AROUND YOUR ATTITUDE, GO TO THE BIG CHART (CHART OF ATTITUDES).

START AT THE BOTTOM PHRASE OF COLUMN ONE OF THE BIG CHART. SCAN EVERY TIME YOU FELT THAT WAY TOWARD THE WORLD, TOWARD YOURSELF, TOWARD GROUPS, TOWARD ANIMALS, TOWARD THE SUPREME BEING.

(In this process, most but not all phrases may have been applied.)

TAKE THE NEXT HIGHER PHRASE IN COLUMN ONE AND SCAN FOR ALL DYNAMICS.

TAKE THE NEXT HIGHER PHRASE IN COLUMN ONE AND SCAN FOR ALL DYNAMICS.

PROGRESS ALL THE WAY TO THE TOP OF COLUMN ONE, SCANNING EACH LINE FOR EACH DYNAMIC.

START AT THE BOTTOM OF COLUMN TWO AND TAKE THE LOWEST PHRASE. SCAN EACH TIME YOU TOLD YOURSELF OR THE WORLD THIS PHRASE. SCAN FOR EVERY DYNAMIC.

TAKE THE NEXT HIGHER PHRASE IN COLUMN TWO AND SCAN FOR EACH DYNAMIC.

CONTINUE ON UP COLUMN TWO, SCANNING EACH PHRASE IN TURN FOR EACH DYNAMIC.

SCAN EACH PHRASE FROM BOTTOM TO TOP IN EVERY COLUMN FOR EVERY DYNAMIC UNTIL YOU HAVE SCANNED EVERY PHRASE ON THE BIG CHART.

COLUMN 1

COLUMN 2

COLUMN 3

COLUMN 4

COLUMN 5

COLUMN 6

COLUMN 7

COLUMN 8

COLUMN 9

COLUMN 10

COLUMN 11

COLUMN 12

the
ninth
act

the Ninth act

N THIS ACT we handle EMOTION and COUNTER-EMOTION with even more understanding.

The technical background of this is a simplicity, but it is a simplicity which took twenty years to discover. All things are complex when they are poorly understood. The evolution of knowledge is toward simplicity, not complexity. An evolution toward complexity is an evolution toward authoritarianism and pomposity. "You couldn't possibly understand this, therefore I, who pretend to, am important" is the attitude which mires learning. The only claim science has on anyone's attention or interest is the ability of a science to make phenomena workable and align those phenomena for better understanding. A body of data which does not accomplish this is not only not a science, it is a pretense and a humbuggery. Thus, if you are working with any idea that the human mind "is too complex to understand," you are taking the stand of those who failed. The problem of resolving the human mind was enormously difficult. The solution of the operation and difficulties of the human mind is very simple.

We have three levels of operation: They are THOUGHT, EMOTION and EFFORT. Thought produces motion or action through the medium of emotion. Motion and effort in general produce thought directly, but also through the medium of emotion. Thought is without time. It is instantaneous. Emotion, where its band rests in thought, is also without time. Effort, action contain time. A motion is a change of position in space. A change of position requires time. The common partner of time and space is motion. To have motion, we have to have space and time. To have emotion, we do not need time. And there is no time whatever in thought. This is the theoretical background. It doesn't much matter whether it is clearly understood or not.

An individual is a collection of "memories" going back to his first appearance on Earth. In other words, he is the composite of all his facsimiles plus his impulse TO BE. Individuality depends upon facsimiles.

The very character and shape of the body—its genetic blueprint which says whether one has one head or two—is a composite of facsimiles, according to theory and evidences.

The facsimiles which occasion behavior were initially counter-efforts. All facsimiles contain counter-efforts. The body and personality are actually old counter-efforts which "I" has turned into efforts. Thoughts are timeless. You can close your eyes and see, in thought, some item which you well know is since vanished in the MEST universe. You have it as a facsimile still. You can, in thought, go back and be a small child. You cannot go back in body and change the past. That you can go back in thought tells us that the thought must be right here in present time too. In other words, you as mind can handle yesterday as thought. Thought is timeless. Thoughts are filed by your concept of when they happened. As long as you know the "time tab" of any thought, it is yours completely. When you do not know the time tab of a thought, you no longer control it.

People are very fond of saying they have "bad memories." They use this as a social excuse and to avoid recalling failures. The memory, by these processes, repairs rapidly until a person can recall things at will. His ability to recall things depends upon his ability to read the time tabs on his facsimiles, so to speak. In other words, so long as he recalls accurately, he is in control of the facsimile. When he cannot recall accurately, he is not in control of the facsimile.

At the Foundation we can repair psychotics, the despair of thousands of years of civilized Man, in a relatively short period of time. For two thousand years they have been giving psychotics shocks, restraints and operations—there has been no change. Freud, alone, suggested a change. But he didn't have the reason why nor the effectiveness. And today, in major institutions, these antique methods pass for "modern" treatment. Out of our present body of knowledge, we are restoring the sanity and effectiveness of psychotics—a thing which has never before been done with regularity or a guarantee of success. We even restore psychotics who have been given "modern" treatments, shock and the rest of it.

How is this done?

Handle it this way: An insane person cannot reason or control himself. That means he cannot handle his facsimiles. By a series of precise steps, the auditor gives the psychotic back the control of the facsimiles. These steps are as follows:

1. By mimicry (a form of communication), tactile (the most direct communication) and by general ARC, we get the psychotic into communication with one human being—the auditor. This is sometimes long and difficult and is the most arduous step. It can be assisted by giving the psychotic MEST—time and space—and removing restraints.

2. The auditor then works to get the psychotic into contact with present time. He calls attention to objects and the general environment until the psychotic sees that these are real. When the auditor knows the psychotic knows the reality of beds and walls, he turns attention to the psychotic himself—as a being. He establishes the fact, with the psychotic, that the psychotic controls his own hands and feet and body.

3. At this stage the auditor may introduce the psychotic into association with other people and a wider environment. This is again more present time. The auditor NEVER evaluates anything for the psychotic.

THE PSYCHOTIC IS INSANE BECAUSE OF TOO MUCH EVALUATION BY OTHERS AND WILL SLUMP IF SOMEBODY STARTS THINKING FOR HIM AGAIN.

4. The next step is to get the psychotic to evaluate something. This may be as mild as whether or not hamburgers are good to eat. The psychotic decides on an evaluation, then many evaluations in present time.

5. Now the psychotic is asked to make minor decisions in present time plus action on those decisions. This includes getting him to decide to accept something and to decide to throw something away. For the handling of MEST is not unlike the handling of thoughts and, to a psychotic, thoughts are as solid as MEST.

6. The next step is to get the psychotic to recall something, no matter how general, about his past. He is asked to recall things until he strikes an incident he REALLY KNOWS IS REAL. It is real to him. It is a real memory. This is another up point in his tone, as each of these steps listed are. But it is the big point. He has recognized as REAL one of his own facsimiles. He isn't coaxed into "admitting" it is real.

He recalls and knows that it really happened. He is then made to recall many such incidents.

HE IS NEVER INVALIDATED OR ARGUED WITH ABOUT WHAT HE THINKS IS REAL. THE AUDITOR SIMPLY IGNORES THE HALLUCINATIONS AND ACCEPTS A REAL MEMORY AT LAST.

7. The succeeding step is to get the psychotic to recall a past evaluation, a time when he made up his mind about the character or quality of something. The specific moment of evaluation is attained. Then the psychotic is made to recall a decision he has made in the past. Many evaluations and decisions are thus recalled.

8. The psychotic is now questioned about the times he has helped people. If possible, heavy failures are avoided. When he has recalled times when he has helped people and knows each incident recalled is real and actually happened, one goes to the next step.

9. The auditor now tries to locate the decision, the exact instant, with all perceptions possible, when the psychotic decided to go crazy. There may be many such decisions. These are recalled many times each.

10. The psychotic is now questioned on the subject of departed or failed relatives or friends until one is discovered who went mad. This is the location of a goal continuation for another.

11. Now the psychotic is worked on the subject of sympathy, what he has had to do to get sympathy, what sympathy he has given others. Probably a grief charge will come into view and can be run.

The individual, about step 8, is no longer classifiable as very psychotic. By step 10, he is at worst neurotic and he can be processed by counter-emotion, regret and other techniques.

This is outlined to give you some sort of an idea of what psychosis is and how sanity is restored. It is the condition of being unable to handle one's facsimiles. Sanity is restored by restoring an individual's ability, little by little, to handle his facsimiles.

But by what mechanism does an individual become unable to handle his memories? There are several answers, but the main one is COUNTER-EMOTION.

Counter-emotion is felt as the "atmosphere" around a person or place. Ask anyone to recall the "feel" of the "atmosphere" of an area or a person and he can re-experience it, at least in part.

Emotion, according to present theory, can be laid down by anyone against anyone. The emotions of A can be infiltrated into the facsimiles of B. The thoughts of A, similarly, can be infiltrated into the thoughts of B. But so far as we are concerned, at this writing, the mechanisms of thought and counter-thought are not well known. Emotion and counter-emotion are easily established.

How does one human being control another? High on the Tone Scale, it is by letting the individual control himself as thoroughly as possible. Below 2.0, in the mis-emotion band, a human being seeks to control or destroy another by COUNTER-EMOTION and COUNTER-THOUGHT.

The atmosphere surrounding a mis-emotion person is easily sensed. When one advances a facsimile to a mis-emotion person, mis-emotion is immediately thrown into that facsimile. Effort is transferred by physical contact. Emotion is simply transferred by anger, fear, argument, sympathy, etc., from a mis-emotion person into the facsimiles of another. You may have noticed how you can become less sure of yourself or uneasy around people who are embarrassed or uneasy or afraid. This is a simple mechanism. You are getting your facsimiles "colored" by a foreign emotion.

Every facsimile you advance, with argument or persuasion, toward a mis-emotional person gets counter-emotion thrown into it.

THAT COUNTER-EMOTION TAKES YOUR FACSIMILE OUT OF YOUR OWN CONTROL AND PUTS IT INTO THE CONTROL OF THE MIS-EMOTIONAL PERSON.

Nothing is easier to prove. You have noticed, probably, in Lock Scanning that certain persons were "occluded" or that the whole track was occluded. That occluded person was mis-emotional. The facsimiles you displayed around that person have *their* emotion on them, not *yours*. Your thought, then, has ceased to control such facsimiles. They do not come to view when called for by you. They are occluded. The facsimiles aren't owned by you any longer, but by the mis-emotional person.

One by one, your facsimiles can be taken out of your control by mis-emotional persons. The end result is no further ownership of your own facsimiles or you. The end result is control by the environment, not self-control; mis-emotion instead of self-confidence; doubt and fear of acting. In short, reactions such as those which appear along the lower band of the Chart of Attitudes. Slowed reaction time and illnesses and chronic pains result from these facsimiles which are no longer under your control. Mis-emotion has swamped them, occluded them and so they can hurt you.

There is another, even simpler subject in COUNTER-THOUGHT.

You think one thing, somebody else thinks another. Their thought is counter to your thought. Live awhile around somebody low on the scale and your thoughts get swamped by counter-thought. This is rehabilitated simply by running the ideas of another and the moment they expressed them.

Counter-emotion and counter-thought can become sufficiently serious so as to give you the illusion of having the facsimiles of another. This is a last extreme. This is hallucination.

Take a person who is normally occluded in your memory. Think back to a time when this person told you a story or an incident. You may have no view of that person telling the story but, instead, a view of the activity in the story. This is a "dub-in" occasioned by their mis-emotion. The end product of this is to have the time track of some mis-emotional person, with fake perceptions upon it. This is hallucination complete.

A mis-emotional person can become occluded not only in recall, but also in present time. Such a person blurs out. When they come into the room, one has the illusion of the light failing slightly.

We all have the ambition to see a bright world. The thing which makes it unbright, in the main, is the mis-emotion we carry on our facsimiles from the atmospheres of mis-emotion in which we have dwelt.

Here is an exercise:

GO TO A PLACE ON THE TRACK WHERE THERE IS AN OCCLUSION. NOW TRY TO FEEL THE MIS-EMOTION WHICH MIGHT BE IN THE ATMOSPHERE. EXPERIENCE THIS COUNTER-EMOTION BY RUNNING THROUGH THE INCIDENT SWIFTLY MANY TIMES.

(A PAIN MIGHT HAVE TURNED ON. IF SO, CONTINUE TO RUN THIS COUNTER-EMOTION UNTIL THE PAIN IS GONE. YOU PROBABLY ARE NOT RUNNING THE FULL LENGTH OF THE INCIDENT.)

New data appeared to you from that occluded area. Your own thoughts and feelings in that area began to brighten. You knew what you were thinking about and saying after you had run it a few times. This exercise is the one necessary to restore recall perception on occluded people and areas.

Another exercise:

GO TO A PLACE IN RECALL WHERE A NORMALLY OCCLUDED PERSON IS TELLING YOU A STORY OR AN INCIDENT. FIND AN AREA WHERE YOU ARE GETTING THE PICTURE OF THE STORY, NOT THE PICTURE OF THE PERSON TELLING IT. RUN THE COUNTER-EMOTION OF THE PICTURE SEVERAL TIMES UNTIL YOU GET A VIEW OF THE PERSON TELLING YOU THE INCIDENT.

This is how people get occluded. A mis-emotional person specializes in telling people what to think and what the people think. Occlusion in childhood and hallucinatory pictures of childhood are occasioned by telling the child what happened to him, often and in detail. This knocks out the facsimile of the child and substitutes either occlusion or a false picture.

RUN THE MIS-EMOTION OR ANY COUNTER-EMOTION OF TIMES WHEN YOU WERE TOLD WHAT HAD HAPPENED TO YOU. RUN THESE UNTIL THE OCCLUSION VANISHES OR THE PICTURE GOES AWAY. DON'T NECESSARILY GO BACK TO THE INCIDENT BEING TALKED ABOUT.

LIST FIVE PEOPLE WHO ARE OCCLUDED ON YOUR TRACK.

1.

2.

3.

4.

5.

RUN THE ATMOSPHERE AROUND THESE OCCLUSIONS UNTIL EACH ONE APPEARS IN VIEW. IF PICTURES OF WHAT THEY SAY TURN UP, RUN THE PICTURES UNTIL THE PERSON TURNS UP INSTEAD.

WARNING: YOU WILL HIT SYMPATHY AND A "DESIRE" FOR SYMPATHY FROM EVERY ONE OF THESE PERSONS. DON'T STOP LOCK SCANNING IN A BURST OF CONTRITION AND FLY TO OR WRITE THESE PEOPLE IF THEY ARE STILL ALIVE. YOUR MIND WILL CHANGE ABOUT THEM.

LIST FIVE PEOPLE IN YOUR LIFE WHO HAD DIFFERENT IDEAS ABOUT THINGS THAN YOURSELF.

1.

2.

3.

4.

5.

NOW LOCK SCAN THROUGH ALL INCIDENTS OR COUNTER-IDEAS FOR EACH PERSON LISTED. PICK UP THEIR THOUGHT AND THEN YOUR THOUGHT IN EACH INCIDENT.

LIST THE NAMES OR LOCATIONS OF ALL THE SCHOOLS YOU ATTENDED.

1.

2.

3.

4.

5.

NOW LOCK SCAN THE ATMOSPHERE OF EVERY CLASSROOM AND TEACHER OF EACH SCHOOL IN TURN AS COUNTER-EMOTION.

NOW LOCK SCAN THE PUPILS, FRIENDS AND ENEMIES OF EACH SCHOOL IN TURN AS COUNTER-EMOTION.

NOW LOCK SCAN THE TEACHERS AND SCHOOLS AS COUNTER-THOUGHT TO YOUR THOUGHT, EACH ONE IN TURN.

NOW LOCK SCAN THE PUPILS, ENEMIES AND FRIENDS AS COUNTER-THOUGHT TO YOUR THOUGHT, EACH ONE IN TURN.

LIST FIVE PERSONS WHOM YOU CONSIDER TO HAVE WRONGED YOU.

1.

2.

3.

4.

5.

LOCK SCAN EACH TIME YOU SAW EACH, WITH ATTENTION TO COUNTER-EMOTION.

LOCK SCAN EACH TIME YOU COMMUNICATED OR SAW EACH, WITH ATTENTION TO COUNTER-THOUGHT.

Let us now consider another phenomena about emotion. This is the EMOTIONAL CURVE.

On the Tone Scale you will find a difference of height between various emotions and mis-emotions. The emotional curve is the drop or rise from one level of emotion to another.

Can you find a time when you were happy and suddenly became sad?

This is easy.

EXPERIENCE OR GET A CONCEPT OF HOW YOU WOULD FEEL IF YOU WERE HAPPY AND THEN HOW YOU WOULD FEEL IF YOU BECAME SAD. THEN EXPERIENCE THE CHANGE FROM HAPPINESS TO SADNESS. NOW FIND A SITUATION WHERE YOU WERE HAPPY AND BECAME SAD. RUN THIS CURVE.

WHO WAS PRESENT? RUN THE DROP IN TONE AS YOUR OWN EMOTION. THEN RUN THE DROP IN TONE AS COUNTER-EMOTION, THE ATMOSPHERE CHANGE.

RUN THE EMOTIONAL CURVE FROM HAPPINESS TO SADNESS SEVERAL TIMES UNTIL YOU HAVE FULL RECOVERY ON YOUR OWN IDEAS AND COUNTER-THOUGHT. WHAT DID YOU THINK? WHAT DID THE OTHER SAY?

There are two EMOTIONAL CURVES: One is the emotional curve you experience directly in yourself. The other is the counter-emotional curve where you feel a change in tone in the atmosphere.

This is an auditor tool and is used to locate the SERVICE FACSIMILE of the preclear.

The
Tenth
Act

the tenth act

FOR THE AUDITOR (if you are being audited part time or full time) the Tenth Act is the running out by THOUGHT, EFFORT and EMOTION the SERVICE FACSIMILE.

He will discover it from the data you have already written in this book, by looking you over for malfunction and by running EMOTIONAL CURVES until you run into the front end of the incident.

An individual with a very thorough knowledge from additional texts on this science might be able to run the service facsimile itself. But several things militate against it: The first of them being that the preclear will try to run it "out of valence" (as somebody else). The second, that he considers it valuable and so doesn't want to lose it. The third being that it takes a preclear so very much longer to run his own service facsimile than it takes an auditor.

the
eleventh
act

The Eleventh Act

THIS ENTIRE ACT is addressed to the subject of SYMPATHY.

Probably you could kill a man with sympathy. It has been done. There are three levels of healing: The first is to do something efficient about the condition. The next, if the first can't be done, is to make the patient comfortable. The third, if he can't be made comfortable, is to give him sympathy. That is in accordance with old medical practice. However, sympathy is a terrible thing, but is considered to be a very valuable thing.

The survival value of sympathy is this: When an individual is hurt or immobilized, he cannot fend for himself, get himself food, defend himself. If he is to survive, he must count upon another or others to care for him. His bid for such care is the enlistment of the sympathy of others. This is practical. The cheerful good-fellowship of the weak, crippled or ill is part of this mechanism. If men weren't sympathetic, none of us would be alive.

The non-survival value of sympathy is this: An individual fails in some activity or effort to help. He then considers himself incapable of surviving by himself. Even though he isn't sick, actually, he makes a bid for sympathy. When a person, not acutely ill or immobilized by injury, is making a bid for sympathy, he considers that he has failed so badly that he cannot by himself continue on in life.

His self-confidence is undermined. He is not able to handle himself well. Counter-emotion and counter-thought have garbled his facsimiles. He feels he has to have sympathy to get along. And he displays an illness or disability to gain sympathy. This is mechanical and is not to be disparaged—the person is actually in need of help. And almost every human being is prone to this error. Almost everyone will make a bid for sympathy by holding out some old facsimile. A psychosomatic illness is at once an "explanation" of failure and a bid for sympathy. That does not make the sympathy, when received, less sweet. And it does not make the ill any less painful.

One is peculiarly liable to sympathy bids around his parents and family. The worst case an auditor can encounter is one which wants auditing only for the auditor's sympathy and wants to retain the service facsimile because it is a sympathy source. The answer to this is to get the preclear far enough up the Tone Scale so that he is sufficiently self-confident not to need any sympathy. Only then, in some cases, will the SERVICE FACSIMILE (the technical term for the facsimile the preclear uses to gain sympathy) surrender to auditing.

The purpose of this Act is to pick up SYMPATHY FACSIMILES.

In other works on this science, you will find in detail the role of SELF-DETERMINISM. We are all self-determined, natively.

NOTHING which we do is beyond self-determined action.

When you make a decision, it is MADE.

A later part of this processing deals thoroughly with this.

Nobody ever became ill without wanting to be ill at some earlier moment in his life. Here is a polio case, in bed two years. She became ill because she felt sorry for another little girl who got polio and so decided to get it herself. It was a clear-cut decision, followed by two long years in bed.

If you doubt that you ever wished to be ill, what about school? Didn't you ever beg off by a plaint of being sick? How many times have you done this?

SCAN THROUGH EACH AND EVERY TIME YOU DECIDED TO GET SICK.

SCAN THROUGH ALL THE REASONS YOU DECIDED TO BE ILL.

When you have completed this exercise until you have extroverted on the subject, begin on the following:

LOCATE A MOMENT WHEN YOU FELT SYMPATHY FOR SOMETHING. SCAN THROUGH THIS MOMENT OVER AND OVER UNTIL IT IS DESENSITIZED.

SCAN NOW THE COUNTER-EMOTION TO YOUR SYMPATHY IN THAT SAME INCIDENT.

SCAN THE SYMPATHETIC THOUGHT IN THAT INCIDENT.

SCAN THE COUNTER-THOUGHT IN THAT INCIDENT IF ANY.

These four steps are a pattern for single incidents. After you have scanned just so many of these incidents, you will find that sympathy all up and down the track seems to be resolving.

ON THE SAME SUBJECT, TAKE UP THE FOLLOWING PEOPLE. SCAN EVERY INCIDENT YOU CAN FIND CONTAINING SYMPATHY BY YOU FOR THEM ON THE ABOVE PATTERN.

(Omit any you did not have.)

MOTHER.

FATHER.

GUARDIAN.

FATHER'S GRANDMOTHER.

FATHER'S MOTHER.

FATHER'S GRANDFATHER.

FATHER'S FATHER.

MOTHER'S GRANDMOTHER.

MOTHER'S MOTHER.

MOTHER'S GRANDFATHER.

MOTHER'S FATHER.

AUNTS.

GREAT-AUNTS.

UNCLES.

GREAT-UNCLES.

PLAYMATES.

MARITAL PARTNERS.

TEACHERS.

DOGS.

CATS.

HORSES.

GOLDFISH.

CHILDREN.

DOLLS.

TOYS.

ANIMALS.

BIRDS.

POSSESSIONS.

SCENES.

HOUSES.

BEDS.

SCAN NOW THE FOLLOWING STORY CHARACTERS FOR SYMPATHY OR OTHER EMOTION. (Omit any you were not acquainted with, but be sure you didn't know them.)

TINY TIM.

LITTLE ORPHAN ANNIE.

ANY EUGENE FIELD POEM.

ANGELS.

LITTLE NELL.

ANY OTHER STORY CHARACTER.

Now we will reverse the process.

SCAN ANY SYMPATHY GIVEN YOU BY ANY OF THE LIST OF RELATIVES AND PEOPLE ABOVE. SCAN EACH INCIDENT IN DETAIL. THE INCIDENT MAY INCLUDE SICKNESS. IF SO, SCAN IT UNTIL ANY SYMPTOMS YOU PICK UP VANISH AGAIN. (By scanning emotion and counter-emotion, facsimiles drop off.)

SCAN SELECTIVELY ON SYMPATHY AND COUNTER-EMOTION THE FOLLOWING:

YOURSELF.

FOR YOUR EYES.

FOR YOUR MOUTH.

FOR YOUR EARS.

FOR YOUR HEAD.

FOR YOUR ARMS.

FOR YOUR HANDS.

FOR YOUR INTERNAL ORGANS.

FOR YOUR STOMACH.

FOR YOUR LEGS.

FOR YOUR FEET.

FOR YOUR BACK.

FOR THE GENITALS.

FOR YOUR LIFE.

SCAN SYMPATHY AND COUNTER-EMOTION FOR EACH OF THE FOLLOWING:

EVERY GROUP.

EVERY STATE OR NATION.

EVERY POPULATION.

FOR MAN IN GENERAL.

FOR THE WORLD.

SCAN SYMPATHY AND COUNTER-EMOTION FOR EACH OF THE FOLLOWING:

TREES.

CHRISTMAS TREES.

ANY LIFE FORM.

THE SUPREME BEING.

Now review all this analytically. You will discover the following: Before you felt sympathy, you offended in some way. You did something. Then you were sorry for it. This offense may have taken place years before your sympathy came about or only minutes. This is the emotional curve of sympathy. It goes from antagonism or anger, down to sympathy.

You know, now, where and on what dynamic you felt the greatest sympathy. Was it for mother? All right, let's find out where we first offended mother, hurt her in fact.

SCAN EVERY SUBJECT OF SYMPATHY EARLY ENOUGH TO FIND WHERE YOU OFFENDED. SCAN OUT THE OFFENSE.

IF IT DOESN'T COME CLEAR, SCAN REGRET AS AN EMOTION UNTIL IT DOES COME CLEAR.

IF YOU ENCOUNTER A GRIEF CHARGE, RUN IT AS A STRAIGHT INCIDENT AS CONTAINED IN THE SIXTH ACT.

LIST NOW THE CHIEF OBJECTS OF SYMPATHY.

CHECK EACH ONE AGAIN AND SCAN IT AGAIN.

This used to be called a "guilt complex." This process undoes them.

the
twelfth
act

the twelfth act

T IS TIME that we took another glance at BUTTONS. There are several things in particular that each human being finds aberrative and has in common.

BY LOCK SCANNING, RUN EACH ONE OF THE FOLLOWING WITH ATTENTION TO COUNTER-EMOTION AND COUNTER-THOUGHT:

HIDING THINGS:

HIDING THINGS FROM SELF.

HIDING THINGS FROM PARENTS.

HIDING THINGS FROM EMPLOYERS.

HIDING THINGS FROM TEACHERS.

HIDING THINGS FROM THE PUBLIC.

TALKING:

THE FEELING THAT PEOPLE WILL TALK.

THE FEAR THAT YOU MAY TALK.

THE SECRETS YOU DARE NOT TELL.

THE SECRETS YOU PROMISED NOT TO TELL.

BEING TALKED TO.

FEAR OF TALKING TO SOMEBODY.

FEAR OF TALKING TO CROWDS.

TALKING BEHIND PEOPLE'S BACKS.

METHODS OF AVOIDING BEING TALKED TO.

BEING TALKED INTO THINGS.

ENDURING:

ENDURING CONVERSATION.

ENDURING SITUATIONS.

WAITING. (AVOID PHYSICAL PAIN INCIDENTS.)

KEEPING THINGS:

KEEPING PETS.

KEEPING TOYS.

KEEPING POSSESSIONS.

YOUR DECISIONS TO KEEP THINGS.

YOUR FAILURE TO KEEP THINGS.

KEEPING PEOPLE.

LOSING THINGS:

LOSING PETS.

LOSING POSSESSIONS.

LOSING PEOPLE.

BEING LEFT (AS A COMMON, NOT A FINAL OCCURRENCE).

TAKING THINGS SERIOUSLY:

TAKING TASKS SERIOUSLY.

TAKING PEOPLE SERIOUSLY.

REGARDING SITUATIONS AS SERIOUS.

REGARDING WORK AS SERIOUS.

WHY YOU REGARDED THESE THINGS SERIOUSLY.

MOMENTS WHEN YOU DECIDED TO TAKE THINGS SERIOUSLY.

NOT TAKING THINGS SERIOUSLY:

EFFORTS NOT TO TAKE THINGS SERIOUSLY.

EFFORTS TO GET OTHERS NOT TO TAKE THINGS SERIOUSLY.

BEING TOLD TO TAKE THINGS SERIOUSLY.

REFUSING TO TAKE THINGS SERIOUSLY.

REGRET AT NOT TAKING SOMETHING SERIOUSLY.

TRYING TO STOP THINGS:

STOPPING PEOPLE.

STOPPING SITUATIONS.

STOPPING MECHANICAL THINGS. (YOU MAY FIND YOU HAVE TRIED TO STOP TIME OFTEN. THAT'S WHEN YOU GET A FIXED VISIO. SIMPLY RUN OFF THE REGRET.)

STARTING THINGS:

STARTING PEOPLE.

STARTING SITUATIONS.

STARTING MECHANICAL THINGS.

STARTING CHILDREN.

CHANGING THINGS:

DECISIONS NOT TO CHANGE THINGS.

DECISIONS TO CHANGE SELF.

DECISIONS TO CHANGE OTHERS.

EFFORTS TO CHANGE OTHERS.

CHANGING DIRECTIONS OF THINGS.

MOVING THINGS:

MOVING PEOPLE.

MOVING HEAVY OBJECTS.

MOVING YOURSELF.

RESISTING BEING MOVED OUT OF BED YOUR ENTIRE LIFETIME.

OWNING THINGS:

EFFORTS TO OWN THINGS.

EFFORTS TO KEEP OTHERS FROM CONTROLLING WHAT YOU OWN.

EFFORTS NOT TO OWN THINGS.

CARE OF CLOTHING:

TIMES YOU COULDN'T SELECT CLOTHING.

TIMES YOU WERE FORCED TO CARE FOR CLOTHING.

TIMES WHEN YOU COULDN'T WEAR CLOTHING YOU OWNED.

TIMES WHEN YOU COULDN'T HAVE CLOTHING.

CARE OF PERSON:

TIMES WHEN YOU WERE FORCED TO CARE FOR PERSON.

TIMES WHEN SOMEBODY ELSE FORCED CARE ON YOU.

TIMES WHEN YOU DECIDED NOT TO TAKE CARE OF YOURSELF.

TO BE:

TIMES WHEN YOU DECIDED TO BE SOMETHING.

TIMES WHEN YOU DECIDED YOU COULDN'T BE SOMETHING.

TIMES WHEN YOU DECIDED TO CHANGE BEING WHAT YOU WERE.

NOT TO BE:

TIMES WHEN YOU DECIDED TO QUIT.

DECISIONS TO STOP BEING WHAT YOU WERE.

HABITS:

TIMES WHEN YOU FIRST DECIDED TO HAVE ANY HABIT YOU HAVE.

TIMES WHEN YOU DECIDED NOT TO HAVE THE HABITS.

TIMES WHEN YOU DECIDED TO HAVE THE HABITS YOU HAVE.

KNOWING:

TIMES WHEN YOU DECIDED YOU KNEW.

NOT KNOWING:

TIMES WHEN YOU DECIDED YOU DID NOT KNOW.

Doubts:

Times when you doubted yourself.

Times when you doubted others.

Decisions that you could not trust.

Decisions that you could trust.

Wrong:

Times when you decided you had been wrong.

Times when you were afraid you were wrong.

Times when another said you were wrong.

Times when evidence turned up that you had been wrong.

Right:

Times when you hoped you weren't right.

Times when you found you were right.

Fear that you would not be right.

Time:

Incidents where you decided you didn't have any time.

Times when you said you didn't have time.

Times when somebody else didn't have time.

Times when you tried to get out of something by saying you didn't have time.

Times when you felt it was too late to start but that it should have been done.

The past:

Times when you decided to put all the past behind you.

Times when you decided the past was too terrible.

THE PRESENT:

YOUR DECISIONS ABOUT THE PRESENT, GOOD OR BAD.

THE FUTURE:

TIMES WHEN YOU DECIDED THE FUTURE WAS DOUBTFUL.

TIMES WHEN YOU WANTED THE FUTURE TO BE LIKE THE PAST.

TIMES WHEN YOU WERE AFRAID OF THE FUTURE.

TIMES WHEN YOU FEARED DYING.

TIMES WHEN YOU WANTED TO DIE.

TIMES WHEN YOU WERE GLAD TO HAVE A BRIGHT FUTURE.

TIMES WHEN YOUR PLANS FOR THE FUTURE HAD TO BE VIOLENTLY CHANGED.

TIMES WHEN SOMEBODY ELSE PLANNED YOUR FUTURE.

TIMES WHEN YOU PLANNED ANOTHER'S FUTURE.

HOPELESSNESS ABOUT THE FUTURE.

HOPE FOR THE FUTURE.

THE HOPELESSNESS OF ANOTHER ABOUT THE FUTURE.

THE HOPES OF ANOTHER FOR THE FUTURE.

FAILURE TO MEASURE UP TO WHAT ANOTHER HOPED FOR YOUR FUTURE.

AGREEMENT:

TIMES WHEN YOU WERE FORCED TO AGREE BUT DIDN'T WANT TO.

TIMES WHEN YOU FORCED OTHERS TO AGREE.

TIMES WHEN YOU WERE PREVENTED FROM AGREEING.

TIMES WHEN YOU PREVENTED OTHERS FROM AGREEING.

TIMES WHEN YOU WERE GLAD TO AGREE.

COMMUNICATION:

TIMES WHEN YOU WERE FORCED TO COMMUNICATE.

TIMES WHEN YOU WERE PREVENTED FROM COMMUNICATING.

TIMES WHEN YOU FORCED OTHERS TO COMMUNICATE.

TIMES WHEN YOU PREVENTED OTHERS FROM COMMUNICATING.

TIMES WHEN YOU WANTED TO COMMUNICATE.

AFFINITY:

TIMES WHEN YOU WERE FORCED TO LIKE SOMEBODY.

TIMES WHEN YOU WERE PREVENTED FROM LIKING SOMEBODY.

TIMES WHEN YOU FORCED ANOTHER TO LIKE YOU.

TIMES WHEN YOU PREVENTED ANOTHER FROM LIKING YOU.

TIMES WHEN YOU DECIDED YOU LIKED SOMEBODY.

INDIVIDUALITY:

TIMES WHEN YOU FELT YOU WEREN'T YOURSELF.

TIMES WHEN YOU DECIDED NOT TO BE YOURSELF.

TIMES WHEN YOU WERE FORCED TO BE YOURSELF.

TIMES WHEN YOU WERE INHIBITED FROM BEING YOURSELF.

TIMES WHEN YOU TRIED TO CHANGE ANOTHER PERSON.

TIMES WHEN YOU DECIDED NOT TO CHANGE SOMEBODY ELSE.

TRUTH:

TIMES WHEN YOU DECIDED TO LIE.

THE REASONS WHY YOU DECIDED TO LIE.

TIMES WHEN YOU FELT BETTER LYING.

TIMES WHEN LYING GOT YOU INTO TROUBLE.

TIMES WHEN YOU DECIDED NEVER TO LIE AGAIN.

FAITH:

TIMES WHEN YOU DECIDED TO HAVE FAITH IN THE SUPREME BEING.

TIMES WHEN YOU DECIDED NOT TO HAVE FAITH IN THE SUPREME BEING.

TIMES WHEN YOU DECIDED NOT TO HAVE FAITH IN YOUR GOVERNMENT.

TIMES WHEN YOU DECIDED TO HAVE FAITH IN YOUR GOVERNMENT.

TIMES WHEN YOU DECIDED TO HAVE FAITH IN YOURSELF.

TIMES WHEN YOU DIDN'T HAVE FAITH IN YOURSELF.

TIMES WHEN ANOTHER DID NOT HAVE ANY FAITH IN YOU.

ANGER:

ALL THE TIMES YOU HAVE BEEN ANGRY, WITH ATTENTION TO YOUR EMOTION AND COUNTER-EMOTION AND THE REASONS YOU WERE ANGRY.

FEAR:

ALL THE TIMES YOU HAVE BEEN AFRAID, WITH ATTENTION TO YOUR EMOTION AND THE ATMOSPHERE IN WHICH YOU WERE AND REASONS WHY YOU WERE AFRAID.

SCAN THE FIRST TIMES YOU DECIDED TO BE AFRAID.

COWARDICE:

SCAN ALL THE TIMES YOU CONSIDERED YOURSELF A COWARD.

SCAN THE TIMES YOU CONSIDERED OTHERS COWARDLY.

EMBARRASSMENT:

SCAN ALL THE TIMES YOU HAVE BEEN EMBARRASSED.

SCAN THE TIMES YOU HAVE BEEN EMBARRASSED FOR OTHERS.

SHAME:

SCAN ALL THE TIMES YOU HAVE BEEN ASHAMED.

SCAN THE TIMES YOU HAVE BEEN ASHAMED FOR OTHERS.

GRIEF:

SPOT AND RUN EVERY GRIEF CHARGE ON YOUR CASE.

LIST THEM IN THE BLANK BELOW, THEN RUN THEM.

RUN COUNTER-EMOTION AND REGRET UNTIL CHARGE COMES INTO VIEW. THEN RUN IT AS A SINGLE INCIDENT.

APATHY:

SCAN EVERY PERSON AROUND YOU WHO HAS EVER BEEN IN APATHY.

SCAN EVERY TIME YOU YOURSELF FELT APATHY.

SCAN THE TIMES WHEN YOU SOUGHT TO LIFT OTHERS OUT OF APATHY.

SCAN THE TIMES WHEN OTHERS SOUGHT TO LIFT YOU OUT OF APATHY.

SCAN ALL THE TIMES WHEN YOU HAVE BEEN SUPREMELY HAPPY.

SCAN THE TIMES YOU HAVE MADE OTHERS HAPPY.

RUN EMOTIONAL CURVES ON THE TIMES WHEN YOU TRIED TO ENTHUSE OTHERS AND FAILED.

RUN THE TIMES YOU ENTHUSED OTHERS AND SUCCEEDED.

The
Thirteenth
Act

the thirteenth act

THE SUBJECT of blame and regret is an interesting one. Blame of self and blame of others produce interesting results in recalls. Facsimiles can become clouded with blame and regret.

This is the subject of CAUSE and EFFECT.

An individual natively desires to be CAUSE.

He tries not to become a bad EFFECT.

You try to help people and people try to help you, because you and they want to be cause. When something bad happens, neither one wishes to be cause.

You want to be an effect. Then you find the effect bad. You try not to be an effect. And then you blame something or somebody.

Blaming yourself or others for being a cause is to deny yourself full control of your facsimiles. You say somebody caused something. You make them RESPONSIBLE. They are then CAUSE.

This is a powerful position. It ends up with your having given them control over a facsimile or many facsimiles. If you blame somebody hard enough and long enough, you have kept on electing them as cause until they are much more powerful than yourself.

If you blame your mother, for instance, you make your mother cause and must then obey her. And your facsimiles relating to her, or to your whole life, are out of your control.

If you blame yourself, this is an admitted failure and again you have facsimiles out of control.

You blame somebody, you elect them as cause. This makes you an effect of their cause. As an effect, you are thus placed well down the Tone Scale.

You desire to be an effect in some quarter and thereafter you may continue to be an effect and will go down the scale to a point where you may develop psychosomatic ills.

There are certain main spheres where one wishes to be an effect. Here we have the importance of aberration on the Second Dynamic, SEX. You wish to have the pleasure of sex. This is yourself electing yourself as an effect. As an effect, you can then be given pain on the Second Dynamic.

You wish to be pleasantly an effect in eating. You elect yourself an effect. You can thereafter be effected by pain in the food department. The basis of ulcers or any stomach trouble, including constipation, is the original desire to eat.

You wish to be amused and entertained. Thus amusement channels—sight, sound, rhythm—can become aberrated by pain.

It is a natural law that one cannot be aberrated without one's own consent. One must wish to be an effect before he can become an effect. If he becomes an effect, then he can later become "effected" unpleasantly by counter-efforts.

If you want to be an effect of your marital or sexual partner, or any sexual act, you open the door to being an unpleasant effect.

Examine the column of the Chart of Attitudes between CAUSE and EFFECT. This is a gradient scale of causes and effects.

Freud was right in selecting sex as being very aberrative. Before him, thousands of years of mystics knew they had to abstain from material or physical pleasures and sex in order to remain high and saintly. They did not know the mechanism at work. We now do. The moment they wanted to be an effect, they could become, in that channel, an unpleasant as well as a pleasant effect and so go down the Tone Scale.

There are several conditions relating to this: One is the desire not to be a cause. One is the desire not to be an effect. One is the desire to prevent something or somebody else from being a cause. One is the desire to prevent somebody or something else from being an effect.

In sex, one may not desire to be the cause of children. This would be for either a man or a woman. Children, in this society, can be embarrassing or expensive. One desires, at the same time, to cause a sexual partner pleasure. Here is desire not to be a cause fighting with the desire to be a cause. The result is conflict, aberration, impotence, sex punishment and irregular practices.

In sex, again, one desires greatly to be an effect for the sake of pleasure. One wishes to experience the pleasure of sex. He does not want to experience the pain of childbirth, for himself or his partner. Nor does he wish the effect of disease. Nor does he wish to be the effect of public antagonism toward sexual practice. Thus, his desire to be effect comes in conflict with his desire not to be effect and the result is aberration, impotence, glandular interruption, marital breakdowns, divorces, suicide and sudden death.

In food, cause and effect work similarly to sex. One wishes to be pleasantly effected by the flavor or substance of food. He may not want to have the effect of the work he has to do to eat or the propitiation he has to give to eat. He wants to be cause.

He is running a carbon-oxygen engine which has to have the effect of food. People low on the Tone Scale use this sure route to making a person into an effect by denying food or forcing people to eat food. The society uses this effect to get work done.

Low-scale mothers are very strict with their children about food. This is a sure method of control. By forcing the child to be a non-self-determined effect about food, the mother can control the child in many other ways. All low-scale control is done by forcing the individual to be an effect where the individual naturally has to be an effect. Where a naturally desired effect can be enforced by command, the enforcer can gain a wide control simply by continual demonstration that the target individual is an effect, not a cause.

The sexual sphere is peculiarly liable to cause and effect action because of the communication. Tactile is the most direct method of sensory communication. It is much more effective than talk. A close communication with a low-scale person brings down, as well, the affinity and the reality levels. If a sexual partner is demanding or insatiable, that partner elects the other into being an unwilling cause and denies his right to the effect and, thus, makes ruin of a personality. An individual aberrated enough about sex will do strange things to be a cause or an effect. He will substitute punishment for sex. He will pervert others.

Homosexuality comes from this manifestation and from the manifestation of life continuation for others. A boy whose mother is dominant will try to continue her life from any failure she has. A girl whose father is dominant will try to continue his life from any failure he has. The mother or the father was cause in the child's eyes. The child elected himself successor to cause. Break this life continuum concept by running sympathy and grief for the dominant parent and then run off the desires to be an effect and their failures and the homosexual is rehabilitated. Homosexuality is about 1.1 on the Tone Scale. So is general promiscuity.

The facsimiles of an individual can become considerably scrambled by masturbation. Practically all the ape family and Man masturbate. Masturbation is a prohibition result. It couldn't drive anyone crazy. But it can make the individual pull old sex facsimiles into present time for self-stimulation and opens the door for him to desire facsimiles to be in present time. After a while, he will be pulling pain facsimiles into present time.

These are the exercises of CAUSE and EFFECT Processing:

SCAN THROUGH EVERY TIME YOU DESIRED NOT TO BE A CAUSE SEXUALLY.

SCAN THROUGH EVERY TIME YOU REGRETTED BEING A SEXUAL CAUSE.

SCAN THROUGH EVERY TIME YOU DESIRED NOT TO BE AN EFFECT SEXUALLY.

SCAN THROUGH EVERY TIME YOU REGRETTED BEING AN EFFECT SEXUALLY.

SCAN THROUGH EVERY TIME YOU DESIRED TO BE A SEXUAL CAUSE.

SCAN THROUGH EVERY TIME YOU DESIRED TO BE A SEXUAL EFFECT.

(Don't forget that scanning is done until you are extroverted on the subject.)

SCAN EVERY TIME YOU CALLED UP AN OLD SEXUAL EXPERIENCE FOR YOUR AMUSEMENT.

SCAN EVERY TIME A SEXUAL PARTNER WAS DEMANDING.

SCAN EVERY TIME A SEXUAL PARTNER REFUSED SEX.

SCAN EVERY TIME SOMEBODY STOLE FROM YOU A MEMBER OF THE OTHER SEX.

SCAN EVERY FAILURE CONCERNING SEX.

SCAN EVERY TIME YOU OBEYED A SEXUAL PARTNER ABOUT ANYTHING.

SCAN EVERY TIME YOU RESENTED SOMEBODY'S SEXUAL CONVERSATION.

SCAN EVERY TIME YOU ENJOYED SOMEBODY'S SEXUAL CONVERSATION.

SCAN EVERY TIME YOU TRIED TO HIDE SOMETHING ABOUT SEX.

Now let us repeat these operations on the subject of food:

SCAN EVERY TIME YOU DESIRED FOOD.

SCAN EVERY TIME YOU WERE FORCED TO EAT.

SCAN EVERY TIME YOU WORRIED ABOUT FOOD.

SCAN EVERY TIME YOU BLAMED FOOD FOR AN ILLNESS.

SCAN EVERY FEELING OF QUEASINESS ABOUT FOOD UNTIL ANY PHYSICAL SENSATION IS GONE.

Now let us go into entertainment:

SCAN EVERY TIME YOU TRIED TO ENTERTAIN SOMEBODY AND FAILED.

SCAN EVERY TIME YOU WANTED TO BE ENTERTAINED AND WEREN'T.

SCAN EVERY TIME SOMEBODY WANTED TO BE ENTERTAINED AND YOU DIDN'T WANT TO.

SCAN EVERY TIME YOU WERE BORED WITH ENTERTAINMENT.

SCAN EVERY TIME YOU WANTED TO RETAIN THE SENSATION OF HAVING BEEN ENTERTAINED.

Now let us go into perceptions in general:

SCAN EVERY TIME YOU DID NOT WANT TO BE TOUCHED.

SCAN EVERY TIME YOU WERE FORCED TO TOUCH SOMETHING.

SCAN EVERY TIME YOU WANTED TO TOUCH SOMETHING AND COULDN'T.

SCAN EVERY TIME YOU TOUCHED A SEXUAL PARTNER.

SCAN EVERY TIME YOU DIDN'T WANT TO LOOK.

SCAN EVERY TIME YOU WANTED TO BE PLEASED BY LOOKING.

SCAN EVERY TIME YOU WISHED THINGS LOOKED AS GOOD AS THEY USED TO.

SCAN EVERY REGRET YOU'VE EVER HAD ABOUT SIGHT.

SCAN EVERY TIME YOU DECIDED YOU COULDN'T SEE WELL.

SCAN EVERY TIME YOU WERE TOLD YOU COULDN'T SEE.

SCAN EVERY TIME YOU AGREED YOU COULDN'T SEE.

SCAN EVERY TIME YOU DIDN'T WANT TO LISTEN.

SCAN EVERY TIME YOU WANTED TO HEAR AND COULDN'T.

SCAN EVERY TIME YOU WANTED TO HEAR SOMETHING PLEASANT.

SCAN EVERY TIME YOUR EARS RANG.

SCAN EVERY TIME YOU DECIDED SOMETHING WAS WRONG WITH YOUR HEARING.

SCAN EVERY TIME YOU TASTED SOMETHING BAD.

SCAN EVERY TIME YOU TASTED SOMETHING GOOD.

SCAN EVERY TIME YOUR MOTHER PUSHED YOU AWAY.

SCAN EVERY TIME YOU WANTED A GOOD EFFECT IN YOUR STOMACH AND FAILED.

SCAN EVERY TIME YOU LOOKED WITH FAVOR ON A BOTTLE. (Get way back early on this one.)

SCAN EVERY TIME YOU TOLD SOMEBODY YOU WERE TIRED.

SCAN EVERY TIME YOU TOLD SOMEBODY YOU DIDN'T FEEL WELL.

SCAN EVERY TIME YOU FELT SYMPATHY FOR A BLIND MAN.

SCAN EVERY TIME YOU FELT SYMPATHY FOR A DEAF MAN.

SCAN EVERY TIME YOU SMELLED SOMETHING BAD AND THE COUNTER-EMOTION.

SCAN ALL THE TIMES YOU SMELLED SOMETHING GOOD.

SCAN ALL THE TIMES YOU HID THE FACT THAT SOME EFFECT PLEASED YOU.

SCAN ALL THE TIMES YOU WANTED TO BE CAUSE.

SCAN ALL THE TIMES YOU CONCLUDED YOU WERE IMPORTANT.

SCAN ALL THE TIMES YOU CONCLUDED YOU WERE NOT IMPORTANT.

SCAN ALL THE TIMES YOU CONCLUDED YOU WERE NOBODY.

SCAN ALL THE TIMES YOU CONCLUDED YOU WERE SOMEBODY.

SCAN ALL THE TIMES YOU THOUGHT YOU WERE NOT VALUABLE.

SCAN ALL THE TIMES YOU THOUGHT YOU WERE VALUABLE.

SCAN ALL THE TIMES YOU TRIED TO CONVINCE SOMEBODY YOU WERE IMPORTANT.

SCAN ALL THE TIMES YOU TRIED TO CONVINCE SOMEBODY YOU WERE SOMEBODY.

SCAN ALL THE TIMES YOU TRIED TO CONVINCE SOMEBODY YOU WERE VALUABLE.

SCAN ALL THE TIMES YOU TRIED TO STOP SOUND DURING SEX.

SCAN ALL THE TIMES YOU STOPPED OR INTERRUPTED SEX.

SCAN ALL THE TIMES YOU STARTED SEX AND FAILED.

SCAN ALL THE TIMES YOU WANTED TO HEAR SOUNDS DURING SEX.

SCAN ALL THE TIMES YOU WANTED SEXUAL CONVERSATION TO EFFECT YOU.

SCAN ALL THE TIMES YOU RESENTED SEXUAL CONVERSATION.

SCAN ALL THE TIMES YOU RESENTED "DIRTY JOKES."

SCAN OFF THE COUNTER-EMOTION OF EACH EXERCISE ABOVE, EACH IN TURN.

As you have read here before and as you have come to suspect in your processing, your own decisions and evaluations are the most important items in the entire process.

What you decide is LAW to you. What you evaluate is evaluation to you.

SELF-CONFIDENCE is nothing more than belief in one's ability to decide and in one's decisions.

MOST PEOPLE THINK THEY HAVE UNCONSCIOUS MINDS OR BACKGROUNDS OF MOTIVATION SIMPLY BECAUSE THEY HAVE REFUSED THEIR OWN POWER TO DECIDE.

Negation of decision, refusal of decision, letting others decide are the most powerful sources of aberration. They apply to any and all subjects.

THIS SECTION IS DEVOTED TO PICKING UP EACH AND EVERY POSTULATE YOU CAN NOW REACH IN YOUR WHOLE LIFETIME.

A POSTULATE is a decision you make to yourself or to others. You make one. Then, afterwards, conditions change and you make a second one. This makes the first one wrong. You make a postulate as cause and then, by having lived through some instants of time, become an effect of your own cause.

A computer could not work if you kept leaving its totals on the calculator for the next problem. That is what you do with decisions. They have to be made. Sweep them up before making more. It is a new method of thinking and one that keeps you happy.

No need to be afraid of making decisions. Simply sweep up old decisions. You make New Year's resolutions. And you make them into the teeth of old resolutions which were different. Then you don't keep your new resolutions and you tell yourself you are weak-willed. You aren't weak-willed. You are simply obeying yourself as of yesterday.

Emotion and effort cover up these postulates. They should be free and clear by now and, indeed, should blow at a glance. There are two parts to every postulate: There is the evaluation of data and the decision itself.

When you pick up an old decision, also pick up the *reason* you made it. They "blow" very quickly.

SCAN THROUGH EVERY DECISION, WITH ITS REASON WHY, YOU HAVE MADE ABOUT WOMEN.

SCAN EVERY DECISION ABOUT MEN.

SCAN EVERY DECISION ABOUT YOURSELF.

SCAN EVERY DECISION ABOUT THE WORLD.

SCAN EVERY DECISION ABOUT DOGS.

SCAN EVERY DECISION ABOUT CATS.

SCAN EVERY DECISION ABOUT HORSES.

SCAN EVERY DECISION ABOUT FISH.

SCAN EVERY DECISION ABOUT FOOD.

SCAN EVERY DECISION ABOUT SEX.

SCAN EVERY DECISION ABOUT CLOTHING.

SCAN EVERY DECISION ABOUT SHOES.

SCAN EVERY DECISION ABOUT HOUSES.

SCAN EVERY DECISION ABOUT CARS.

SCAN EVERY DECISION ABOUT SCENERY.

SCAN EVERY DECISION ABOUT CRIMINALS.

SCAN EVERY DECISION ABOUT NEWSPAPERS.

SCAN EVERY DECISION ABOUT YOUR MOTHER.

SCAN EVERY DECISION ABOUT YOUR FATHER.

SCAN EVERY DECISION ABOUT PHILOSOPHY.

SCAN EVERY DECISION ABOUT PSYCHOLOGY.

SCAN EVERY DECISION ABOUT EDUCATION.

SCAN EVERY DECISION ABOUT MONEY.

SCAN EVERY DECISION ABOUT WORK.

SCAN EVERY DECISION ABOUT LIFE.

SCAN EVERY DECISION ABOUT GOD.

SCAN EVERY DECISION ABOUT FIGHTING.

SCAN EVERY DECISION ABOUT SIN.

SCAN EVERY DECISION ABOUT OBEYING.

SCAN EVERY DECISION ABOUT MAKING OTHERS OBEY.

SCAN EVERY DECISION ABOUT GOVERNMENT.

SCAN EVERY DECISION TO APOLOGIZE.

SCAN EVERY DECISION TO BE JEALOUS.

SCAN EVERY DECISION TO BE ANGRY.

SCAN EVERY DECISION TO HELP.

SCAN EVERY CONCLUSION THAT YOU HAVE FAILED.

SCAN EVERY DECISION THAT YOU HAVE SUCCEEDED.

SCAN EVERY DECISION THAT YOU ARE A GOOD SEXUAL PARTNER.

SCAN EVERY DECISION THAT YOU ARE A POOR SEXUAL PARTNER.

SCAN EVERY DECISION THAT ANY OTHER IS A GOOD SEXUAL PARTNER.

SCAN EVERY DECISION THAT ANY OTHER IS A BAD SEXUAL PARTNER.

SCAN EVERY DECISION TO REGRET SOMETHING.

SCAN EVERY DECISION TO ENJOY SOMETHING.

SCAN EVERY TIME A CONTRIBUTION HAS BEEN REJECTED.

SCAN EVERY TIME A CONTRIBUTION HAS BEEN ACCEPTED.

SCAN EVERY DECISION TO RESENT CRITICISM.

SCAN EVERY DECISION TO WORK FOR PRAISE.

SCAN EVERY DECISION TO QUIT.

SCAN EVERY DECISION TO START.

SCAN EVERY DECISION TO STOP.

SCAN EVERY DECISION TO CHANGE.

SCAN EVERY DECISION TO WAIT.

SCAN EVERY DECISION TO MOVE.

SCAN EVERY CONCLUSION THAT YOU ARE ILL.

SCAN EVERY CONCLUSION THAT YOU ARE WELL.

SCAN EVERY DECISION TO RESENT SOMETHING.

SCAN EVERY DECISION TO BE HUMAN.

the
Fourteenth
act

the fourteenth act

IRST REVIEW the earlier data about CONTROL CENTERS. Then do the following:

WRITE DOWN EVERY TIME YOU CONSIDERED YOURSELF TO HAVE HAD A MAJOR FAILURE.

RUN EACH SINGLE INCIDENT CONSECUTIVELY FROM THE MOMENT YOU PLANNED THE ACTION, THROUGH THE MOMENT YOU REALIZED YOU HAD FAILED, THROUGH THE POSSIBLE RESULTING ILLNESS AND TO THE MOMENT WHEN YOU FELT CHEERFUL AGAIN. GO THROUGH EACH INCIDENT IN COMPLETE DETAIL WITH COUNTER-THOUGHT, COUNTER-EMOTION AND BLAME AND REGRET, WITH ALL AVAILABLE PERCEPTICS UNTIL THE ENTIRE INCIDENT IS IN TONE 4.0. THAT TONE IS LAUGHTER. DO NOT QUIT IN BOREDOM: THAT'S ONLY PARTWAY THERE.

SCAN OFF ALL LOCKS FROM EACH FAILURE.

Now the next step.

RUN EVERY DEATH OF EVERYONE YOU HAVE KNOWN IN THIS LIFETIME. RUN REGRET AND BLAME OF SELF OR OTHERS UNTIL THE DEATH SHOWS UP IN COMPLETE DETAIL. RUN THE DEATH COMPLETELY OUT. IF YOU HAVE DIFFICULTY, RUN EVERY TIME YOU OFFENDED THE DEAD PERSON, EVERY TIME YOU FELT SYMPATHY FOR THE DEAD PERSON, UNTIL THE INCIDENT IS IN FULL VIEW. THEN RUN IT COMPLETELY. REMEMBER TO FIND AND RUN ANY DECISION TO TRY TO MAKE THIS PERSON LIVE OR ANY REGRET THAT YOU DIDN'T MAKE THIS PERSON LIVE.

RUN OFF THE DEATH OF EVERY PET SIMILARLY TO PEOPLE.

This should rehabilitate all CONTROL CENTERS for this lifetime.

The
Fifteenth
Act

the fifteenth act

THIS IS A REVIEW ACT and is very necessary to a completion of processing.

Turn back to the beginning of the book and read all the text up to the Processing Section. That text will mean a great deal more to you now than it did before.

NOW TAKE THE SECOND ACT AND REVIEW EVERYTHING YOU DID IN IT. THERE WILL BE MUCH MORE DATA FOR IT AND MUCH MORE UNDERSTANDING.

TAKE EACH ACT CONSECUTIVELY AND DO THE COMPLETE ACT AGAIN. READ THE TEXTS FOR THE ACTS AND REPEAT ALL THE EXERCISES. NEW DATA WILL BE FOUND ALL UP AND DOWN THE LINE.

defir
Log

tions,
cs and
axioms

Definitions,
Logics and Axioms

THESE ARE THE DEFINITIONS, LOGICS AND AXIOMS of this science. It should be borne in mind that these actually form epistemology, the science of knowledge. These cannot but embrace various fields and sciences. They are listed in this volume without further elucidation, but will be found to be self-explanatory for the most part. Adequate phenomena exist to demonstrate the self-evidence of these Definitions, Postulates, Logics and Axioms.

The first section, the Logics, is separate from the Axioms only in that from the system of thinking so evaluated, the Axioms themselves flow. The word "logics" is used here to mean postulates pertaining to the organizational structure of alignment.

the Logics

LOGIC 1:

KNOWLEDGE IS A WHOLE GROUP OR SUBDIVISION OF A GROUP OF DATA OR SPECULATIONS OR CONCLUSIONS ON DATA OR METHODS OF GAINING DATA.

LOGIC 2:

A BODY OF KNOWLEDGE IS A BODY OF DATA, ALIGNED OR UNALIGNED, OR METHODS OF GAINING DATA.

LOGIC 3:

ANY KNOWLEDGE WHICH CAN BE SENSED, MEASURED OR EXPERIENCED BY ANY ENTITY IS CAPABLE OF INFLUENCING THAT ENTITY.

> COROLLARY: THAT KNOWLEDGE WHICH CANNOT BE SENSED, MEASURED OR EXPERIENCED BY ANY ENTITY OR TYPE OF ENTITY CANNOT INFLUENCE THAT ENTITY OR TYPE OF ENTITY.

LOGIC 4:

A DATUM IS A FACSIMILE OF STATES OF BEING, STATES OF NOT BEING, ACTIONS OR INACTIONS, CONCLUSIONS OR SUPPOSITIONS IN THE PHYSICAL OR ANY OTHER UNIVERSE.

LOGIC 5:

A DEFINITION OF TERMS IS NECESSARY TO THE ALIGNMENT, STATEMENT AND RESOLUTION OF SUPPOSITIONS, OBSERVATIONS, PROBLEMS AND SOLUTIONS AND THEIR COMMUNICATION.

> DEFINITION—DESCRIPTIVE DEFINITION: *One which classifies by characteristics, by describing existing states of being.*

> DEFINITION—DIFFERENTIATIVE DEFINITION: *One which compares unlikeness to existing states of being or not being.*

DEFINITION–ASSOCIATIVE DEFINITION: *One which declares likeness to existing states of being or not being.*

DEFINITION–ACTION DEFINITION: *One which delineates cause and potential change of state of being by cause of existence, inexistence, action, inaction, purpose or lack of purpose.*

LOGIC 6:

ABSOLUTES ARE UNOBTAINABLE.

LOGIC 7:

GRADIENT SCALES ARE NECESSARY TO THE EVALUATION OF PROBLEMS AND THEIR DATA.

This is the tool of infinity-valued logic: Absolutes are unobtainable. Terms such as good and bad, alive and dead, right and wrong, are used only in conjunction with gradient scales. On the scale of right and wrong, everything above zero or center would be more and more right, approaching an infinite rightness, and everything below center would be more and more wrong, approaching infinite wrongness. All things assisting the survival of the survivor are considered to be *right* for the survivor. All things inhibiting survival from the viewpoint of the survivor can be considered *wrong* for the survivor. The more a thing assists survival, the more it can be considered right for the survivor; the more a thing or action inhibits survival, the more it is wrong from the viewpoint of the intended survivor.

COROLLARY: ANY DATUM HAS ONLY RELATIVE TRUTH.

COROLLARY: TRUTH IS RELATIVE TO ENVIRONMENTS, EXPERIENCE AND TRUTH.

LOGIC 8:

A DATUM CAN BE EVALUATED ONLY BY A DATUM OF COMPARABLE MAGNITUDE.

LOGIC 9:
A DATUM IS AS VALUABLE AS IT HAS BEEN EVALUATED.

LOGIC 10:
THE VALUE OF A DATUM IS ESTABLISHED BY THE AMOUNT OF ALIGNMENT (relationship) IT IMPARTS TO OTHER DATA.

LOGIC 11:
THE VALUE OF A DATUM OR FIELD OF DATA CAN BE ESTABLISHED BY ITS DEGREE OF ASSISTANCE IN SURVIVAL OR ITS INHIBITION TO SURVIVAL.

LOGIC 12:
THE VALUE OF A DATUM OR A FIELD OF DATA IS MODIFIED BY THE VIEWPOINT OF THE OBSERVER.

LOGIC 13:
PROBLEMS ARE RESOLVED BY COMPARTMENTING THEM INTO AREAS OF SIMILAR MAGNITUDE AND DATA, COMPARING THEM TO DATA ALREADY KNOWN OR PARTIALLY KNOWN, AND RESOLVING EACH AREA. DATA WHICH CANNOT BE KNOWN IMMEDIATELY MAY BE RESOLVED BY ADDRESSING WHAT IS KNOWN AND USING ITS SOLUTION TO RESOLVE THE REMAINDER.

LOGIC 14:
FACTORS INTRODUCED INTO A PROBLEM OR SOLUTION WHICH DO NOT DERIVE FROM NATURAL LAW BUT ONLY FROM AUTHORITARIAN COMMAND ABERRATE THAT PROBLEM OR SOLUTION.

LOGIC 15:
THE INTRODUCTION OF AN ARBITRARY INTO A PROBLEM OR SOLUTION INVITES THE FURTHER INTRODUCTION OF ARBITRARIES INTO PROBLEMS AND SOLUTIONS.

LOGIC 16:
AN ABSTRACT POSTULATE MUST BE COMPARED TO THE UNIVERSE TO WHICH IT APPLIES AND BROUGHT INTO THE CATEGORY OF

THINGS WHICH CAN BE SENSED, MEASURED OR EXPERIENCED IN THAT UNIVERSE BEFORE SUCH POSTULATE CAN BE CONSIDERED WORKABLE.

LOGIC 17:

THOSE FIELDS WHICH MOST DEPEND UPON AUTHORITATIVE OPINION FOR THEIR DATA LEAST CONTAIN KNOWN NATURAL LAW.

LOGIC 18:

A POSTULATE IS AS VALUABLE AS IT IS WORKABLE.

LOGIC 19:

THE WORKABILITY OF A POSTULATE IS ESTABLISHED BY THE DEGREE TO WHICH IT EXPLAINS EXISTING PHENOMENA ALREADY KNOWN, BY THE DEGREE THAT IT PREDICTS NEW PHENOMENA WHICH WHEN LOOKED FOR WILL BE FOUND TO EXIST, AND BY THE DEGREE THAT IT DOES NOT REQUIRE THAT PHENOMENA WHICH DO NOT EXIST IN FACT BE CALLED INTO EXISTENCE FOR ITS EXPLANATION.

LOGIC 20:

A SCIENCE MAY BE CONSIDERED TO BE A LARGE BODY OF ALIGNED DATA WHICH HAS SIMILARITY IN APPLICATION AND WHICH HAS BEEN DEDUCED OR INDUCED FROM BASIC POSTULATES.

LOGIC 21:

MATHEMATICS ARE METHODS OF POSTULATING OR RESOLVING REAL OR ABSTRACT DATA IN ANY UNIVERSE AND INTEGRATING BY SYMBOLIZATION OF DATA, POSTULATES AND RESOLUTIONS.

LOGIC 22:

THE HUMAN MIND* IS AN OBSERVER, POSTULATOR, CREATOR AND STORAGE PLACE OF KNOWLEDGE.

---

*The human mind by definition includes the awareness unit of the living organism, the observer, the computer of data, the spirit, the memory storage, the life force and the individual motivator of the living organism. It is used as distinct from the brain which can be considered to be motivated by the mind. —LRH

LOGIC 23:

THE HUMAN MIND IS A SERVOMECHANISM TO ANY MATHEMATICS EVOLVED OR EMPLOYED BY THE HUMAN MIND.

POSTULATE: THE HUMAN MIND AND INVENTIONS OF THE HUMAN MIND ARE CAPABLE OF RESOLVING ANY AND ALL PROBLEMS WHICH CAN BE SENSED, MEASURED OR EXPERIENCED DIRECTLY OR INDIRECTLY.

COROLLARY: THE HUMAN MIND IS CAPABLE OF RESOLVING THE PROBLEM OF THE HUMAN MIND.

The borderline of solution of this science lies between *why* life is surviving and *how* life is surviving. It is possible to resolve *how* life is surviving without resolving *why* life is surviving.

LOGIC 24:

THE RESOLUTION OF THE PHILOSOPHICAL, SCIENTIFIC AND HUMAN STUDIES (such as economics, politics, sociology, medicine, criminology, etc.) DEPENDS PRIMARILY UPON THE RESOLUTION OF THE PROBLEMS OF THE HUMAN MIND.

NOTE: The primary step in resolving the broad activities of Man could be considered to be the resolving of the activities of the mind itself. Hence, the Logics carry to this point and then proceed as Axioms concerning the human mind, such Axioms being substantiated as relative truths by much newly discovered phenomena. The ensuing Axioms, from Logic 24, apply no less to the various -ologies than they do to de-aberrating or improving the operation of the mind. It should not be thought that the following Axioms are devoted to the construction of anything as limited as a therapy, which is only incidental to the resolution of human aberration and such things as psychosomatic illnesses. These Axioms are capable of such solution, as has been demonstrated, but such a narrow application would indicate a very narrow scope of view.

axioms

AXIOM 1:

THE SOURCE OF LIFE IS A STATIC OF PECULIAR AND PARTICULAR PROPERTIES.

AXIOM 2:

AT LEAST A PORTION OF THE STATIC CALLED LIFE IS IMPINGED UPON THE PHYSICAL UNIVERSE.

AXIOM 3:

THAT PORTION OF THE STATIC OF LIFE WHICH IS IMPINGED UPON THE PHYSICAL UNIVERSE HAS FOR ITS DYNAMIC GOAL, SURVIVAL AND ONLY SURVIVAL.

AXIOM 4:

THE PHYSICAL UNIVERSE IS REDUCIBLE TO MOTION OF ENERGY OPERATING IN SPACE THROUGH TIME.

AXIOM 5:

THAT PORTION OF THE STATIC OF LIFE CONCERNED WITH THE LIFE ORGANISMS OF THE PHYSICAL UNIVERSE IS CONCERNED WHOLLY WITH MOTION.

AXIOM 6:

THE LIFE STATIC HAS AS ONE OF ITS PROPERTIES THE ABILITY TO MOBILIZE AND ANIMATE MATTER INTO LIVING ORGANISMS.

AXIOM 7:

THE LIFE STATIC IS ENGAGED IN A CONQUEST OF THE PHYSICAL UNIVERSE.

AXIOM 8:

THE LIFE STATIC CONQUERS THE MATERIAL UNIVERSE BY LEARNING AND APPLYING THE PHYSICAL LAWS OF THE PHYSICAL UNIVERSE.

SYMBOL: The symbol for the *Life Static* in use hereafter is the Greek letter *theta* (θ).

AXIOM 9:

A FUNDAMENTAL OPERATION OF *THETA* IN SURVIVING IS BRINGING ORDER INTO THE CHAOS OF THE PHYSICAL UNIVERSE.

AXIOM 10:

THETA BRINGS ORDER INTO CHAOS BY CONQUERING WHATEVER IN *MEST* MAY BE PRO-SURVIVAL AND DESTROYING WHATEVER IN *MEST* MAY BE CONTRA-SURVIVAL, AT LEAST THROUGH THE MEDIUM OF LIFE ORGANISMS.

SYMBOL: The symbol for the *physical universe* in use hereafter is *MEST*, from the first letters of the words Matter, Energy, Space and Time, or the Greek letter *phi* (ϕ).

AXIOM 11:

A LIFE ORGANISM IS COMPOSED OF MATTER AND ENERGY IN SPACE AND TIME, ANIMATED BY *THETA*.

SYMBOL: Living organism or organisms will hereafter be represented by the Greek letter *lambda* (λ).

AXIOM 12:

THE *MEST* PART OF THE ORGANISM FOLLOWS THE LAWS OF THE PHYSICAL SCIENCES. ALL *LAMBDA* IS CONCERNED WITH MOTION.

AXIOM 13:

THETA OPERATING THROUGH *LAMBDA* CONVERTS THE FORCES OF THE PHYSICAL UNIVERSE INTO FORCES TO CONQUER THE PHYSICAL UNIVERSE.

AXIOM 14:

THETA WORKING UPON PHYSICAL UNIVERSE MOTION MUST
MAINTAIN A HARMONIOUS RATE OF MOTION.

The limits of *lambda* are narrow, both as to thermal and mechanical
motion.

AXIOM 15:

LAMBDA IS THE INTERMEDIATE STEP IN THE CONQUEST OF THE
PHYSICAL UNIVERSE.

AXIOM 16:

THE BASIC FOOD OF ANY ORGANISM CONSISTS OF LIGHT AND
CHEMICALS.

Organisms can exist only as higher levels of complexities because
lower levels of converters exist.

Theta evolves organisms from lower to higher forms and supports
them by the existence of lower converter forms.

AXIOM 17:

THETA, VIA *LAMBDA*, EFFECTS AN EVOLUTION OF *MEST*.

In this we have the waste products of organisms on the one hand
as those very complex chemicals which bacteria make and, on the
other hand, we have the physical face of the Earth being changed
by animals and men, such changes as grass holding mountains
from eroding or roots causing boulders to break, buildings being
built, and rivers being dammed. There is obviously an evolution
in *MEST* in progress under the incursion of *theta*.

AXIOM 18:

LAMBDA, EVEN WITHIN A SPECIES, VARIES IN ITS ENDOWMENT
OF *THETA*.

AXIOM 19:

THE EFFORT OF *LAMBDA* IS TOWARD SURVIVAL.

THE GOAL OF *LAMBDA* IS SURVIVAL.

THE PENALTY OF FAILURE TO ADVANCE TOWARD THAT GOAL IS TO SUCCUMB.

> DEFINITION: *Persistence is the ability to exert continuance of effort toward survival goals.*

AXIOM 20:

LAMBDA CREATES, CONSERVES, MAINTAINS, ACQUIRES, DESTROYS, CHANGES, OCCUPIES, GROUPS AND DISPERSES *MEST*. *LAMBDA* SURVIVES BY ANIMATING AND MOBILIZING OR DESTROYING MATTER AND ENERGY IN SPACE AND TIME.

AXIOM 21:

LAMBDA IS DEPENDENT UPON OPTIMUM MOTION. MOTION WHICH IS TOO SWIFT AND MOTION WHICH IS TOO SLOW ARE EQUALLY CONTRA-SURVIVAL.

AXIOM 22:

THETA AND THOUGHT ARE SIMILAR ORDERS OF STATIC.

AXIOM 23:

ALL THOUGHT IS CONCERNED WITH MOTION.

AXIOM 24:

THE ESTABLISHMENT OF AN OPTIMUM MOTION IS A BASIC GOAL OF REASON.

> DEFINITION: Lambda *is a chemical heat engine existing in space and time motivated by the Life Static and directed by thought.*

AXIOM 25:

THE BASIC PURPOSE OF REASON IS THE CALCULATION OR ESTIMATION OF EFFORT.

AXIOM 26:

THOUGHT IS ACCOMPLISHED BY *THETA FACSIMILES* OF PHYSICAL UNIVERSE, ENTITIES OR ACTIONS.

AXIOM 27:

THETA IS SATISFIED ONLY WITH HARMONIOUS ACTION OR OPTIMUM MOTION AND REJECTS OR DESTROYS ACTION OR MOTION ABOVE OR BELOW ITS TOLERANCE BAND.

AXIOM 28:

THE MIND IS CONCERNED WHOLLY WITH THE ESTIMATION OF EFFORT.

DEFINITION: *Mind is the* theta *command post of any organism or organisms.*

AXIOM 29:

THE BASIC ERRORS OF REASON ARE FAILURE TO DIFFERENTIATE AMONGST MATTER, ENERGY, SPACE AND TIME.

AXIOM 30:

RIGHTNESS IS PROPER CALCULATION OF EFFORT.

AXIOM 31:

WRONGNESS IS ALWAYS MISCALCULATION OF EFFORT.

AXIOM 32:

THETA CAN EXERT ITSELF DIRECTLY OR EXTENSIONALLY.

Theta can direct physical application of the organism to the environment or, through the mind, can first calculate the action or extend, as in language, ideas.

AXIOM 33:

CONCLUSIONS ARE DIRECTED TOWARD THE INHIBITION, MAINTENANCE OR ACCELERATIONS OF EFFORTS.

AXIOM 34:

THE COMMON DENOMINATOR OF ALL LIFE ORGANISMS IS MOTION.

AXIOM 35:

EFFORT OF AN ORGANISM TO SURVIVE OR SUCCUMB IS PHYSICAL MOTION OF A LIFE ORGANISM AT A GIVEN MOMENT IN TIME THROUGH SPACE.

DEFINITION: *Motion is any change in orientation in space.*

DEFINITION: *Force is random effort.*

DEFINITION: *Effort is directed force.*

AXIOM 36:

AN ORGANISM'S EFFORT CAN BE TO REMAIN AT REST OR PERSIST IN A GIVEN MOTION.

Static state has position in time, but an organism which is remaining positionally in a static state, if alive, is still continuing a highly complex pattern of motion, such as the heartbeat, digestion, etc.

The efforts of organisms to survive or succumb are assisted, compelled or opposed by the efforts of other organisms, matter, energy, space and time.

DEFINITION: *Attention is a motion which must remain at an optimum effort.*

Attention is aberrated by becoming unfixed and sweeping at random or becoming too fixed without sweeping.

Unknown threats to survival when sensed cause attention to sweep without fixing.

Known threats to survival when sensed cause attention to fix.

AXIOM 37:

THE ULTIMATE GOAL OF *LAMBDA* IS INFINITE SURVIVAL.

AXIOM 38:

DEATH IS ABANDONMENT BY *THETA* OF A LIFE ORGANISM OR RACE OR SPECIES WHERE THESE CAN NO LONGER SERVE *THETA* IN ITS GOALS OF INFINITE SURVIVAL.

AXIOM 39:

THE REWARD OF AN ORGANISM ENGAGING UPON SURVIVAL ACTIVITY IS PLEASURE.

AXIOM 40:

THE PENALTY OF AN ORGANISM FAILING TO ENGAGE UPON SURVIVAL ACTIVITY, OR ENGAGING IN NON-SURVIVAL ACTIVITY, IS PAIN.

AXIOM 41:

THE CELL AND/OR VIRUS ARE THE PRIMARY BUILDING BLOCKS OF LIFE ORGANISMS.

AXIOM 42:

THE VIRUS AND CELL ARE MATTER AND ENERGY ANIMATED AND MOTIVATED IN SPACE AND TIME BY *THETA*.

AXIOM 43:

THETA MOBILIZES THE VIRUS AND CELL IN COLONIAL AGGREGATIONS TO INCREASE POTENTIAL MOTION AND ACCOMPLISH EFFORT.

AXIOM 44:

THE GOAL OF VIRUSES AND CELLS IS SURVIVAL IN SPACE THROUGH TIME.

AXIOM 45:

THE TOTAL MISSION OF HIGHER ORGANISMS, VIRUSES AND CELLS IS THE SAME AS THAT OF THE VIRUS AND CELL.

AXIOM 46:

COLONIAL AGGREGATIONS OF VIRUSES AND CELLS CAN BE IMBUED WITH MORE *THETA* THAN THEY INHERENTLY CONTAINED.

Life energy joins any group whether a group of organisms or group of cells composing an organism. Here we have personal entity, individuation, etc.

AXIOM 47:

EFFORT CAN BE ACCOMPLISHED BY *LAMBDA* ONLY THROUGH THE COORDINATION OF ITS PARTS TOWARD GOALS.

AXIOM 48:

AN ORGANISM IS EQUIPPED TO BE GOVERNED AND CONTROLLED BY A MIND.

AXIOM 49:

THE PURPOSE OF THE MIND IS TO POSE AND RESOLVE PROBLEMS RELATING TO SURVIVAL AND TO DIRECT THE EFFORT OF THE ORGANISM ACCORDING TO THESE SOLUTIONS.

AXIOM 50:

ALL PROBLEMS ARE POSED AND RESOLVED THROUGH ESTIMATIONS OF EFFORT.

AXIOM 51:

THE MIND CAN CONFUSE POSITION IN SPACE WITH POSITION IN TIME. (Counter-efforts producing action phrases.)

AXIOM 52:

AN ORGANISM PROCEEDING TOWARD SURVIVAL IS DIRECTED BY THE MIND OF THAT ORGANISM IN THE ACCOMPLISHMENT OF SURVIVAL EFFORT.

AXIOM 53:

AN ORGANISM PROCEEDING TOWARD SUCCUMB IS DIRECTED BY THE MIND OF THAT ORGANISM IN THE ACCOMPLISHMENT OF DEATH.

AXIOM 54:

SURVIVAL OF AN ORGANISM IS ACCOMPLISHED BY THE OVERCOMING OF EFFORTS OPPOSING ITS SURVIVAL. (Note: Corollary for other dynamics.)

> **DEFINITION:** *Dynamic is the ability to translate solutions into action.*

AXIOM 55:

SURVIVAL EFFORT FOR AN ORGANISM INCLUDES THE DYNAMIC THRUST BY THAT ORGANISM FOR THE SURVIVAL OF ITSELF, ITS PROCREATION, ITS GROUP, ITS SUBSPECIES, ITS SPECIES, ALL LIFE ORGANISMS, MATERIAL UNIVERSE, THE LIFE STATIC AND, POSSIBLY, A SUPREME BEING. (Note: List of dynamics.)

AXIOM 56:

THE CYCLE OF AN ORGANISM, A GROUP OF ORGANISMS OR A SPECIES IS INCEPTION, GROWTH, RE-CREATION, DECAY AND DEATH.

AXIOM 57:

THE EFFORT OF AN ORGANISM IS DIRECTED TOWARD THE CONTROL OF THE ENVIRONMENT FOR ALL THE DYNAMICS.

AXIOM 58:

CONTROL OF AN ENVIRONMENT IS ACCOMPLISHED BY THE SUPPORT OF PRO-SURVIVAL FACTORS ALONG ANY DYNAMIC.

AXIOM 59:

ANY TYPE OF HIGHER ORGANISM IS ACCOMPLISHED BY THE EVOLUTION OF VIRUSES AND CELLS INTO FORMS CAPABLE OF BETTER EFFORTS TO CONTROL OR LIVE IN AN ENVIRONMENT.

AXIOM 60:

THE USEFULNESS OF AN ORGANISM IS DETERMINED BY ITS ABILITY TO CONTROL THE ENVIRONMENT OR TO SUPPORT ORGANISMS WHICH CONTROL THE ENVIRONMENT.

AXIOM 61:

AN ORGANISM IS REJECTED BY *THETA* TO THE DEGREE THAT IT FAILS IN ITS GOALS.

AXIOM 62:

HIGHER ORGANISMS CAN EXIST ONLY IN THE DEGREE THAT THEY ARE SUPPORTED BY THE LOWER ORGANISMS.

AXIOM 63:

THE USEFULNESS OF AN ORGANISM IS DETERMINED BY THE ALIGNMENT OF ITS EFFORTS TOWARD SURVIVAL.

AXIOM 64:

THE MIND PERCEIVES AND STORES ALL DATA OF THE ENVIRONMENT AND ALIGNS OR FAILS TO ALIGN THESE ACCORDING TO THE TIME THEY WERE PERCEIVED.

DEFINITION: *A conclusion is the* theta facsimiles *of a group of combined data.*

DEFINITION: *A datum is a* theta facsimile *of physical action.*

AXIOM 65:

THE PROCESS OF THOUGHT IS THE PERCEPTION OF THE PRESENT AND THE COMPARISON OF IT TO THE PERCEPTIONS AND CONCLUSIONS OF THE PAST IN ORDER TO DIRECT ACTION IN THE IMMEDIATE OR DISTANT FUTURE.

COROLLARY: THE ATTEMPT OF THOUGHT IS TO PERCEIVE REALITIES OF THE PAST AND PRESENT IN ORDER TO PREDICT OR POSTULATE REALITIES OF THE FUTURE.

AXIOM 66:

THE PROCESS BY WHICH LIFE EFFECTS ITS CONQUEST OF THE MATERIAL UNIVERSE CONSISTS IN THE CONVERSION OF THE POTENTIAL EFFORT OF MATTER AND ENERGY IN SPACE AND THROUGH TIME TO EFFECT WITH IT THE CONVERSION OF FURTHER MATTER AND ENERGY IN SPACE AND THROUGH TIME.

AXIOM 67:

THETA CONTAINS ITS OWN *THETA UNIVERSE* EFFORT WHICH TRANSLATES INTO *MEST* EFFORT.

AXIOM 68:

THE SINGLE ARBITRARY IN ANY ORGANISM IS TIME.

AXIOM 69:

PHYSICAL UNIVERSE PERCEPTIONS AND EFFORTS ARE RECEIVED BY AN ORGANISM AS FORCE WAVES, CONVERT BY FACSIMILE INTO *THETA* AND ARE THUS STORED.

> DEFINITION: *Randomity is the misalignment through the internal or external efforts by other forms of life or the material universe of the efforts of an organism, and is imposed on the physical organism by counter-efforts in the environment.*

AXIOM 70:

ANY CYCLE OF ANY LIFE ORGANISM IS FROM STATIC TO MOTION TO STATIC.

AXIOM 71:

THE CYCLE OF RANDOMITY IS FROM STATIC, THROUGH OPTIMUM, THROUGH RANDOMITY SUFFICIENTLY REPETITIOUS OR SIMILAR TO CONSTITUTE ANOTHER STATIC.

AXIOM 72:

THERE ARE TWO SUBDIVISIONS TO RANDOMITY: DATA RANDOMITY AND FORCE RANDOMITY.

AXIOM 73:

THE THREE DEGREES OF RANDOMITY CONSIST OF MINUS RANDOMITY, OPTIMUM RANDOMITY AND PLUS RANDOMITY.

DEFINITION: *Randomity is a component factor and necessary part of motion, if motion is to continue.*

AXIOM 74:

OPTIMUM RANDOMITY IS NECESSARY TO LEARNING.

AXIOM 75:

THE IMPORTANT FACTORS IN ANY AREA OF RANDOMITY ARE EFFORT AND COUNTER-EFFORT. (Note: As distinguished from near-perceptions of effort.)

AXIOM 76:

RANDOMITY AMONGST ORGANISMS IS VITAL TO CONTINUOUS SURVIVAL OF ALL ORGANISMS.

AXIOM 77:

THETA AFFECTS THE ORGANISM, OTHER ORGANISMS AND THE PHYSICAL UNIVERSE BY TRANSLATING *THETA FACSIMILES* INTO PHYSICAL EFFORTS OR RANDOMITY OF EFFORTS.

DEFINITION: *The degree of randomity is measured by the randomness of effort vectors within the organism, amongst organisms, amongst races or species of organisms or between organisms and the physical universe.*

AXIOM 78:

RANDOMITY BECOMES INTENSE IN INDIRECT RATIO TO THE TIME IN WHICH IT TAKES PLACE, MODIFIED BY THE TOTAL EFFORT IN THE AREA.

AXIOM 79:

INITIAL RANDOMITY CAN BE REINFORCED BY RANDOMITIES OF GREATER OR LESSER MAGNITUDE.

AXIOM 80:

AREAS OF RANDOMITY EXIST IN CHAINS OF SIMILARITY PLOTTED AGAINST TIME. THIS CAN BE TRUE OF WORDS AND ACTIONS CONTAINED IN RANDOMITIES. EACH MAY HAVE ITS OWN CHAIN PLOTTED AGAINST TIME.

AXIOM 81:

SANITY CONSISTS OF OPTIMUM RANDOMITY.

AXIOM 82:

ABERRATION EXISTS TO THE DEGREE THAT PLUS OR MINUS RANDOMITY EXISTS IN THE ENVIRONMENT OR PAST DATA OF AN ORGANISM, GROUP OR SPECIES MODIFIED BY THE ENDOWED SELF-DETERMINISM OF THAT ORGANISM, GROUP OR SPECIES.

AXIOM 83:

THE SELF-DETERMINISM OF AN ORGANISM IS DETERMINED BY ITS *THETA* ENDOWMENT, MODIFIED BY MINUS OR PLUS RANDOMITY IN ITS ENVIRONMENT OR ITS EXISTENCE.

AXIOM 84:

THE SELF-DETERMINISM OF AN ORGANISM IS INCREASED BY OPTIMUM RANDOMITY OF COUNTER-EFFORTS.

AXIOM 85:

THE SELF-DETERMINISM OF AN ORGANISM IS REDUCED BY PLUS OR MINUS RANDOMITY OF COUNTER-EFFORTS IN THE ENVIRONMENT.

AXIOM 86:

RANDOMITY CONTAINS BOTH THE RANDOMNESS OF EFFORTS AND THE VOLUME OF EFFORTS. (Note: An area of randomity can have a great deal of confusion but, without volume of energy, the confusion itself is negligible.)

AXIOM 87:

THAT COUNTER-EFFORT IS MOST ACCEPTABLE TO AN ORGANISM WHICH MOST CLOSELY APPEARS TO ASSIST ITS ACCOMPLISHMENT OF ITS GOAL.

AXIOM 88:

AN AREA OF SEVERE PLUS OR MINUS RANDOMITY CAN OCCLUDE DATA ON ANY OF THE SUBJECTS OF THAT PLUS OR MINUS RANDOMITY WHICH TOOK PLACE IN A PRIOR TIME. (Note: Shut-off mechanisms of earlier lives, perceptics, specific incidents, etc.)

AXIOM 89:

RESTIMULATION OF PLUS, MINUS OR OPTIMUM RANDOMITY CAN PRODUCE INCREASED PLUS, MINUS OR OPTIMUM RANDOMITY RESPECTIVELY IN THE ORGANISM.

AXIOM 90:

AN AREA OF RANDOMITY CAN ASSUME SUFFICIENT MAGNITUDE SO AS TO APPEAR TO THE ORGANISM AS PAIN, ACCORDING TO ITS GOALS.

AXIOM 91:

PAST RANDOMITY CAN IMPOSE ITSELF UPON THE PRESENT ORGANISM AS *THETA FACSIMILES*.

AXIOM 92:

THE ENGRAM IS A SEVERE AREA OF PLUS OR MINUS RANDOMITY OF SUFFICIENT VOLUME TO CAUSE UNCONSCIOUSNESS.

AXIOM 93:

UNCONSCIOUSNESS IS AN EXCESS OF RANDOMITY IMPOSED BY A COUNTER-EFFORT OF SUFFICIENT FORCE TO CLOUD THE AWARENESS AND DIRECT FUNCTION OF THE ORGANISM THROUGH THE MIND'S CONTROL CENTER.

AXIOM 94:

ANY COUNTER-EFFORT WHICH MISALIGNS THE ORGANISM'S COMMAND OF ITSELF OR ITS ENVIRONMENT ESTABLISHES PLUS OR MINUS RANDOMITY OR, IF OF SUFFICIENT MAGNITUDE, IS AN ENGRAM.

AXIOM 95:

PAST ENGRAMS ARE RESTIMULATED BY THE CONTROL CENTER'S PERCEPTION OF CIRCUMSTANCES SIMILAR TO THAT ENGRAM IN THE PRESENT ENVIRONMENT.

AXIOM 96:

AN ENGRAM IS A *THETA FACSIMILE* OF ATOMS AND MOLECULES IN MISALIGNMENT.

AXIOM 97:

ENGRAMS FIX EMOTIONAL RESPONSE AS THAT EMOTIONAL RESPONSE OF THE ORGANISM DURING THE RECEIPT OF THE COUNTER-EFFORT.

AXIOM 98:

FREE EMOTIONAL RESPONSE DEPENDS ON OPTIMUM RANDOMITY. IT DEPENDS UPON ABSENCE OF OR NON-RESTIMULATION OF ENGRAMS.

AXIOM 99:

THETA FACSIMILES CAN RECOMBINE INTO NEW SYMBOLS.

AXIOM 100:

LANGUAGE IS THE SYMBOLIZATION OF EFFORT.

AXIOM 101:

LANGUAGE DEPENDS FOR ITS FORCE UPON THE FORCE WHICH ACCOMPANIED ITS DEFINITION. (Note: Counter-effort, not language, is aberrative.)

AXIOM 102:

THE ENVIRONMENT CAN OCCLUDE THE CENTRAL CONTROL OF ANY ORGANISM AND ASSUME CONTROL OF THE MOTOR CONTROLS OF THAT ORGANISM. (Engram, restimulation, locks, hypnotism.)

AXIOM 103:

INTELLIGENCE DEPENDS ON THE ABILITY TO SELECT ALIGNED OR MISALIGNED DATA FROM AN AREA OF RANDOMITY AND SO DISCOVER A SOLUTION TO REDUCE ALL RANDOMITY IN THAT AREA.

AXIOM 104:

PERSISTENCE OBTAINS IN THE ABILITY OF THE MIND TO PUT SOLUTIONS INTO PHYSICAL ACTION TOWARD THE REALIZATION OF GOALS.

AXIOM 105:

AN UNKNOWN DATUM CAN PRODUCE DATA OF PLUS OR MINUS RANDOMITY.

AXIOM 106:

THE INTRODUCTION OF AN ARBITRARY FACTOR OR FORCE WITHOUT RECOURSE TO NATURAL LAWS OF THE BODY OR THE AREA INTO WHICH THE ARBITRARY IS INTRODUCED BRINGS ABOUT PLUS OR MINUS RANDOMITY.

AXIOM 107:

DATA OF PLUS OR MINUS RANDOMITY DEPENDS FOR ITS CONFUSION ON FORMER PLUS OR MINUS RANDOMITY OR ABSENT DATA.

AXIOM 108:

EFFORTS WHICH ARE INHIBITED OR COMPELLED BY EXTERIOR EFFORTS EFFECT A PLUS OR MINUS RANDOMITY OF EFFORTS.

AXIOM 109:

BEHAVIOR IS MODIFIED BY COUNTER-EFFORTS WHICH HAVE
IMPINGED ON THE ORGANISM.

AXIOM 110:

THE COMPONENT PARTS OF *THETA* ARE AFFINITY, REALITY AND
COMMUNICATION.

AXIOM 111:

SELF-DETERMINISM CONSISTS OF MAXIMAL AFFINITY, REALITY
AND COMMUNICATION.

AXIOM 112:

AFFINITY IS THE COHESION OF *THETA*.

Affinity manifests itself as the recognition of similarity of efforts
and goals amongst organisms by those organisms.

AXIOM 113:

REALITY IS THE AGREEMENT UPON PERCEPTIONS AND DATA IN THE
PHYSICAL UNIVERSE.

All that we can be sure is real is that on which we have agreed is
real. Agreement is the essence of reality.

AXIOM 114:

COMMUNICATION IS THE INTERCHANGE OF PERCEPTION
THROUGH THE MATERIAL UNIVERSE BETWEEN ORGANISMS OR THE
PERCEPTION OF THE MATERIAL UNIVERSE BY SENSE CHANNELS.

AXIOM 115:

SELF-DETERMINISM IS THE *THETA* CONTROL OF THE ORGANISM.

AXIOM 116:

A SELF-DETERMINED EFFORT IS THAT COUNTER-EFFORT WHICH HAS
BEEN RECEIVED INTO THE ORGANISM IN THE PAST AND INTEGRATED
INTO THE ORGANISM FOR ITS CONSCIOUS USE.

AXIOM 117:

THE COMPONENTS OF SELF-DETERMINISM ARE AFFINITY, COMMUNICATION AND REALITY.

Self-determinism is manifested along each dynamic.

AXIOM 118:

AN ORGANISM CANNOT BECOME ABERRATED UNLESS IT HAS AGREED UPON THAT ABERRATION, HAS BEEN IN COMMUNICATION WITH A SOURCE OF ABERRATION AND HAS HAD AFFINITY FOR THE ABERRATOR.

AXIOM 119:

AGREEMENT WITH ANY SOURCE CONTRA- OR PRO-SURVIVAL POSTULATES A NEW REALITY FOR THE ORGANISM.

AXIOM 120:

NON-SURVIVAL COURSES, THOUGHTS AND ACTIONS REQUIRE NON-OPTIMUM EFFORT.

AXIOM 121:

EVERY THOUGHT HAS BEEN PRECEDED BY PHYSICAL ACTION.

AXIOM 122:

THE MIND DOES WITH THOUGHT AS IT HAS DONE WITH ENTITIES IN THE PHYSICAL UNIVERSE.

AXIOM 123:

ALL EFFORT CONCERNED WITH PAIN IS CONCERNED WITH LOSS.

Organisms hold pain and engrams to them as a latent effort to prevent loss of some portion of the organism.

All loss is a loss of motion.

AXIOM 124:

THE AMOUNT OF COUNTER-EFFORT THE ORGANISM CAN
OVERCOME IS PROPORTIONAL TO THE *THETA* ENDOWMENT OF THE
ORGANISM, MODIFIED BY THE PHYSIQUE OF THAT ORGANISM.

AXIOM 125:

EXCESSIVE COUNTER-EFFORT TO THE EFFORT OF A LIFE ORGANISM
PRODUCES UNCONSCIOUSNESS.

COROLLARY: UNCONSCIOUSNESS GIVES THE SUPPRESSION OF AN
ORGANISM'S CONTROL CENTER BY COUNTER-EFFORT.

DEFINITION: *The control center of the organism can be defined as
the contact point between* theta *and the physical universe and is
that center which is aware of being aware and which has charge of
and responsibility for the organism along all its dynamics.*

AXIOM 126:

PERCEPTIONS ARE ALWAYS RECEIVED IN THE CONTROL CENTER OF
AN ORGANISM WHETHER THE CONTROL CENTER IS IN CONTROL
OF THE ORGANISM AT THE TIME OR NOT.

This is an explanation for the assumption of valences.

AXIOM 127:

ALL PERCEPTIONS REACHING THE ORGANISM'S SENSE CHANNELS
ARE RECORDED AND STORED BY *THETA FACSIMILE.*

DEFINITION: *Perception is the process of recording data from the
physical universe and storing it as a* theta facsimile.

DEFINITION: *Recall is the process of regaining perceptions.*

AXIOM 128:

ANY ORGANISM CAN RECALL EVERYTHING WHICH IT HAS
PERCEIVED.

AXIOM 129:

AN ORGANISM DISPLACED BY PLUS OR MINUS RANDOMITY IS THEREAFTER REMOTE FROM THE PERCEPTION RECORDING CENTER.

Increased remoteness brings about occlusions of perceptions. One can perceive things in present time and then, because they are being recorded after they passed *theta* perception of the awareness unit, they are recorded but cannot be recalled.

AXIOM 130:

THETA FACSIMILES OF COUNTER-EFFORT ARE ALL THAT INTERPOSE BETWEEN THE CONTROL CENTER AND ITS RECALLS.

AXIOM 131:

ANY COUNTER-EFFORT RECEIVED INTO A CONTROL CENTER IS ALWAYS ACCOMPANIED BY ALL PERCEPTICS.

AXIOM 132:

THE RANDOM COUNTER-EFFORTS TO AN ORGANISM AND THE INTERMINGLED PERCEPTIONS IN THE RANDOMITY CAN RE-EXERT THAT FORCE UPON AN ORGANISM WHEN RESTIMULATED.

DEFINITION: *Restimulation is the reactivation of a past counter-effort by appearance in the organism's environment of a similarity toward the content of the past randomity area.*

AXIOM 133:

SELF-DETERMINISM ALONE BRINGS ABOUT THE MECHANISM OF RESTIMULATION.

AXIOM 134:

A REACTIVATED AREA OF THE PAST RANDOMITY IMPINGES THE EFFORT AND THE PERCEPTIONS UPON THE ORGANISM.

AXIOM 135:

ACTIVATION OF A RANDOMITY AREA IS ACCOMPLISHED FIRST BY THE PERCEPTIONS, THEN BY THE PAIN, FINALLY BY THE EFFORT.

AXIOM 136:

THE MIND IS PLASTICALLY CAPABLE OF RECORDING ALL EFFORTS
AND COUNTER-EFFORTS.

AXIOM 137:

A COUNTER-EFFORT ACCOMPANIED BY SUFFICIENT (ENRANDOMED)
FORCE IMPRESSES THE FACSIMILE OF THE COUNTER-EFFORT
PERSONALITY INTO THE MIND OF AN ORGANISM.

AXIOM 138:

ABERRATION IS THE DEGREE OF RESIDUAL PLUS OR MINUS
RANDOMITY ACCUMULATED BY COMPELLING, INHIBITING, OR
UNWARRANTED ASSISTING OF EFFORTS ON THE PART OF OTHER
ORGANISMS OR THE PHYSICAL (MATERIAL) UNIVERSE.

Aberration is caused by what is done to the individual, not what
the individual does, plus his self-determinism about what has been
done to him.

AXIOM 139:

ABERRATED BEHAVIOR CONSISTS OF DESTRUCTIVE EFFORT TOWARD
PRO-SURVIVAL DATA OR ENTITIES ON ANY DYNAMIC, OR EFFORT
TOWARD THE SURVIVAL OF CONTRA-SURVIVAL DATA OR ENTITIES
FOR ANY DYNAMIC.

AXIOM 140:

A VALENCE IS A FACSIMILE PERSONALITY MADE CAPABLE OF FORCE
BY THE COUNTER-EFFORT OF THE MOMENT OF RECEIPT INTO THE
PLUS OR MINUS RANDOMITY OF UNCONSCIOUSNESS.

Valences are assistive, compulsive or inhibitive to the organism.

A CONTROL CENTER IS NOT A VALENCE.

AXIOM 141:

A CONTROL CENTER EFFORT IS ALIGNED TOWARD A GOAL
THROUGH DEFINITE SPACE AS A RECOGNIZED INCIDENT IN TIME.

AXIOM 142:

AN ORGANISM IS AS HEALTHY AND SANE AS IT IS SELF-DETERMINED.

The environmental control of the organism motor controls inhibits the organism's ability to change with the changing environment, since the organism will attempt to carry forward with one set of responses when it needs by self-determinism to create another to survive in another environment.

AXIOM 143:

ALL LEARNING IS ACCOMPLISHED BY RANDOM EFFORT.

AXIOM 144:

A COUNTER-EFFORT PRODUCING SUFFICIENT PLUS OR MINUS RANDOMITY TO RECORD IS RECORDED WITH AN INDEX OF SPACE AND TIME AS HIDDEN AS THE REMAINDER OF ITS CONTENT.

AXIOM 145:

A COUNTER-EFFORT PRODUCING SUFFICIENT PLUS OR MINUS RANDOMITY WHEN ACTIVATED BY RESTIMULATION EXERTS ITSELF AGAINST THE ENVIRONMENT OR THE ORGANISM WITHOUT REGARD TO SPACE AND TIME, EXCEPT REACTIVATED PERCEPTIONS.

AXIOM 146:

COUNTER-EFFORTS ARE DIRECTED OUT FROM THE ORGANISM UNTIL THEY ARE FURTHER ENRANDOMED BY THE ENVIRON AT WHICH TIME THEY AGAIN ACTIVATE AGAINST THE CONTROL CENTER.

AXIOM 147:

AN ORGANISM'S MIND EMPLOYS COUNTER-EFFORTS EFFECTIVELY ONLY SO LONG AS INSUFFICIENT PLUS OR MINUS RANDOMITY EXISTS TO HIDE DIFFERENTIATION OF THE FACSIMILES CREATED.

AXIOM 148:

PHYSICAL LAWS ARE LEARNED BY LIFE ENERGY ONLY BY IMPINGEMENT OF THE PHYSICAL UNIVERSE PRODUCING RANDOMITY, AND A WITHDRAWAL FROM THAT IMPINGEMENT.

AXIOM 149:

LIFE DEPENDS UPON AN ALIGNMENT OF FORCE VECTORS IN THE DIRECTION OF SURVIVAL AND THE NULLIFICATION OF FORCE VECTORS IN THE DIRECTION OF SUCCUMB IN ORDER TO SURVIVE.

COROLLARY: LIFE DEPENDS UPON AN ALIGNMENT OF FORCE VECTORS IN THE DIRECTION OF SUCCUMB AND THE NULLIFICATION OF FORCE VECTORS IN THE DIRECTION OF SURVIVE IN ORDER TO SUCCUMB.

AXIOM 150:

ANY AREA OF RANDOMITY GATHERS TO IT SITUATIONS SIMILAR TO IT WHICH DO NOT CONTAIN ACTUAL EFFORTS BUT ONLY PERCEPTIONS.

AXIOM 151:

WHETHER AN ORGANISM HAS THE GOAL OF SURVIVING OR SUCCUMBING DEPENDS UPON THE AMOUNT OF PLUS OR MINUS RANDOMITY IT HAS REACTIVATED. (NOT RESIDUAL.)

AXIOM 152:

SURVIVAL IS ACCOMPLISHED ONLY BY MOTION.

AXIOM 153:

IN THE PHYSICAL UNIVERSE THE ABSENCE OF MOTION IS VANISHMENT.

AXIOM 154:

DEATH IS THE EQUIVALENT TO LIFE OF TOTAL LACK OF LIFE-MOTIVATED MOTION.

AXIOM 155:

ACQUISITION OF PRO-SURVIVAL MATTER AND ENERGY OR
ORGANISMS IN SPACE AND TIME MEANS INCREASED MOTION.

AXIOM 156:

LOSS OF PRO-SURVIVAL MATTER AND ENERGY OR ORGANISMS IN
SPACE AND TIME MEANS DECREASED MOTION.

AXIOM 157:

ACQUISITION OR PROXIMITY OF MATTER, ENERGY OR ORGANISMS
WHICH ASSIST THE SURVIVAL OF AN ORGANISM INCREASE THE
SURVIVAL POTENTIALS OF AN ORGANISM.

AXIOM 158:

ACQUISITION OR PROXIMITY OF MATTER, ENERGY OR ORGANISMS
WHICH INHIBIT THE SURVIVAL OF AN ORGANISM DECREASE ITS
SURVIVAL POTENTIAL.

AXIOM 159:

GAIN OF SURVIVAL ENERGY, MATTER OR ORGANISMS INCREASES
THE FREEDOM OF AN ORGANISM.

AXIOM 160:

RECEIPT OR PROXIMITY OF NON-SURVIVAL ENERGY, MATTER OR
TIME DECREASES THE FREEDOM OF MOTION OF AN ORGANISM.

AXIOM 161:

THE CONTROL CENTER ATTEMPTS THE HALTING OR LENGTHENING
OF TIME, THE EXPANSION OR CONTRACTION OF SPACE AND THE
DECREASE OR INCREASE OF ENERGY AND MATTER.

This is a primary source of invalidation, and it is also a primary
source of aberration.

AXIOM 162:

PAIN IS THE BALK OF EFFORT BY COUNTER-EFFORT IN GREAT INTENSITY, WHETHER THAT EFFORT IS TO REMAIN AT REST OR IN MOTION.

AXIOM 163:

PERCEPTION, INCLUDING PAIN, CAN BE EXHAUSTED FROM AN AREA OF PLUS OR MINUS RANDOMITY STILL LEAVING THE EFFORT AND COUNTER-EFFORT OF THAT PLUS OR MINUS RANDOMITY.

AXIOM 164:

THE RATIONALITY OF THE MIND DEPENDS UPON AN OPTIMUM REACTION TOWARD TIME.

DEFINITION: *Sanity, the computation of futures.*

DEFINITION: *Neurotic, the computation of present time only.*

DEFINITION: *Psychotic, computation only of past situations.*

AXIOM 165:

SURVIVAL PERTAINS ONLY TO THE FUTURE.

COROLLARY: SUCCUMB PERTAINS ONLY TO THE PRESENT AND PAST.

AXIOM 166:

AN INDIVIDUAL IS AS HAPPY AS HE CAN PERCEIVE SURVIVAL POTENTIALS IN THE FUTURE.

AXIOM 167:

AS THE NEEDS OF ANY ORGANISM ARE MET IT RISES HIGHER AND HIGHER IN ITS EFFORTS ALONG THE DYNAMICS.

An organism which achieves ARC with itself can better achieve ARC with sex in the future; having achieved this it can achieve ARC with groups; having achieved this, it can achieve ARC with Mankind, etc.

AXIOM 168:

AFFINITY, REALITY AND COMMUNICATION CO-EXIST IN AN INEXTRICABLE RELATIONSHIP.

The co-existent relationship between Affinity, Reality and Communication is such that none can be increased without increasing the other two and none can be decreased without decreasing the other two.

AXIOM 169:

ANY AESTHETIC PRODUCT IS A SYMBOLIC FACSIMILE OR COMBINATION OF FACSIMILES OF *THETA* OR PHYSICAL UNIVERSES IN VARIED RANDOMITIES AND VOLUMES OF RANDOMITIES WITH THE INTERPLAY OF TONES.

AXIOM 170:

AN AESTHETIC PRODUCT IS AN INTERPRETATION OF THE UNIVERSES BY AN INDIVIDUAL OR GROUP MIND.

AXIOM 171:

DELUSION IS THE POSTULATION BY THE IMAGINATION OF OCCURRENCES IN AREAS OF PLUS OR MINUS RANDOMITY.

AXIOM 172:

DREAMS ARE THE IMAGINATIVE RECONSTRUCTION OF AREAS OF RANDOMITY OR THE RE-SYMBOLIZATION OF THE EFFORTS OF *THETA*.

AXIOM 173:

A MOTION IS CREATED BY THE DEGREE OF OPTIMUM RANDOMITY INTRODUCED BY THE COUNTER-EFFORT TO AN ORGANISM'S EFFORT.

AXIOM 174:

MEST, WHICH HAS BEEN MOBILIZED BY LIFE FORMS, IS IN MORE AFFINITY WITH LIFE ORGANISMS THAN NON-MOBILIZED *MEST*.

AXIOM 175:

ALL PAST PERCEPTION, CONCLUSION AND EXISTENCE MOMENTS, INCLUDING THOSE OF PLUS OR MINUS RANDOMITY, ARE RECOVERABLE TO THE CONTROL CENTER OF THE ORGANISM.

AXIOM 176:

THE ABILITY TO PRODUCE SURVIVAL EFFORT ON THE PART OF AN ORGANISM IS AFFECTED BY THE DEGREES OF RANDOMITY EXISTING IN ITS PAST. (This includes learning.)

AXIOM 177:

AREAS OF PAST PLUS OR MINUS RANDOMITY CAN BE READDRESSED BY THE CONTROL CENTER OF AN ORGANISM AND THE PLUS OR MINUS RANDOMITY EXHAUSTED.

AXIOM 178:

THE EXHAUSTION OF PAST PLUS OR MINUS RANDOMITIES PERMITS THE CONTROL CENTER OF AN ORGANISM TO EFFECT ITS OWN EFFORTS TOWARD SURVIVAL GOALS.

AXIOM 179:

THE EXHAUSTION OF SELF-DETERMINED EFFORT FROM A PAST AREA OF PLUS OR MINUS RANDOMITY NULLIFIES THE EFFECTIVENESS OF THAT AREA.

AXIOM 180:

PAIN IS THE RANDOMITY PRODUCED BY SUDDEN OR STRONG COUNTER-EFFORTS.

AXIOM 181:

PAIN IS STORED AS PLUS OR MINUS RANDOMITY.

AXIOM 182:

PAIN, AS AN AREA OF PLUS OR MINUS RANDOMITY, CAN REINFLICT ITSELF UPON THE ORGANISM.

AXIOM 183:

PAST PAIN BECOMES INEFFECTIVE UPON THE ORGANISM WHEN THE RANDOMITY OF ITS AREA IS ADDRESSED AND ALIGNED.

AXIOM 184:

THE EARLIER THE AREA OF PLUS OR MINUS RANDOMITY, THE GREATER SELF-PRODUCED EFFORT EXISTED TO REPEL IT.

AXIOM 185:

LATER AREAS OF PLUS OR MINUS RANDOMITY CANNOT BE REALIGNED EASILY UNTIL EARLIER AREAS ARE REALIGNED.

AXIOM 186:

AREAS OF PLUS OR MINUS RANDOMITY BECOME INCREASED IN ACTIVITY WHEN PERCEPTIONS OF SIMILARITY ARE INTRODUCED INTO THEM.

AXIOM 187:

PAST AREAS OF PLUS OR MINUS RANDOMITY CAN BE REDUCED AND ALIGNED BY ADDRESS TO THEM IN PRESENT TIME.

AXIOM 188:

ABSOLUTE GOOD AND ABSOLUTE EVIL DO NOT EXIST IN THE *MEST* UNIVERSE.

AXIOM 189:

THAT WHICH IS GOOD FOR AN ORGANISM MAY BE DEFINED AS THAT WHICH PROMOTES THE SURVIVAL OF THAT ORGANISM.

COROLLARY: EVIL MAY BE DEFINED AS THAT WHICH INHIBITS OR BRINGS PLUS OR MINUS RANDOMITY INTO THE ORGANISM, WHICH IS CONTRARY TO THE SURVIVAL MOTIVES OF THE ORGANISM.

AXIOM 190:

HAPPINESS CONSISTS IN THE ACT OF BRINGING ALIGNMENT INTO HITHERTO RESISTING PLUS OR MINUS RANDOMITY. NEITHER THE ACT OR ACTION OF ATTAINING SURVIVAL, NOR THE ACCOMPLISHMENT OF THIS ACT ITSELF, BRINGS ABOUT HAPPINESS.

AXIOM 191:

CONSTRUCTION IS AN ALIGNMENT OF DATA.

> COROLLARY: DESTRUCTION IS A PLUS OR MINUS RANDOMITY OF DATA.

> The effort of construction is the alignment toward the survival of the aligning organism.

> Destruction is the effort of bringing randomity into an area.

AXIOM 192:

OPTIMUM SURVIVAL BEHAVIOR CONSISTS OF EFFORT IN THE MAXIMUM SURVIVAL INTEREST IN EVERYTHING CONCERNED IN THE DYNAMICS.

AXIOM 193:

THE OPTIMUM SURVIVAL SOLUTION OF ANY PROBLEM WOULD CONSIST OF THE HIGHEST ATTAINABLE SURVIVAL FOR EVERY DYNAMIC CONCERNED.

AXIOM 194:

THE WORTH OF ANY ORGANISM CONSISTS OF ITS VALUE TO THE SURVIVAL OF ITS OWN *THETA* ALONG ANY DYNAMIC.

Handbook for Preclears
LRH Glossary

Handbook for Preclears
LRH Glossary

(In writing Handbook for Preclears, *L. Ron Hubbard provided a glossary of all technical terms, defined as they are used in this book and in the sequence they should be learned. As such, the* LRH Glossary *forms a vital component of this text to be studied in full for a thorough comprehension of the nomenclature and subject itself.)*

ACT:

A stage of processing. Applies solely to the particular process in use at a certain case level.

FIFTEEN:

(noun) A designation to denote a finished case. Solely for case recording to designate a case advanced to current completion. This is a Foundation number system for preclears. A case is noted on record by the Act number to which it has been advanced.

AUDITOR:

One who listens and computes. A technician of this science.

PRECLEAR:

One who has entered processing en route to becoming a Fifteen.

CLEAR:

(verb) The act of desensitizing or releasing a thought impression or a series of impressions or observations in the past or a postulate or an emotion or an effort or an entire facsimile. The preclear either releases his hold on the facsimile (memory) or the facsimile itself is desensitized. The word is taken from electronic computers or common office adding machines and describes an action similar to clearing past computations from the machines.

CLEAR:

(noun) A much misunderstood state of being. The word has been used before with other meanings. It has been mistaken as an absolute. It is still used. It is used here as electronics slang and can apply to a chain, an incident or a computation.

CENTER OF CONTROL:

The awareness of awareness unit of the mind. This is not part of the brain, but part of the mind, the brain being physiological. The mind has two control centers possible, by definition, the right and the left. One is an actual genetic control center. The other is a sub-control center, subservient to the control center.

STRAIGHTWIRE:

A process of recalling from present time, with some perception or at least a concept, a past incident. The name Straightwire derives from the MEST communications process of connecting two points of a communications system. It is essentially memory work. It is applied to postulates, evaluations, incidents, scenes, emotions, or any data which may be in the storage banks of the mind without "sending the preclear" into the incident itself. It is done with the preclear sitting up, eyes open or shut. The auditor is very alert. Straightwire is done rapidly. The preclear is not permitted to wander or reminisce. He responds to questions on the part of the auditor. MANY PRECLEARS DISLIKE BEING QUESTIONED. THE AUDITOR MUST THEN FIRST RESOLVE THE POSTULATES AGAINST BEING QUESTIONED. This would be called "Clearing for Broad Straightwire."

POSTULATE:

(verb) To conclude, decide or resolve a problem or to set a pattern for the future or to nullify a pattern of the past.

POSTULATE:

(noun) A conclusion, decision or resolution made by the individual himself on his own self-determinism on data of the past, known or unknown. The postulate is always known. It is made upon the evaluation of data by the individual or on impulse without data. It resolves a problem of the past, decides on problems or observations in the present or sets a pattern for the future.

PAST POSTULATES:

Decisions or conclusions the preclear has made in the past and to which he is still subjected in the present. Past postulates are uniformly invalid since they cannot resolve present environment.

FACSIMILES:

A facsimile is a memory recording for a finite period of time. It is considered that memory is a static without wavelength, weight, mass or position in space (in other words, a true static) which yet receives the impression of time, space, energy and matter. A careful examination of the phenomena of thought and the behavior of the human mind leads one to this conclusion. The conclusion is itself a postulate, used because it is extremely useful and workable. This is a point of echelon in research that a facsimile can be so described. The description is mathematical and an abstract and may or may not be actual. When a thought recording is so regarded, the problems of the mind rapidly resolve. Facsimiles are said to be "stored." They act upon the physical universe switchboard, called the brain and nervous and glandular system, to monitor action. They appear to have motion and weight only because motion and weight are recorded into them. They are not stored in the cells. They impinge upon the cells. Proof of this matter rests in the fact that an energy which became a facsimile a long time ago can be recontacted and is found to be violent on the contact. Pain is stored as a facsimile. Old pain can be recontacted. Old pain in facsimile form, old emotion in facsimile form, can reimpose itself on present time in such a wise as to deform or otherwise physically effect the body. You can go back to the last time you hurt yourself and find there and re-experience the pain of that hurt unless you are very occluded. You can recover efforts and exertions you have made or which have been made against you in the past. Yet the cells themselves, which have finite life, are long since replaced although the body goes on. Hence, the facsimile theory. The word facsimile is used, as bluntly as one uses it, in connection with a drawing of a box top instead of the actual box top. It means a similar article rather than the article itself. You can recall a memory picture of an elephant or a photograph. The elephant and the photograph are no longer present. A facsimile of them is stored in your mind. A facsimile is complete with every perception of the environment present when that facsimile was made, including sight, sound, smell, taste, weight, joint position and so on through half a hundred perceptions. Just because you cannot recall motion or these perceptions does not mean they were not recorded fully and in motion with every perception channel you had at the time. It does mean that you have interposed a stop between the facsimile and the recall mechanisms of your control centers. There are facsimiles of everything you have experienced in your entire lifetime and everything you have imagined.

HEAVY FACSIMILE:

A heavy facsimile used to be known as an "engram." In view of the fact that it has been found to be stored elsewhere than in the cells, the term "heavy facsimile" has now come into use. A heavy facsimile is an experience, complete with all perceptions and emotions and thoughts and efforts, occupying a precise place in space and a moment in time. It can be an operation, an injury, a term of heavy physical exertion or even a death. It is composed of the preclear's own effort and the effort of the environment (counter-effort).

ENVIRONMENT:

The surroundings of the preclear from moment to moment, in particular or in general, including people, pets, mechanical objects, weather, culture, clothing or the Supreme Being. Anything he perceives or believes he perceives. The objective environment is the environment everyone agrees is there. The subjective environment is the environment the individual himself believes is there. They may not agree.

ACCESSIBILITY:

The state of being willing to be processed (technical sense in this science). The state of being willing to have interpersonal relations (social sense). For the individual himself, accessibility with self means whether or not an individual can recontact his past experiences or data. A man with a "bad memory" (interposed blocks between control center and facsimiles) has memories which are not accessible to him.

PSYCHOTIC:

An individual who is out of contact to a thorough extent with his present time environment and who does not compute into the future. He may be an acute psychotic, wherein he becomes psychotic for only a few minutes at a time and only occasionally in certain environments (as in rages or apathies), or he may be a chronic psychotic (or in a continual disconnect with the future and present). Psychotics who are dramatically harmful to others are considered dangerous enough to be put away. Psychotics who are harmful on a less dramatic basis are no less harmful to their environment and are no less psychotic.

COMPUTING PSYCHOTIC:

One who is running on a circuit, a circuit being a pseudo-personality out of a facsimile strong enough to dictate to the individual and BE the individual.

DRAMATIZING PSYCHOTIC:

One who dramatizes one type of facsimile only.

BROKEN:

Slang used in the wise of "breaking a case," meaning that one breaks the hold of the preclear on a non-survival facsimile. Used in greater or lesser magnitude, such as "breaking a circuit" or "breaking into a chain" or "breaking a computation." Never breaking the preclear or his spirit, but breaking what is breaking the preclear.

ASSISTS:

The straight perception-by-perception running, over and over, of an accident or incident, until it is desensitized as a facsimile and cannot affect the preclear. The assist is used immediately after accidents or operations. It takes away shock and most of the harmful effects of the incident and promotes healing. It is done by starting the individual at the beginning of the incident, with the first awareness of the incident, just as though the preclear were living it all the way through again with full perception of sight, sound, etc., as nearly as they can be obtained. An assist run, for instance, immediately after a dental operation takes all the shock out of the operation. One concludes an assist by picking up the auditing as another incident and running through the auditing and the decision to be audited. An assist saves lives and materially speeds healing.

RECOVERY:

Recovery of one's own ability to determine one's existence.

ASSESSMENT:

An inventory, an examination or a calculation or evaluation of a case.

THOUGHT:

The facsimiles one has recorded of his various environments and the facsimiles he has created with his imaginings, their recombination and evaluations and conclusions, for the purpose of determining action or no action or potential action or no action. Thought is used also to mean a process treating awareness level recordings, as distinct from non-awareness level recordings.

EMOTION:

The catalyst used by the control center to monitor physical action. The relay system, via glands, interposed between "I" and self and, by thought, others. The main emotions are Happiness in which one has confidence and enjoyment in his goals and a belief in his control of environment; Boredom in which one has lost confidence and direction but is not defeated; Antagonism wherein one feels his control threatened; Anger wherein one seeks to destroy that which threatens and seeks without good direction beyond destruction; Covert Hostility wherein one seeks to destroy while reassuring his target that he is not so seeking; Fear wherein one is catalyzed to flee; Grief in which one recognizes loss; Apathy in which one accepts failure on all dynamics and pretends Death. Other emotions are a volume or lack of volume of those named.

Shame or Embarrassment are emotions peculiar to groups or interpersonal relations and are on a level with Grief, denoting loss of position in a group. Emotion is the glandular system parallel of motion and each emotion reflects action to gain or lose motion. At a high level, one is sending back motion; at a mid level, one is holding motion; at a lower level, motion is sweeping through and over one.

PSYCHOSOMATIC ILLNESS:

A term used in common parlance to denote a condition "resulting from a state of mind." Such illnesses account for about 70 percent of all ills, by popular report. Technically, in this science, "a chronic or continuing painful facsimile to which the preclear is holding to account for failures." Arthritis, bursitis, tendonitis, myopia, astigmatism, bizarre aches and pains, sinusitis, colds, ulcers, migraine headaches, toothache, poliomyelitis deformities, fatness, skin malformations, etc., etc., etc., etc., are a few of these legion of chronic somatics. They are traceable to service facsimiles.

REPETITIVE STRAIGHTWIRE:

Attention called to an incident over and over, amongst other incidents, until it is desensitized. Used on conclusions or incidents which do not easily surrender.

LOCK SCANNING:

A process which starts the preclear from a point in the past, with which he has made solid contact, up through all similar incidents, without verbalization. This is done over and over, each time trying to start at an earlier incident of the same kind, until the preclear extroverts on the subject of the chain. "Boil-off" often results, wherein the preclear seems to go to sleep. Avoid boil-off, for it is not therapeutic and will eventually result in reduced tone.

Boil-off is a lazy auditor's excuse to be idle and facsimiles are in such severe conflict that they will not resolve without resolving postulates first.

Lock Scanning is a standardized drill, started on signal and ended with the preclear saying he is again in present time. It can be done on any subject. ABOVE 2.0 only.

SERVICE FACSIMILE:

A definitely non-survival situation contained in a facsimile which is called into action by the individual to explain his failures. A service facsimile may be one of an illness, an injury, an inability. The facsimile begins with a down emotional curve and ends with an upward emotional curve. Between these it has pain. A service facsimile *is* the pattern which is the chronic "psychosomatic illness." It may contain coughs, fever, aches, rashes, any manifestation of a non-survival character, mental or physical. It may even be a suicide effort. It is complete with all perceptions. It has many similar facsimiles. It has many locks. The possession and use of a service facsimile distinguishes a Homo sapiens.

A service facsimile is that facsimile which the preclear uses to apologize for his failures. In other words, it is used to make others wrong and procure their cooperation in the survival of the preclear.

SERVICE FACSIMILE CHAIN:

The entire chain of similar incidents which comprise the total repertoire of the individual who is explaining his failure and thus seeking support.

RELEASE:

(verb) The act of taking the perceptions or effort or effectiveness out of a heavy facsimile, or taking away the preclear's hold on the facsimile.

EFFORT:

The physical-force manifestation of motion. A sharp effort against an individual produces pain. A strenuous effort produces discomfort. Effort can be recalled and re-experienced by the preclear. No preclear below 2.0 should be called upon to use effort as such, as he is incapable of handling it and will stick in it. The essential part of a painful facsimile is its effort, not its perceptions.

COUNTER-EFFORT:

The individual's own effort is simply called EFFORT. The efforts of the environment are called COUNTER-EFFORTS.

EFFORT PROCESSING:

Effort Processing is done by running moments of physical stress. These are run either as simple efforts or counter-efforts or as whole precise incidents. Such incidents as those which contain physical pain or heavy stress of motion (such as injuries, accidents or illnesses) are addressed by Effort Processing.

GENETIC:

By line of protoplasm and by facsimiles and by MEST forms, the individual has arrived in the present age from a past beginning. Genetic applies to the protoplasm line of father and mother to child, grown child to new child and so forth.

EMOTIONAL CURVE:

The drop from any position (on the Tone Scale) above 2.0 to a position below 2.0 on the realization of failure or inadequacy. It is easily recovered by preclears.

SYMPATHY:

The posing of an emotional state similar to the emotional state of an individual in Grief or Apathy.

DYNAMICS:

The central drives of an individual. They are numbered from one to eight as follows: (1) Self survival; (2) Survival through children (includes sexual act); (3) Survival by groups including social and political as well as commercial; (4) Survival through Mankind as a whole; (5) Survival through Life including any species, vegetable or animal; (6) Survival through MEST; (7) Survival through theta or the static itself; (8) (Written as infinity—∞) Survival through a Supreme Being. Each individual is surviving for all eight.

THETA:

The mathematical symbol—θ—for the static of thought. By theta is meant the static itself. By "facsimile" is meant theta which contains impressions by perception.

MEST:

A compound word made up of the first letters of MATTER, ENERGY, SPACE and TIME. A coined word for the PHYSICAL UNIVERSE.

THETA IS NOT CONSIDERED AS PART OF THE PHYSICAL UNIVERSE, BUT IS NOT CONSIDERED ABSOLUTELY AS NOT PART OF THE PHYSICAL UNIVERSE.

PERCEPTIONS:

By means of physical waves, rays and particles of the physical universe, impressions of the environment enter through the "sense channels," such as the eyes and optic nerves, the nose and olfactory nerves, the ears and aural nerves, interbody nerves for interbody perceptions, etc., etc. These are all "perceptions" up to the instant they record as facsimiles, at which moment they become "recordings." When recalled they are perceptions again, being again entered into sense channels from the recall side. There are over half a hundred separate perceptions all being recorded at once.

TEN:

A case advanced to the point of released service facsimile.

appendix

Further Study	315
Guide to the Materials	328
Addresses	330
Editor's Glossary of Words, Terms & Phrases	335
Index	409

Further Study
books & Lectures by L. Ron Hubbard

The materials of Dianetics and Scientology comprise the largest body of information ever assembled on the mind, spirit and life, rigorously refined and codified by L. Ron Hubbard through five decades of research, investigation and development. The results of that work are contained in hundreds of books and more than 3,000 recorded lectures. A full listing and description of them all can be obtained from any Scientology Church or Publications Organization. (See *Guide to the Materials.*)

The books and lectures below form the foundation upon which the Bridge to Freedom is built. They are listed in the sequence Ron wrote or delivered them. In many instances, Ron gave a series of lectures immediately following the release of a new book to provide further explanation and insight of these milestones. Through monumental restoration efforts, those lectures are now available and are listed herein with their companion book.

While Ron's books contain the summaries of breakthroughs and conclusions as they appeared in the developmental research track, his lectures provide the running day-to-day record of research and explain the thoughts, conclusions, tests and demonstrations that lay along that route. In that regard, they are the complete record of the entire research track, providing not only the most important breakthroughs in Man's history, but the *why* and *how* Ron arrived at them.

Not the least advantage of a chronological study of these books and lectures is the inclusion of words and terms which, when originally used, were defined by LRH with considerable exactitude. Far beyond a mere "definition," entire lectures are devoted to a full description of each new Dianetic or Scientology term—what made the breakthrough possible, its application in auditing as well as its application to life itself. As a result, one leaves behind no misunderstoods, obtains a full conceptual understanding of Dianetics and Scientology and grasps the subjects at a level not otherwise possible.

Through a sequential study, you can see how the subject progressed and recognize the highest levels of development. The listing of books and lectures below shows where *Handbook for Preclears* fits within the developmental line. From there you can determine your *next* step or any earlier books and lectures you may have missed. You will then be able to fill in missing gaps, not only gaining knowledge of each breakthrough, but greater understanding of what you've already studied.

This is the path to knowing how to know, unlocking the gates to your future eternity. Follow it.

DIANETICS: THE ORIGINAL THESIS • Ron's *first* description of Dianetics. Originally circulated in manuscript form, it was soon copied and passed from hand to hand. Ensuing word of mouth created such demand for more information, Ron concluded the only way to answer the inquiries was with a book. That book was Dianetics: The Modern Science of Mental Health, now the all-time self-help bestseller. Find out what started it all. For here is the bedrock foundation of Dianetic discoveries: the *Original Axioms,* the *Dynamic Principle of Existence,* the *Anatomy of the Analytical* and *Reactive Mind,* the *Dynamics,* the *Tone Scale,* the *Auditor's Code* and the first description of a *Clear.* Even more than that, here are the primary laws describing *how* and *why* auditing works. It's only here in Dianetics: The Original Thesis.

DIANETICS: THE EVOLUTION OF A SCIENCE • This is the story of *how* Ron discovered the reactive mind and developed the procedures to get rid of it. Originally written for a national magazine—published to coincide with the release of Dianetics: The Modern Science of Mental Health—it started a wildfire movement virtually overnight upon that book's publication. Here then are both the fundamentals of Dianetics as well as the only account of Ron's two-decade journey of discovery and how he applied a scientific methodology to the problems of the human mind. He wrote it so you would know. Hence, this book is a must for every Dianeticist and Scientologist.

DIANETICS: THE MODERN SCIENCE OF MENTAL HEALTH • The bolt from the blue that began a worldwide movement. For while Ron had previously announced his discovery of the reactive mind, it had only fueled the fire of those wanting more information. More to the point—it was humanly impossible for one man to clear an entire planet. Encompassing all his previous discoveries and case histories of those breakthroughs in application, Ron provided the complete handbook of Dianetics procedure to train auditors to use it everywhere. A bestseller for more than half a century and with tens of millions of copies in print, Dianetics: The Modern Science of Mental Health has been translated in more than fifty languages, and used in more than 100 countries of Earth—indisputably, the most widely read and influential book about the human mind ever written. And that is why it will forever be known as *Book One.*

DIANETICS LECTURES AND DEMONSTRATIONS • Immediately following the publication of *Dianetics,* LRH began lecturing to packed auditoriums across America. Although addressing thousands at a time, demand continued to grow. To meet that demand, his presentation in Oakland, California, was recorded. In these four lectures, Ron related the events that sparked his investigation and his personal journey to his groundbreaking discoveries. He followed it all with a personal demonstration of Dianetics auditing—the only such demonstration of Book One available. *4 lectures.*

DIANETICS PROFESSIONAL COURSE LECTURES—*A SPECIAL COURSE FOR BOOK ONE AUDITORS* • Following six months of coast-to-coast travel, lecturing to the first Dianeticists, Ron assembled auditors in Los Angeles for a new Professional Course. The subject was his next sweeping discovery on life—the *ARC Triangle,* describing the interrelationship of *Affinity, Reality* and *Communication.* Through a series of fifteen lectures, LRH announced many firsts, including the *Spectrum of Logic,* containing an infinity of gradients from right to wrong; *ARC and the Dynamics;* the *Tone Scales of ARC;* the *Auditor's Code* and how it relates to ARC; and the *Accessibility Chart* that classifies a case and how to process it. Here, then, is both the final statement on Book One Auditing Procedures and the discovery upon which all further research would advance. The data in these lectures was thought to be lost for over fifty years and only available in student notes published in Notes on the Lectures. The original recordings have now been discovered making them broadly available for the first time. Life in its highest state, *Understanding,* is composed of Affinity, Reality and Communication. And, as LRH said, the best description of the ARC Triangle to be found anywhere is in these lectures. *15 lectures.*

SCIENCE OF SURVIVAL—*PREDICTION OF HUMAN BEHAVIOR* • The most useful book you will ever own. Built around the *Hubbard Chart of Human Evaluation,* Science of Survival provides the first accurate prediction of human behavior. Included on the chart are all the manifestations of an individual's survival potential graduated from highest to lowest, making this the complete book on the Tone Scale. Knowing only one or two characteristics of a person and using this chart, you can plot his or her position on the Tone Scale and thereby know the rest, obtaining an accurate index of their *entire* personality, conduct and character. Before this book the world was convinced that cases could not improve but only deteriorate. Science of Survival presents the idea of different states of case and the brand-new idea that one can progress upward on the Tone Scale. And therein lies the basis of today's Grade Chart.

THE SCIENCE OF SURVIVAL LECTURES • Underlying the development of the Tone Scale and Chart of Human Evaluation was a monumental breakthrough: The *Theta-MEST Theory,* containing the explanation of the interaction between Life—*theta*—with the physical universe of Matter, Energy, Space and Time—*MEST.* In these lectures, delivered to students immediately following publication of the book, Ron gave the most expansive description of all that lies behind the Chart of Human Evaluation and its application in life itself. Moreover, here also is the explanation of how the ratio of *theta* and *en(turbulated)-theta* determines one's position on the Tone Scale and the means to ascend to higher states. *4 lectures.*

SELF ANALYSIS • The barriers of life are really just shadows. Learn to know yourself—not just a shadow of yourself. Containing the most complete description of consciousness, Self Analysis takes you through your past, through your potentials, your life. First, with a series of self-examinations and using a special version of the Hubbard Chart of Human Evaluation, you plot yourself on the Tone Scale. Then, applying a series of light yet powerful processes, you embark on the great adventure of self-discovery. This book further contains embracive principles that reach *any* case, from the lowest to the highest—including auditing techniques so effective they are referred to by Ron again and again through all following years of research into the highest states. In sum, this book not only moves one up the Tone Scale but can pull a person out of almost anything.

ADVANCED PROCEDURE AND AXIOMS • With new breakthroughs on the nature and anatomy of engrams—"Engrams are effective only when the individual himself determines that they will be effective"—came the discovery of the being's use of a *Service Facsimile:* a mechanism employed to explain away failures in life, but which then locks a person into detrimental patterns of behavior and further failure. In consequence came a new type of processing addressing *Thought, Emotion* and *Effort* detailed in the "Fifteen Acts" of Advanced Procedure and oriented to the rehabilitation of the preclear's *Self-determinism.* Hence, this book also contains the all-encompassing, no-excuses-allowed explanation of *Full Responsibility,* the key to unlocking it all. Moreover, here is the codification of *Definitions, Logics,* and *Axioms,* providing both the summation of the entire subject and direction for all future research. *See Handbook for Preclears, written as a companion self-processing manual to Advanced Procedure and Axioms.*

THOUGHT, EMOTION AND EFFORT • With the codification of the Axioms came the means to address key points on a case that could unravel all aberration. *Basic Postulates, Prime Thought, Cause and Effect* and their effect on everything from *memory* and *responsibility* to an individual's own role in empowering *engrams*—these matters are only addressed in this series. Here, too, is the most complete description of the *Service Facsimile* found anywhere—and why its resolution removes an individual's self-imposed disabilities. *21 lectures.*

HANDBOOK FOR PRECLEARS • *(This current volume.)* The "Fifteen Acts" of Advanced Procedure and Axioms are paralleled by the fifteen Self-processing Acts given in Handbook for Preclears. Moreover, this book contains several essays giving the most expansive description of the *Ideal State of Man*. Discover why behavior patterns become so solidly fixed; why habits seemingly can't be broken; how decisions long ago have more power over a person than his decisions today; and why a person keeps past negative experiences in the present. It's all clearly laid out on the Chart of Attitudes—a milestone breakthrough that complements the Chart of Human Evaluation—plotting the ideal state of being and one's *attitudes* and *reactions* to life. *In self-processing, Handbook for Preclears is used in conjunction with Self Analysis.*

THE LIFE CONTINUUM • Besieged with requests for lectures on his latest breakthroughs, Ron replied with everything they wanted and more at the Second Annual Conference of Dianetic Auditors. Describing the technology that lies behind the self-processing steps of the *Handbook*—here is the *how* and *why* of it all: the discovery of *Life Continuum*—the mechanism by which an individual is compelled to carry on the life of another deceased or departed individual, generating in his own body the infirmities and mannerisms of the departed. Combined with auditor instruction on use of the Chart of Attitudes in determining how to enter every case at the proper gradient, here, too, are directions for dissemination of the Handbook and hence, the means to begin wide-scale clearing. *10 lectures.*

SCIENTOLOGY: MILESTONE ONE • Ron began the first lecture in this series with six words that would change the world forever: "This is a course in *Scientology*." From there, Ron not only described the vast scope of this, a then brand-new subject, he also detailed his discoveries on past lives. He proceeded from there to the description of the first E-Meter and its initial use in uncovering the *theta line* (the entire track of a thetan's existence), as entirely distinct from the *genetic body line* (the time track of bodies and their physical evolution), shattering the "one-life" lie and revealing the *whole track* of spiritual existence. Here, then, is the very genesis of Scientology. *22 lectures.*

THE ROUTE TO INFINITY: TECHNIQUE 80 LECTURES • As Ron explained, "Technique 80 is the *To Be or Not To Be* Technique." With that, he unveiled the crucial foundation on which ability and sanity rest: *the being's capacity to make a decision.* Here, then, is the anatomy of "maybe," the *Wavelengths of ARC*, the *Tone Scale of Decisions,* and the means to rehabilitate a being's ability *To Be*... almost *anything. 7 lectures. (Knowledge of Technique 80 is required for Technique 88 as described in Scientology: A History of Man—below.)*

SCIENTOLOGY: A HISTORY OF MAN • "A cold-blooded and factual account of your last 76 trillion years." So begins A History of Man, announcing the revolutionary *Technique 88*—revealing for the first time the truth about whole track experience and the exclusive address, in auditing, to the thetan. Here is history unraveled with the first E-Meter, delineating and describing the principal incidents on the whole track to be found in any human being: *Electronic implants, entities, the genetic track, between-lives incidents, how bodies evolved* and *why you got trapped in them*—they're all detailed here.

TECHNIQUE 88: INCIDENTS ON THE TRACK BEFORE EARTH • "Technique 88 is the most hyperbolical, effervescent, dramatic, unexaggeratable, high-flown, superlative, grandiose, colossal and magnificent technique which the mind of Man could conceivably embrace. It is as big as the whole track and all the incidents on it. It's what you apply it to; it's what's been going on. It contains the riddles and secrets, the mysteries of all time. You could bannerline this technique like they do a sideshow, but nothing you could say, no adjective you could use, would adequately describe even a small segment of it. It not only batters the imagination, it makes you ashamed to imagine anything," is Ron's introduction to you in this never-before-available lecture series, expanding on all else contained in History of Man. What awaits you is the whole track itself. *15 lectures.*

SCIENTOLOGY 8-80 • The *first* explanation of the electronics of human thought and the energy phenomena in any being. Discover how even physical universe laws of motion are mirrored in a being, not to mention the electronics of aberration. Here is the link between theta and MEST revealing what energy *is*, and how you *create* it. It was this breakthrough that revealed the subject of a thetan's *flows* and which, in turn, is applied in *every* auditing process today. In the book's title, "8-8" stands for *Infinity-Infinity*, and "0" represents the static, *theta*. Included are the *Wavelengths of Emotion, Aesthetics, Beauty and Ugliness, Inflow and Outflow* and the *Sub-zero Tone Scale*—applicable only to the thetan.

SOURCE OF LIFE ENERGY • Beginning with the announcement of his new book—Scientology 8-80—Ron not only unveiled his breakthroughs of theta as the Source of Life Energy, but detailed the *Methods of Research* he used to make that and every other discovery of Dianetics and Scientology: the Qs and *Logics*—methods of *thinking* applicable to any universe or thinking process. Here, then, is both *how to think* and *how to evaluate all data and knowledge,* and thus, the linchpin to a full understanding of both Scientology and life itself. *14 lectures.*

THE COMMAND OF THETA • While in preparation of his newest book and the Doctorate Course he was about to deliver, Ron called together auditors for a new Professional Course. As he said, "For the first time with this class we are stepping, really, beyond the scope of the word *Survival*." From that vantage point, the Command of Theta gives the technology that bridges the knowledge from 8-80 to 8-8008, and provides the first full explanation of the subject of *Cause* and a permanent shift of orientation in life from MEST to *Theta*. *10 lectures.*

SCIENTOLOGY 8-8008 • The complete description of the behavior and potentials of a *thetan,* and textbook for the Philadelphia Doctorate Course and The Factors: Admiration and the Renaissance of Beingness lectures. As Ron said, the book's title serves to fix in the mind of the individual a route by which he can rehabilitate himself, his abilities, his ethics and his goals—the attainment of *infinity* (8) by the reduction of the apparent *infinity* (8) of the MEST universe to *zero* (0) and the increase of the apparent *zero* (0) of one's own universe to *infinity* (8). Condensed herein are more than 80,000 hours of investigation, with a summarization and amplification of every breakthrough to date—and the full significance of those discoveries form the new vantage point of *Operating Thetan*.

THE PHILADELPHIA DOCTORATE COURSE LECTURES • This renowned series stands as the largest single body of work on the anatomy, behavior and potentials of the spirit of Man ever assembled, providing the very fundamentals which underlie the route to Operating Thetan. Here it is in complete detail—the thetan's relationship to the *creation, maintenance* and *destruction of universes.* In just those terms, here is the *anatomy* of matter, energy, space and time, and *postulating* universes into existence. Here, too, is the thetan's fall from whole track abilities and the *universal laws* by which they are restored. In short, here is Ron's codification of the upper echelon of theta beingness and behavior. Lecture after lecture fully expands every concept of the course text, Scientology 8-8008, providing the total scope of *you* in native state. *76 lectures and accompanying reproductions of the original 54 LRH hand-drawn lecture charts.*

THE FACTORS: ADMIRATION AND THE RENAISSANCE OF BEINGNESS • With the *potentials* of a thetan fully established came a look outward resulting in Ron's monumental discovery of a *universal solvent* and the basic laws of the theta *universe*—laws quite literally senior to anything: *The Factors: Summation of the Considerations of the Human Spirit and Material Universe.* So dramatic were these breakthroughs, Ron expanded the book Scientology 8-8008, both clarifying previous discoveries and adding chapter after chapter which, studied with these lectures, provide a postgraduate level to the Doctorate Course. Here then are lectures containing the knowledge of *universal truth* unlocking the riddle of creation itself. *18 lectures.*

THE CREATION OF HUMAN ABILITY—*A HANDBOOK FOR SCIENTOLOGISTS* • On the heels of his discoveries of Operating Thetan came a year of intensive research, exploring the realm of a *thetan exterior.* Through auditing and instruction, including 450 lectures in this same twelve-month span, Ron codified the entire subject of Scientology. And it's all contained in this handbook, from a *Summary of Scientology* to its basic *Axioms* and *Codes.* Moreover, here is *Intensive Procedure,* containing the famed Exteriorization Processes of *Route 1* and *Route 2*—processes drawn right from the Axioms. Each one is described in detail—*how* the process is used, *why* it works, the axiomatic technology that underlies its use, and the complete explanation of how a being can break the *false agreements* and *self-created barriers* that enslave him to the physical universe. In short, this book contains the ultimate summary of thetan exterior OT ability and its permanent accomplishment.

PHOENIX LECTURES: FREEING THE HUMAN SPIRIT • Here is the panoramic view of Scientology complete. Having codified the subject of Scientology in Creation of Human Ability, Ron then delivered a series of half-hour lectures to specifically accompany a full study of the book. From the *essentials* that underlie the technology—*The Axioms, Conditions of Existence* and *Considerations and Mechanics,* to the processes of *Intensive Procedure,* including twelve lectures describing one-by-one the thetan exterior processes of *Route 1*—it's all covered in full, providing a conceptual understanding of the *science of knowledge* and *native state OT ability.* Here then are the bedrock principles upon which everything in Scientology rests, including the embracive statement of the religion and its heritage—*Scientology, Its General Background.* Hence, this is the watershed lecture series on Scientology itself, and the axiomatic foundation for all future research. *42 lectures.*

DIANETICS 55!—*THE COMPLETE MANUAL OF HUMAN COMMUNICATION* • With all breakthroughs to date, a single factor had been isolated as crucial to success in every type of auditing. As LRH said, "Communication is so thoroughly important today in Dianetics and Scientology (as it always has been on the whole track) that it could be said if you were to get a preclear into communication, you would get him well." And this book delineates the *exact,* but previously unknown, anatomy and formulas for *perfect* communication. The magic of the communication cycle is *the* fundamental of auditing and the primary reason auditing works. The breakthroughs here opened new vistas of application—discoveries of such magnitude, LRH called Dianetics 55! the *Second Book* of Dianetics.

THE UNIFICATION CONGRESS: COMMUNICATION! FREEDOM & ABILITY • The historic Congress announcing the reunification of the subjects of Dianetics and Scientology with the release of *Dianetics 55!* Until now, each had operated in their own sphere: Dianetics addressed Man *as Man*—the first four dynamics, while Scientology addressed life *itself*—the Fifth to Eighth Dynamics. The formula which would serve as the foundation for all future development was contained in a single word: *Communication.* It was a paramount breakthrough Ron would later call, "the great discovery of Dianetics and Scientology." Here, then, are the lectures, as it happened. *16 lectures and accompanying reproductions of the original LRH hand-drawn lecture charts.*

SCIENTOLOGY: THE FUNDAMENTALS OF THOUGHT—*THE BASIC BOOK OF THE THEORY AND PRACTICE OF SCIENTOLOGY FOR BEGINNERS* • Designated by Ron as the *Book One of Scientology*. After having fully unified and codified the subjects of Dianetics and Scientology came the refinement of their *fundamentals*. Originally published as a résumé of Scientology for use in translations into non-English tongues, this book is of inestimable value to both the beginner and advanced student of the mind, spirit and life. Equipped with this book alone, one can begin a practice and perform seeming miracle changes in the states of well-being, ability and intelligence of people. Contained within are the *Conditions of Existence, Eight Dynamics, ARC Triangle, Parts of Man,* the full analysis of *Life as a Game,* and more, including exact processes for individual application of these principles in processing. Here, then, in one book, is the starting point for bringing Scientology to people everywhere.

HUBBARD PROFESSIONAL COURSE LECTURES • While Fundamentals of Thought stands as an introduction to the subject for beginners, it also contains a distillation of fundamentals for every Scientologist. Here are the in-depth descriptions of those fundamentals, each lecture one-half hour in length and providing, one-by-one, a complete mastery of a single Scientology breakthrough—*Axioms 1–10; The Anatomy of Control; Handling of Problems; Start, Change and Stop; Confusion and Stable Data; Exteriorization; Valences* and more—the *why* behind them, *how* they came to be and their mechanics. And it's all brought together with the *Code of a Scientologist,* point by point, and its use in actually creating a new civilization. In short, here are the LRH lectures that make a *Professional Scientologist*—one who can apply the subject to every aspect of life. *21 lectures.*

Additional Books Containing Scientology Essentials

Work

THE PROBLEMS OF WORK—*SCIENTOLOGY APPLIED TO THE WORKADAY WORLD* •
Having codified the entire subject of Scientology, Ron immediately set out to
provide the *beginning* manual for its application by anyone. As he described it:
life is composed of seven-tenths work, one-tenth familial, one-tenth political and
one-tenth relaxation. Here, then, is Scientology applied to that seven-tenths of
existence including the answers to *Exhaustion* and the *Secret of Efficiency*. Here,
too, is the analysis of life itself—a game composed of exact rules. Know them and
you succeed. Problems of Work contains technology no one can live without, and
that can immediately be applied by both the Scientologist and those new to the
subject.

Life Principles

SCIENTOLOGY: A NEW SLANT ON LIFE • Scientology essentials for every aspect of
life. Basic answers that put you in charge of your existence, truths to consult again
and again: *Is It Possible to Be Happy?*, *Two Rules for Happy Living*, *Personal Integrity*,
The Anti-Social Personality and many more. In every part of this book you will find
Scientology truths that describe conditions in your life and furnish *exact* ways to
improve them. Scientology: A New Slant on Life contains essential knowledge for
every Scientologist and a perfect introduction for anyone new to the subject.

Axioms, Codes and Scales

SCIENTOLOGY 0-8: THE BOOK OF BASICS • The companion to all Ron's books,
lectures and materials. This is *the* Book of Basics, containing indispensable data
you will refer to constantly: the *Axioms of Dianetics and Scientology; The Factors;* a
full compilation of all *Scales*—more than 100 in all; listings of the *Perceptics* and
Awareness Levels; all *Codes* and *Creeds* and much more. The senior laws of existence
are condensed into this single volume, distilled from more than 15,000 pages of
writings, 3,000 lectures and scores of books.

Scientology Ethics: Technology of Optimum Survival

INTRODUCTION TO SCIENTOLOGY ETHICS • A new hope for Man arises with the first workable technology of ethics—technology to help an individual pull himself out of the downward skid of life and to a higher plateau of survival. This is the comprehensive handbook providing the crucial fundamentals: *Basics of Ethics & Justice; Honesty; Conditions of Existence; Condition Formulas* from Confusion to Power; the *Basics of Suppression* and its handling; as well as *Justice Procedures* and their use in Scientology Churches. Here, then, is the technology to overcome any barriers in life and in one's personal journey up the Bridge to Total Freedom.

Purification

CLEAR BODY, CLEAR MIND—*THE EFFECTIVE PURIFICATION PROGRAM* • We live in a biochemical world, and this book is the solution. While investigating the harmful effects that earlier drug use had on preclears' cases, Ron made the major discovery that many street drugs, particularly LSD, remained in a person's body long after ingested. Residues of the drug, he noted, could have serious and lasting effects, including triggering further "trips." Additional research revealed that a wide range of substances—medical drugs, alcohol, pollutants, household chemicals and even food preservatives—could also lodge in the body's tissues. Through research on thousands of cases, he developed the *Purification Program* to eliminate their destructive effects. Clear Body, Clear Mind details every aspect of the all-natural regimen that can free one from the harmful effects of drugs and other toxins, opening the way for spiritual progress.

Reference Handbooks

What Is Scientology?

The complete and essential encyclopedic reference on the subject and practice of Scientology. Organized for use, this book contains the pertinent data on every aspect of the subject:

• The life of L. Ron Hubbard and his path of discovery

• The Spiritual Heritage of the religion

• A full description of Dianetics and Scientology

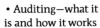

• Auditing—what it is and how it works

• Courses—what they contain and how they are structured

• The Grade Chart of Services and how one ascends to higher states

• The Scientology Ethics and Justice System

• The Organizational Structure of the Church

• A complete description of the many Social Betterment programs supported by the Church, including: Drug Rehabilitation, Criminal Reform, Literacy and Education and the instilling of real values for morality

Over 1,000 pages in length, with more than 500 photographs and illustrations, this text further includes Creeds, Codes, a full listing of all books and materials as well as a Catechism with answers to virtually any question regarding the subject.

You Ask and This Book Answers.

The Scientology Handbook

Scientology fundamentals for daily use in every part of life. Encompassing 19 separate bodies of technology, here is the most comprehensive manual on the basics of life ever published. Each chapter contains key principles and technology for your continual use:

• Study Technology

• The Dynamics of Existence

• The Components of Understanding— Affinity, Reality and Communication

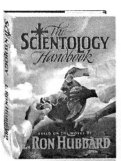

• The Tone Scale

• Communication and its Formulas

• Assists for Illnesses and Injuries

• How to Resolve Conflicts

• Integrity and Honesty

• Ethics and Condition Formulas

• Answers to Suppression and a Dangerous Environment

• Marriage

• Children

• Tools for the Workplace

More than 700 photographs and illustrations make it easy for you to learn the procedures and apply them at once. This book is truly the indispensable handbook for every Scientologist.

The Technology to Build a Better World.

about L. Ron Hubbard

o really know life," L. Ron Hubbard wrote, "you've got to be part of life. You must get down and look, you must get into the nooks and crannies of existence. You have to rub elbows with all kinds and types of men before you can finally establish what he is."

Through his long and extraordinary journey to the founding of Dianetics and Scientology, Ron did just that. From his adventurous youth in a rough and tumble American West to his far-flung trek across a still mysterious Asia; from his two-decade search for the very essence of life to the triumph of Dianetics and Scientology—such are the stories recounted in the L. Ron Hubbard Biographical Publications.

Presenting the photographic overview of Ron's greater journey is *L. Ron Hubbard: Images of a Lifetime*. Drawn from his own archival collection, this is Ron's life as he himself saw it.

While for the many aspects of that rich and varied life, stands the Ron Series. Each issue focuses on a specific LRH profession: *Auditor, Humanitarian, Philosopher, Artist, Poet, Music Maker, Photographer* and many more including his published articles on *Freedom* and his personal *Letters & Journals*. Here is the life of a man who lived at least twenty lives in the space of one.

FOR FURTHER INFORMATION VISIT
www.lronhubbard.org

Guide to the Materials

You're on an Adventure! Here's the Map.

- All books
- All lectures
- All reference books

All of it laid out in chronological sequence with descriptions of what each contains.

Uour journey to a full understanding of Dianetics and Scientology is the greatest adventure of all. But you need a map that shows you where you are and where you are going.

That map is the Materials Guide Chart. It shows all Ron's books and lectures with a full description of their content and subject matter so you can find exactly what *you* are looking for and precisely what *you* need.

Since each book and lecture is laid out in chronological sequence, you can see *how* the subjects of Dianetics and Scientology were developed. And what that means is by simply studying this chart you are in for cognition after cognition!

New editions of all books include extensive glossaries, containing definitions for every technical term. And as a result of a monumental restoration program, the entire library of Ron's lectures are being made available on compact disc, with complete transcripts, glossaries, lecture graphs, diagrams and issues he refers to in the lectures. As a result, you get *all* the data, and can learn with ease, gaining a full *conceptual* understanding.

And what that adds up to is a new Golden Age of Knowledge every Dianeticist and Scientologist has dreamed of.

To obtain your FREE Materials Guide Chart and Catalog, or to order L. Ron Hubbard's books and lectures, contact:

WESTERN HEMISPHERE:
**Bridge
Publications, Inc.**
4751 Fountain Avenue
Los Angeles, CA 90029 USA
www.bridgepub.com
Phone: 1-800-722-1733
Fax: 1-323-953-3328

EASTERN HEMISPHERE:
**New Era Publications
International ApS**
Store Kongensgade 53
1264 Copenhagen K, Denmark
www.newerapublications.com
Phone: (45) 33 73 66 66
Fax: (45) 33 73 66 33

Books and lectures are also available direct from Churches of Scientology.
*See **Addresses**.*

addresses

D ianetics is a forerunner and substudy of Scientology, the fastest-growing religion in the world today. Centers and Churches exist in cities throughout the world, and new ones are continually forming.

To obtain more information or to locate the Church or Center nearest you, visit the Scientology website:

www.scientology.org
e-mail: info@scientology.org

or

Phone: 1-800-334-LIFE
(for US and Canada)

You can also write to any one of the Continental Organizations, listed on the following page, who can direct you to one of the thousands of Churches and Centers world over.

L. Ron Hubbard's books and lectures may be obtained from any of these addresses or direct from the publishers on the previous page.

CONTINENTAL
CHURCH ORGANIZATIONS:

UNITED STATES
**CHURCH OF SCIENTOLOGY
CONTINENTAL LIAISON OFFICE
WESTERN UNITED STATES**
1308 L. Ron Hubbard Way
Los Angeles, California 90027 USA
info@wus.scientology.org

**CHURCH OF SCIENTOLOGY
CONTINENTAL LIAISON OFFICE
EASTERN UNITED STATES**
349 W. 48th Street
New York, New York 10036 USA
info@eus.scientology.org

CANADA
**CHURCH OF SCIENTOLOGY
CONTINENTAL LIAISON OFFICE
CANADA**
696 Yonge Street, 2nd Floor
Toronto, Ontario
Canada M4Y 2A7
info@scientology.ca

LATIN AMERICA
**CHURCH OF SCIENTOLOGY
CONTINENTAL LIAISON OFFICE
LATIN AMERICA**
Federacion Mexicana de Dianetica
Calle Puebla #31
Colonia Roma, Mexico D.F.
C.P. 06700, Mexico
info@scientology.org.mx

UNITED KINGDOM
**CHURCH OF SCIENTOLOGY
CONTINENTAL LIAISON OFFICE
UNITED KINGDOM**
Saint Hill Manor
East Grinstead, West Sussex
England, RH19 4JY
info@scientology.org.uk

AFRICA
**CHURCH OF SCIENTOLOGY
CONTINENTAL LIAISON OFFICE AFRICA**
5 Cynthia Street
Kensington
Johannesburg 2094, South Africa
info@scientology.org.za

AUSTRALIA, NEW ZEALAND & OCEANIA
CHURCH OF SCIENTOLOGY
CONTINENTAL LIAISON OFFICE ANZO
16 Dorahy Street
Dundas, New South Wales 2117
Australia
info@scientology.org.au

**Church of Scientology
Liaison Office of Taiwan**
1st, No. 231, Cisian 2nd Road
Kaoshiung City
Taiwan, ROC
info@scientology.org.tw

EUROPE
CHURCH OF SCIENTOLOGY
CONTINENTAL LIAISON OFFICE EUROPE
Store Kongensgade 55
1264 Copenhagen K, Denmark
info@scientology.org.dk

**Church of Scientology
Liaison Office of Commonwealth
of Independent States**
Management Center of Dianetics
and Scientology Dissemination
Pervomajskaya Street, House 1A
Korpus Grazhdanskoy Oboroni
Losino-Petrovsky Town
141150 Moscow, Russia
info@scientology.ru

**Church of Scientology
Liaison Office of Central Europe**
1082 Leonardo da Vinci u. 8-14
Budapest, Hungary
info@scientology.hu

**Church of Scientology
Liaison Office of Iberia**
C/Miguel Menendez Boneta, 18
28460 – Los Molinos
Madrid, Spain
info@spain.scientology.org

**Church of Scientology
Liaison Office of Italy**
Via Cadorna, 61
20090 Vimodrone
Milan, Italy
info@scientology.it

Become a Member
of the International
Association of Scientologists

The International Association of Scientologists is the membership organization of all Scientologists united in the most vital crusade on Earth.

A free Six-Month Introductory Membership is extended to anyone who has not held a membership with the Association before.

As a member, you are eligible for discounts on Scientology materials offered only to IAS Members. You also receive the Association magazine, *IMPACT*, issued six times a year, full of Scientology news from around the world.

The purpose of the IAS is:

"To unite, advance, support and protect Scientology and Scientologists in all parts of the world so as to achieve the Aims of Scientology as originated by L. Ron Hubbard."

Join the strongest force for positive change on the planet today, opening the lives of millions to the greater truth embodied in Scientology.

JOIN THE INTERNATIONAL ASSOCIATION OF SCIENTOLOGISTS.

To apply for membership,
write to the International
Association of Scientologists
c/o Saint Hill Manor, East Grinstead
West Sussex, England, RH19 4JY

www.iasmembership.org

Editor's Glossary
of Words, Terms & Phrases

Words often have several meanings. The definitions used here only give the meaning that the word has as it is used in this book. Dianetics terms appear in bold type. Beside each definition you will find the page on which it first appears, so you can refer back to the text if you wish.

This glossary is not meant to take the place of standard language or Dianetics and Scientology dictionaries, which should be referred to for any words, terms or phrases that do not appear below.

The chapter LRH Glossary should be read, in full, for a proper grounding in the nomenclature of this subject. Definitions from that chapter are, however, included below for ease of reference and are noted where they occur.

—The Editors

As: grades indicating the highest excellence. In US schools, a grade refers to a letter meant to reflect the quality of a student's work. The system consists of a scale starting at the bottom with F (failing) and moving up through D (poor or barely passing), C (average or satisfactory), B (good or above average), with A (excellent) at the top. Such grades are based on exams, written by teachers, which test whether a student remembers the data he was made to study during the school period. Page 98.

abdicate: renounce or give up power, responsibility or the like. Used in the book to describe the action of the control center turning over direction to the sub-control center after being confronted with a major failure. Page 164.

aberrated: affected by aberration. Page 37.

aberrated, the: persons affected by aberration. Page 2.

aberration: a departure from rational thought or behavior. From the Latin, *aberrare*, to wander from; Latin, *ab*, away, *errare*, to wander. It means basically to err, to make mistakes, or more specifically to have fixed ideas which are not true. The word is also used in its scientific sense. It means departure from a straight line. If a line should go from A to B, then if it is "aberrated" it would go from A to some other point, to some other point, to some other point, to some other point, to some other point and finally arrive at B. Taken in its scientific sense, it would also mean the lack of straightness or to see crookedly as, for example, a man sees a horse but thinks he sees an elephant. Page 2.

absolutes: those things, conditions, etc., which are perfect and complete and are completely free from restriction or condition. Page 263.

abstain: hold oneself back, by one's own choice, especially from something regarded as improper or unhealthy. Page 233.

abstract: pertaining to an idea or term considered apart from what can be sensed, measured or experienced. Page 264.

ACCESSIBILITY: THE STATE OF BEING WILLING TO BE PROCESSED (TECHNICAL SENSE IN THIS SCIENCE). THE STATE OF BEING WILLING TO HAVE INTERPERSONAL RELATIONS (SOCIAL SENSE). FOR THE INDIVIDUAL HIMSELF, ACCESSIBILITY WITH SELF MEANS WHETHER OR NOT AN INDIVIDUAL CAN RECONTACT HIS PAST EXPERIENCES OR DATA. A MAN WITH A "BAD MEMORY" (INTERPOSED BLOCKS BETWEEN CONTROL CENTER AND FACSIMILES) HAS MEMORIES WHICH ARE NOT ACCESSIBLE TO HIM. (From *LRH Glossary*.)

account for: 1. to be the cause, agent or source of. Page 60.
2. give a satisfactory reason or explanation for something. Page 140.

ACT: A STAGE OF PROCESSING. APPLIES SOLELY TO THE PARTICULAR PROCESS IN USE AT A CERTAIN CASE LEVEL. (From *LRH Glossary*.) Page 65.

action phrases: words or phrases in engrams or locks which cause the individual to perform involuntary actions on the time track. Action phrases cause the preclear to go somewhere or stay somewhere or not get in touch with something, in terms of space and time. Examples: "stay here," "don't move." See *Science of Survival*. Page 274.

acutely: in a manner or way that is brief or has a short course or occurs occasionally, as opposed to chronic (long-lasting or happening continually, said of a condition that lasts over a long period). Page 207.

adding machines: machines capable of adding numbers and sometimes other simple arithmetic functions. Such machines were operated manually through large keys which displayed numbers or descriptive words on their surface. One of the keys was labeled "clear" and removed all past computations, allowing the operator a fresh start on a calculation. Page 300.

address: the action of aiming or directing one's words to a particular person, group, etc. Page 2.

addressed: aimed; directed. Page 2.

address (to): the direction of efforts, energies or attention toward something. Page 16.

add up: exist as a particular result or effect, as in *"That's the way the pressure or pain in the stomach may add up."* Page 177.

adept: one who is completely skilled or knowledgeable in all the secrets of his art. Page 130.

Adler: psychologist Alfred Adler (1870-1937), who first collaborated with Sigmund Freud but parted company and founded his own independent school of thought as he disagreed with Freud's emphasis on sex as a driving force. Adler thought people were primarily motivated to overcome inherent feelings of inferiority. Page 130.

admit to: allow, permit or accept as possible to occur. Page 47.

adorn: to lend beauty to or make more pleasing, attractive, impressive, etc.; decorate. Page 98.

advance: to present something for consideration, discussion or as the basis of some action, such as a theory. Page 15.

advisability: the condition of being correct or proper to recommend or suggest; the condition of being desirable or wise. Page 19.

aesthetic: artistically pleasing or beautiful; relating to the beautiful as distinguished from the merely nice, the useful, etc. Page 292.

affair(s): 1. a thing or matter; something of a particular kind, usually with a descriptive or qualifying term, as in *an amazing affair.* Page 82.
2. a romantic and sexual relationship, sometimes one of brief duration, between two people who are not married to each other. Page 99.
3. matters of public interest or concern; matters concerning men or nations collectively. Page 133.

after all: after considering any indications or expectations to the contrary. Page 17.

against one's wishes: in opposition or contrary to what one desires or believes in. Page 81.

aggregations, colonial: groups of organisms formed together into a connected structure and living or growing in close association with each other. *Colonies* in this sense means groups or masses of individual animals or plants, of the same kind, living or growing in close association. *Aggregation* is used in its biological sense, the act or process of organisms coming together to form a group. Page 273.

Alcoholics Anonymous: an international organization of men and women who attempt to help each other with their problem of alcoholism. They believe alcoholism is incurable and encourage members to stay away from alcohol, as their motto states, "one day at a time." Page 111.

alga: singular form of *algae,* any of several types of simple organisms having no true root, stem or leaf. Algae are found in water or damp places and include seaweed and pond scum (a layer of green, freshwater organisms on the surface of stagnant water). Page 17.

alike: in a similar way; to the same degree; equally. Page 25.

all out: with all available means or effort; using or involving all one's resources. Page 132.

amassed: gathered (a large amount of something) over a period of time. Page 109.

amnesia: a partial or total loss of memory. Page 165.

amply: large in amount or degree or extent. Page 39.

analogy: a similarity between like features of two things on which a comparison may be based. Also the comparison so made. Page 35.

anesthetic: a drug that reduces sensitivity to pain and may produce unconsciousness. Page 37.

anthropoid: a man-like ape, such as the gorilla and chimpanzee. Page 33.

anthropologist: a person who specializes in the science that deals with the origins, physical and cultural development, biological characteristics and social customs and beliefs of humankind. Page 39.

apathies: attitudes or feelings of apathy manifested by a lack of feeling or emotion; absences of interest or concern. Page 304.

apology: 1. a defense, excuse or justification, as for a course of action or behavior. Page 39.
2. a written or spoken expression of one's regret, remorse or sorrow for having insulted, failed, injured or wronged another. Page 99.

appendage: something added or attached to something else. Page 39.

approximate: come near or close to, as in degree, nature or quality; approach closely. Page 28.

arbitrary: a factor introduced in a problem's solution when that factor does not derive from a known natural law but only from an opinion or authoritarian command. Page 264.

arduous: requiring great exertion, energy or strong effort. Page 189.

arms, with open: literally, with arms outspread as if to hug someone. Hence, to receive someone or something with great willingness or eagerness. Page 95.

arthritis: acute or chronic inflammation of the joints, causing pain, swelling and stiffness. Page 60.

arts major: a *major* in this sense means a subject or field of study chosen by a student (usually attending a university) to represent his or her main interest and upon which a large share of his or her efforts are concentrated. Hence, an *arts major* is a student whose specialization is the subject of art (painting or sculpture or drawing, etc.), with most of his courses of instruction being in that field. Page 110.

as in: as regards, with respect or reference to. Page 28.

aspect(s): nature; quality; character. Page 79.

assay: an examination or analysis as to the characteristics of something. Page 137.

asserts: puts (oneself) forward boldly or forcefully in doing or saying something. Page 17.

assess: *see* ASSESSMENT. Page 96.

ASSESSMENT: AN INVENTORY, AN EXAMINATION OR A CALCULATION OR EVALUATION OF A CASE. (From *LRH Glossary.*) Page 91.

ASSISTS: THE STRAIGHT PERCEPTION-BY-PERCEPTION RUNNING, OVER AND OVER, OF AN ACCIDENT OR INCIDENT, UNTIL IT IS DESENSITIZED AS A FACSIMILE AND CANNOT AFFECT THE PRECLEAR. THE ASSIST IS USED IMMEDIATELY AFTER ACCIDENTS OR OPERATIONS. IT TAKES AWAY SHOCK AND MOST OF THE HARMFUL EFFECTS OF THE INCIDENT AND PROMOTES HEALING. IT IS DONE BY STARTING THE INDIVIDUAL AT THE BEGINNING OF THE INCIDENT, WITH THE FIRST AWARENESS OF THE INCIDENT, JUST AS THOUGH THE PRECLEAR WERE LIVING IT ALL THE WAY THROUGH AGAIN WITH FULL PERCEPTION OF SIGHT, SOUND, ETC., AS NEARLY AS THEY CAN BE OBTAINED. AN ASSIST RUN, FOR INSTANCE, IMMEDIATELY AFTER A DENTAL OPERATION TAKES ALL THE SHOCK OUT OF THE OPERATION. ONE CONCLUDES AN ASSIST BY PICKING UP THE AUDITING AS ANOTHER INCIDENT AND RUNNING THROUGH THE AUDITING AND THE DECISION TO BE AUDITED. AN ASSIST SAVES LIVES AND MATERIALLY SPEEDS HEALING. (From *LRH Glossary.*)

assume: 1. take on a particular state, quality, character or the like, as in *"To assume a STATE OF BEINGNESS."* Page 19.
2. take upon oneself as a responsibility, obligation, etc., as in *"assume FULL RESPONSIBILITY."* Page 20.
3. take over or seize something that properly belongs to someone else, as in *"assume control."* Page 282.

assumption: the act of taking on (something) as if one's own, as particular characteristics, qualities or the like. Page 285.

astigmatism: a fault in the lens of the eye which reduces the quality of sight, especially a fault which stops the eye from focusing. Page 307.

atmosphere: the feeling that an event or place gives one. Smell, taste, tactile, sound and various sensory messages considered as a unit of feeling. Page 175.

atomic and molecular phenomena: the subject or study of the structure and energy of *atoms* and *molecules* and the relationship between them. An atom is a very small particle which is considered the building block of physical matter. All the material on Earth is composed of various combinations of atoms which unite in an infinite number of ways into more complex structures called molecules. A molecule is one of the basic units of matter, consisting of one or more atoms held together by chemical forces. *Phenomena* is the plural of *phenomenon,* an occurrence, a circumstance or a fact that is perceptible by the senses, and sometimes viewed as significant or in need of explanation. Page 131.

atomic fission: the splitting of the central part of an atom (nucleus) into fragments which is accompanied by a significant release of energy. The pieces of the nucleus then strike other nuclei (centers of atoms) and cause them to fission (split), thus creating a chain reaction. Page 28.

atoms: very small particles which are considered the building blocks of physical matter. All physical material on Earth is composed of various combinations of atoms. An atom is said to be more than a million times smaller than the thickness of a human hair. Page 131.

attainment: an act of arriving at or obtaining something. Page 21.

attain to: to gain as an objective or to arrive at, as through persistence or over time. Page 16.

attributed to: regarded as possessed, owned or originated by; assigned as a characteristic or condition of. Page 141.

at will: just as or when one wishes. Page 37.

at worst: even under the most unfavorable or negative view or circumstances. Page 191.

auditing: same as *processing,* the application of a set of exact verbal procedures and exercises which raise tone and increase perception and memory. Page 21.

AUDITOR: ONE WHO LISTENS AND COMPUTES. A TECHNICIAN OF THIS SCIENCE. (From *LRH Glossary.*) Page 1.

aural: of or relating to the ear or the sense of hearing. Page 311.

authoritarian: 1. one who considers himself an "authority" on a given subject. An *authority* in this sense is a supposed expert or one whose opinion on a subject is likely to be accepted without question and without reference to facts or results. Page 29.
2. of or having to do with an authority. *Authority* here refers to one who has power to determine, pass judgment, dictate or command without reference to data, facts or observation. Page 264.

authoritarianism: the system or practice of an *authority* (or *authorities*), one who is a supposed expert or one whose opinion on a subject is likely to be accepted without question and without reference to facts or results. Under authoritarianism individual freedom of judgment and action would be neglected in favor of absolute obedience to "experts." Page 187.

authorities: persons who think of themselves as experts on a given subject. An *authority* in this sense is a supposed expert or one whose opinion on a subject is likely to be accepted without question and without reference to facts or results. Page 16.

axiomatic text: a reference to the chapter *Definitions, Logics and Axioms.* Page 46.

axioms: statements of natural laws on the order of those of the physical sciences. Page 16.

backgrounds of motivation: *background* means the part of something toward the back. Specifically it refers here to the past personal circumstances and experiences that have shaped an individual's life. *Motivation* means a force or influence that causes a person to do something or act in a certain way. *Backgrounds of motivation* are forces which are thought to come from an unknown source and cause a person to act in a certain way or want to do particular things. Page 241.

Bacon: Francis Bacon (1561–1626), English philosopher and essayist who helped develop the scientific method, a method of experimentation and research that takes its conclusions from observed facts rather than from previous conclusions or theories. Page 98.

bad taste: failure to conform with generally held views concerning what is offensive or acceptable socially; thought of as inappropriate for a particular occasion. Page 111.

balk: that which restrains, hinders or stops something. Page 291.

balked: stopped, as at an obstacle, and refused to proceed or do something specified. Page 136.

banalities: things, such as ideas, concepts, thoughts, which are very commonplace and predictable or not new or fresh. Page 18.

band: 1. a group of individuals acting or functioning together in a common activity. Page 9.
2. a more or less well-defined range of something, as a level on a scale. Page 26.

barest necessity: of or pertaining to the absolute minimum level of things that one cannot do without, such as food, clothing and shelter, and nothing more. *Bare* means just what is needed without being in excess. Page 18.

battle that was lost all for the loss of a horseshoe nail: a reference to a proverb: "For want of a nail the shoe was lost, For want of a shoe the horse was lost, For want of a horse the rider was lost, For want of a rider the battle was lost, For want of a battle the kingdom was lost, And all for the want of a horseshoe nail." Page 19.

bawls (someone) out: criticizes or scolds (someone) loudly, severely or harshly. Page 175.

bear: to accept or have, with the sense of having to endure something difficult or painful. Page 137.

bearable: able to be endured. Page 16.

bedridden: forced to remain in bed because of illness, weakness or injury. Page 135.

beg off: ask to be excused from something; request or obtain release from something. Page 209.

being: the fact or condition of having existence; substance, nature or essence. Page 10.

beingness: the state of cause. You are trying to continue to be cause on all dynamics. Cause is "to be," "I am." That is the state of cause. A person goes all through his life trying to be cause. Page 19.

bicker: engage in a bad-tempered quarrel over something unimportant. Page 16.

bid(s): an earnest effort or attempt to attain or achieve something, as in *"His bid for such care"* or *"sympathy bids."* Page 207.

biologist: one who studies the life and structure of plants and animals. Page 39.

birth to, given: brought into existence; originated. Page 8.

bizarre: very strange and unusual. Page 307.

blast: to criticize or attack sharply. Page 132.

bless (someone): an expression used to wish someone well as in showing approval and support. Page 131.

blink: be startled or surprised, shown through the rapid closing of one's eyelids. Page 99.

blocker: something that obstructs or interrupts (movement, progress, etc.). Page 149.

blood: the killing or injuring of people. Page 7.

blood-soaked: drenched or saturated with blood, referring to newspaper stories filled with murder, war and destruction. Page 110.

bloom: grow or flourish with health, vigor, beauty, etc., likened to a plant opening (blooming) into a flower. Page 130.

blow: leave, depart, disappear or go, as if by an explosive action. Page 242.

blow out one's brains: to shoot oneself in the head. Page 152.

blueprinting: referring to *genetic blueprinting,* the planning of construction of a new body (in the orthodox manner of conception, birth and growth). Page 47.

blunt: 1. make weak or impaired in force; make less effective. Page 26. **2.** plain-spoken, honest or frank. Page 99.

blunted: weakened or impaired in force; made less effective. Page 26.

bluntly: in a manner that is plain-spoken, honest and without delicacy. Page 110.

blur, vague: something that is indistinct or hazy to the mind and so difficult to recall. Page 179.

blurs out: becomes hazy or indistinct in outline or shape. Page 194.

bolt: flee (suddenly); break away, get free or get clear. Page 149.

books, light: not profound or serious; having little importance. *Light books* refers to self-help works purporting to advise on how to win friends and influence people which advocate agreeing with *anything* anybody says. *Friends* means people whom one knows; acquaintances, particularly with the idea of entering into friendly relations with. Page 176.

borne in mind: carried in the mind; remembered, as of a fact or piece of information that is important or could be useful in the future. Page 261.

bound them, ties which: literally, ties are cord or rope used to securely fasten something. Hence, situations, conditions, states of mind, etc., that are firmly connected, brought together or restrained, as if tied by a rope. *Bound* means tied or secured, as with a rope or cord. Page 137.

box top: the very top part of a box containing a commercial product, such as a breakfast cereal, usually bearing the brand name of the product. This is in reference to promotions run to attract consumers where a free gift, prize, etc., is offered in exchange for a designated number of box tops or a certain number of box tops with a small amount of money. To receive the advertised item, the consumer must tear off the box top(s) and send it or "a reasonable facsimile thereof" (an acceptable copy of it) to the manufacturer. Page 303.

branded: labeled or marked as if with a *brand,* a mark formerly put upon criminals with a hot iron. Page 151.

break the habit: manage to get rid of an acquired behavior pattern that has been repeated so often by an individual that it has become automatic with him. Page 46.

bric-a-brac: odds and ends of any sort; miscellaneous items or things of the same sort as mentioned. Page 18.

BROKEN: SLANG USED IN THE WISE OF "BREAKING A CASE," MEANING THAT ONE BREAKS THE HOLD OF THE PRECLEAR ON A NON-SURVIVAL FACSIMILE. USED IN GREATER OR LESSER MAGNITUDE, SUCH AS "BREAKING A CIRCUIT" OR "BREAKING INTO A CHAIN" OR "BREAKING A COMPUTATION." NEVER BREAKING THE PRECLEAR OR HIS SPIRIT, BUT BREAKING WHAT IS BREAKING THE PRECLEAR. (From *LRH Glossary.*)

brotherhood: literally, the state or relationship of being brothers. Hence, a feeling of friendship, understanding and closeness with other people and things. Page 17.

Buck Rogers: a science fiction comic strip, originally appearing in 1929, that tells the adventures of a twentieth-century American Air Force officer (Buck Rogers) who awakens after being caught in suspended animation for five centuries. With the help of superscientific equipment and futuristic weapons, Buck travels through space fighting the forces of evil. Page 131.

building blocks: literally, large blocks of concrete or similar hard material used for building houses and other large structures. Hence, anything thought of as a basic unit of construction such as an element or component regarded as contributing to the growth or development of something. Page 25.

bursitis: inflammation of a fluid-filled sac (bursa) of the body, particularly at the elbow, knee or shoulder joint. A *bursa* is a fluid-filled sac that reduces friction around joints or between other parts that rub against one another. Page 307.

burst: a sudden, intense expression of an emotion, likened to something coming open or flying apart suddenly or violently, especially from internal pressure. Page 196.

but: only, as in the phrase, *"for Man is but recently a food animal"* meaning, because Man until just recently was food for animals. Page 53.

button: that computation or foible or quirk of the human mind which can be made right by merely touching one factor. This term comes from the idea of pushing a button to activate something, as in an electrical or mechanical device. Page 66.

buying (someone) off: giving somebody money or the like in order to ensure cooperation, especially in doing something illegal or dishonest. Page 80.

by and by: before long, soon, shortly. Page 153.

bypassed: avoided (something) by using an alternative channel, passage or route. Page 45.

bypaths: secondary roads as opposed to the chief or main road or highway. Used figuratively. Page 8.

by reason of: because of, due to. Page 2.

by the way: used to introduce something that is not strictly part of the subject at hand; in passing as a side topic. Page 82.

called too late: a humorous reference to psychiatrists who, after failing to help a patient, explain it by saying "they came to me too late." Page 16.

calls up: summons or brings to mind as by remembering. Page 47.

carbon-oxygen motor: a motor (a machine that imparts motion) which operates on carbon and oxygen. The material body of a human is a low-heat engine that runs on a carbon-oxygen system—oxygen from the air and carbon from food are mixed together to form energy. The body runs at 98.6 degrees Fahrenheit (37 centigrade), and the combustion makes it possible for the body to carry out various functions including movement of the muscles. Page 45.

carry straight on through: continue all the way through to the end of some action or activity. Page 1.

case: 1. a general term for a person being or about to be audited. Page 3.
2. the entire accumulation of effort, thought content, pain, painful emotion, failures, etc., residing in the facsimiles of a person's mind. Page 61.
3. of or concerning the state of a person's case, the entire accumulation of effort, thought content, pain, painful emotion, failures, etc., residing in facsimiles of a person's mind. Page 299.

case(s): an instance of something; an occurrence; an example. Page 28.

case, in: if it happens that; if; used to introduce a piece of information and to explain one's reason for giving it. Page 18.

catalyst: something that stimulates a reaction, development or change. Page 53.

catalyzed: driven or urged into action, as by reaction to a stimulus. Page 306.

cell(s): the smallest structural unit of an organism that is capable of independent functioning. All plants and animals are materially made up of one or more cells that usually combine to form various tissues. For instance the human body has more than 10 trillion cells. Page 35.

CENTER OF CONTROL: THE AWARENESS OF AWARENESS UNIT OF THE MIND. THIS IS NOT PART OF THE BRAIN, BUT PART OF THE MIND, THE BRAIN BEING PHYSIOLOGICAL. THE MIND HAS TWO CONTROL CENTERS POSSIBLE, BY DEFINITION, THE RIGHT AND THE LEFT. ONE IS AN ACTUAL GENETIC CONTROL CENTER. THE OTHER IS A SUB-CONTROL CENTER, SUBSERVIENT TO THE CONTROL CENTER. (From *LRH Glossary*.)

challenge forth: summon or invite to action or effort. A *challenge* is something that by its nature or character serves as a call to some special effort. *Forth* is used with the idea of out and into view, as from inaction. Page 25.

charge: suffusion (the state of being spread through or over), as with emotion such as anger, fear, grief, apathy, etc. Page 150.

charge: rush forward in attack. Page 119.

chary: cautious or careful. Page 17.

chatter over fences: *chatter* means to engage in purposeless or foolish talk and here refers to the tradition of neighbors spreading rumor or gossip to each other across a fence such as that separating their properties. Page 99.

chemical heat engine: a reference to the body of a living organism which converts chemical energy (from food or other fuel) into heat and provides mechanical energy, such as to move the body's muscles. Page 270.

chronic: long-lasting or happening continually, as of an illness, medical condition, etc. Page 179.

chronically: always or continually; repeatedly. Page 54.

circuit: a pseudo-personality (false personality) out of a facsimile strong enough to dictate to the individual and BE the individual. See *Dianetics: The Modern Science of Mental Health.* Page 305.

circuit(s): routes or paths around which something can flow and carry out a function. Page 45.

circulatory system: the parts of the body (heart, blood and blood vessels) that act together to perform the function of *circulation,* the movement of blood through the body, supplying nutrients (food) and oxygen to the cells and removing waste products. *Circulate* means to move or cause to move continuously or freely through a closed path which is in, or thought to be in, the shape of a circle. Page 45.

clandestine: secret or hidden, with an intent to conceal. Page 99.

clay: earthy material; the physical as opposed to the spiritual. Page 34.

clean slate: a new start or fresh chance. A *slate* is a thin piece or plate of rock used for writing on with chalk. From the practice in nineteenth-century taverns of recording a customer's debts on a slate with a chalk. Once the debt was paid, the record would be wiped off and the customer had a "clean slate." A person's experiences, especially his mistakes, faults or bad experiences and their effect on his mind or life have often been compared to the writing accumulated on a slate. Page 137.

clean up the slate: remove past mistakes, faults or bad experiences. A *slate* is a thin piece or plate of rock used for writing on with chalk. From the practice in nineteenth-century taverns of recording a customer's debts on a slate with a chalk. Once the debt was paid, the record would be wiped off and the customer had a "clean slate." A person's experiences, especially his mistakes, faults or bad experiences and their effect on his mind or life have often been compared to the writing accumulated on a slate. Page 138.

CLEAR: (*VERB*) THE ACT OF DESENSITIZING OR RELEASING A THOUGHT IMPRESSION OR A SERIES OF IMPRESSIONS OR OBSERVATIONS IN THE PAST OR A POSTULATE OR AN EMOTION OR AN EFFORT OR AN ENTIRE FACSIMILE. THE PRECLEAR EITHER RELEASES HIS HOLD ON THE FACSIMILE (MEMORY) OR THE FACSIMILE ITSELF IS DESENSITIZED. THE WORD IS TAKEN FROM ELECTRONIC COMPUTERS OR COMMON OFFICE ADDING MACHINES AND DESCRIBES AN ACTION SIMILAR TO CLEARING PAST COMPUTATIONS FROM THE MACHINES. (From *LRH Glossary.*)

CLEAR: (*NOUN*) A MUCH MISUNDERSTOOD STATE OF BEING. THE WORD HAS BEEN USED BEFORE WITH OTHER MEANINGS. IT HAS BEEN MISTAKEN AS AN ABSOLUTE. IT IS STILL USED. IT IS USED HERE AS ELECTRONICS SLANG AND CAN APPLY TO A CHAIN, AN INCIDENT OR A COMPUTATION. (From *LRH Glossary.*)

clear-cut: so definite as to leave no possibility of doubt; marked by certainty. Page 208.

cliques: small and exclusive groups of people associated for unworthy or selfish ends, such as to impose themselves as supreme authority in a particular field. Page 131.

closed: concluded; brought to an end; finished, completed. Page 61.

coaxed: get someone to do something by gentle means. Page 190.

cohesion(s): 1. the force(s) between particles within a body or substance that acts to unite them. Page 77.
2. the act or state of cohering, uniting or sticking together; figuratively, a nonmaterial union. Page 283.

coined: describing a formed or created new word or phrase. Page 17.

cold: not affected by passion, emotion or bias; objective. Page 105.

collectivism: a political and economic system in which the people as a group own the land, factories and other means of production, and all is paid for by the state, as in communism. As used in this book, it refers to the communist state of Russia (Union of Soviet Socialist Republics—USSR) that followed the 1917 Russian Revolution. Page 9.

colon(s): a punctuation mark (:) consisting of two dots placed one above the other, used to mark a major division in a sentence without ending the sentence itself, as a period (.) would. Summed up it means "note what follows." It is used to indicate that what follows in the sentence is an example, definition, elaboration, summation, something implied, etc., of what precedes it. For example, "The items we need are as follows: a shovel, a bucket and a jacket." Page 99.

colonial aggregations: groups of organisms formed together into a connected structure and living or growing in close association with each other. *Colonies* in this sense means groups or masses of individual animals or plants, of the same kind, living or growing in close association. *Aggregation* is used in its biological sense, the act or process of organisms coming together to form a group. Page 273.

colored: given an unfavorable or negative modification or influence. Page 192.

Commander Thompson: Joseph Cheesman Thompson (1874–1943), a commander and surgeon in the United States Navy, who studied Freudian analysis with Sigmund Freud (1856–1939) in Vienna for the purpose of introducing the theory and practice of psychoanalysis into the US Navy. Page 131.

commentators: people who report, analyze and evaluate world events and trends, often using newspaper, radio or television. Page 133.

common denominator: something common to or characteristic of a number of people, things, situations, etc.; shared characteristic. Page 272.

company: the lowest administrative military unit, consisting of forty-eight or more soldiers. Page 28.

comparable magnitude: *comparable* means capable of being compared; having features in common with something else to permit or suggest comparison. *Magnitude* means relative size, amount, importance, extent or influence. A datum can be evaluated only by a datum of comparable magnitude. Page 263.

compelled: forced or driven into a course of action; effected by a strong force or influence. Page 272.

complex compounds: *complex* means composed of two or more items or parts. *Complex compounds* are special substances that make up the cells of the body. Page 134.

compound(s): a substance containing two or more elements (substances that themselves cannot be broken down into simpler substances) in exact proportions. A compound can be made up of many elements and usually has properties unlike those of the elements it is made up of. Page 53.

compound word: a word made up of two or more other words. For example, teapot, from *tea* and *pot* or blackbird, from *black* and *bird*. MEST is a compound word made up from (the first letters) of four other words: *matter, energy, space* and *time*. Page 310.

computation(s): technically is that aberrated evaluation and postulate that one must be consistently in a certain state in order to succeed. The computation thus may mean that one must entertain in order to be alive or that one must be dignified in order to succeed or that one must own much in order to live. Page 300.

computation(s): the action or result of calculating or processing data (to come up with answers); thinking. Page 109.

COMPUTING PSYCHOTIC: ONE WHO IS RUNNING ON A CIRCUIT, A CIRCUIT BEING A PSEUDO-PERSONALITY OUT OF A FACSIMILE STRONG ENOUGH TO DICTATE TO THE INDIVIDUAL AND *BE* THE INDIVIDUAL. (From *LRH Glossary.*)

conclusively: in a manner that serves to put an end to doubt, question or uncertainty; decisively; finally. Page 34.

conduits: literally, pipes, tubes or the like, for conveying water or other fluid. Hence, passages or channels. Page 35.

conquest: the action or process of overcoming or mastering, as by physical or mental force. Page 9.

considerable: a rather large or great amount. Page 1.

consists in: exists in; lies or resides in. Page 277.

constitute: to be equivalent in effect or value to; have the form or characteristic of (a specified thing). Page 277.

consult long with: to think or consider carefully, as about a choice to be made, over an extended period of time. Page 137.

contact(s): establish a connection, communication or the like through the mind such as by recall of past events. Page 150.

continuation, goal: *continuation* means the causing of anything to go on; the continued maintenance of a condition or a repetition of an action. A *goal continuation* for another person or thing would be attempting, oneself, to carry on the goal, the purpose or aim, of others who have failed, departed or are dead. Page 191.

contra-survival: from *contra,* against, in opposition to, and *survival.* Hence, *contra-survival* is something in opposition to, against or contrary to survival. Page 268.

contrition: remorse or expressed sorrow for a wrongdoing and inclination to make amends. Page 196.

control sphere: the area or region (thought of as moving outward from a person or source), that someone or something directs, manages or influences. Page 46.

conversely: in a way that is reversed, as in position, order or action, yet implying a connection or linked relationship. Page 17.

converters: organisms such as algae that convert units of light from the sun and minerals from the sea into energy they need to survive. In Axiom 16, *"Organisms can exist only as higher levels of complexities because lower levels of converters exist"* refers to the fact that the largest animals, unable to live on soil and sunlight, live on vegetable forms which are themselves the converters of soil and sunlight into comestibles (things which can be eaten as food) for higher forms. (*Algae* are any of several simple plantlike organisms having no true root, stem or leaf and which use the energy of sunlight to make their own food.) Page 269.

cooling planets: a reference to an early stage in the formation of planets in which they cool. Scientists believe that a planet forms from clouds of dust and gas that gather together through the attraction of gravity. As the planet forms, it heats up. Later, as the gathering mass of the young planet moves through space it cools, changing from gas to liquid and eventually becoming mainly solid. Page 33.

cooperative effort: mental or physical energy exerted by many acting or working together in order to achieve a common purpose. Page 18.

corn: a reference to the practice in ancient Rome where the government provided mass public entertainment and gave the people free food (corn) as a means of keeping the populace happy. In ancient Rome, *corn* was used in its most general meaning of wheat, rye, barley, oats, etc. Page 110.

corollary: a proposition that follows upon one just demonstrated and that requires no additional proof. For an example, see the chapter *Definitions, Logics and Axioms*. Page 262.

cost: to cause to lose, suffer or sacrifice (something). Page 133.

counter-: a word used in combination with another with the meaning of against, in opposition or response to; opposite. Page 54.

COUNTER-EFFORT: THE INDIVIDUAL'S OWN EFFORT IS SIMPLY CALLED *EFFORT*. THE EFFORTS OF THE ENVIRONMENT ARE CALLED *COUNTER-EFFORTS*. (From *LRH Glossary*.) Page 59.

counter-emotion: *counter-* means against, in opposition or response to; opposite. *Counter-emotion* is the emotion of others toward one or the emotion one discharges at people. For example: live around a person who is continually angry and one will begin to emotionally react toward that anger, for the anger seeks to stop one whatever one does. Counter-emotion is fully described in Chapter Eight, The Eighth Act and The Ninth Act. Page 54.

counter-thought: you think one thing, somebody else thinks another. Their thought is counter to your thought. Page 192.

count on: look for or expect; make the basis of one's calculations or plans. Page 66.

course(s): a route, direction, action or series of actions. Page 19.

course of action: a particular manner of proceeding. Also, a chosen path of activity. Page 118.

course of, in the: while doing; during the progress or length of. Page 7.

court: a *court of law,* a person or body of persons appointed to hear and submit a decision on law proceedings. Used figuratively to refer to anything viewed as a court of law that has the capacity to make decisions concerning guilt or innocence and to impose punishment. Page 99.

covert: concealed, hidden or disguised; not openly practiced or shown. Page 79.

cowardice: overwhelming fear and lack of strength when confronted with danger, difficulty or opposition. Page 226.

cracking (cases): discovering the solutions to; breaking through the difficulties of and managing to solve, likened to breaking (cracking) open something to reveal its contents. Page 147.

cracking (one's) heels: a variation of *clicking one's heels,* meaning to be greatly delighted or happy, so much so that to express it, one jumps in the air and clicks one's heels together. Page 133.

criminology: the scientific study of crime, criminals, criminal behavior, punishment and correction. (A *crime* is any illegal act, one forbidden by law, or a failure to act as required by law.) Page 266.

Crusades: a series of wars fought from the late eleventh through the thirteenth centuries, in which European kings and warriors set out to gain control of the lands in which Jesus lived, known as the Holy Land (modern-day Palestine). At that time, these areas were held by Muslims. The Crusaders conquered Jerusalem (now a city in Israel) in 1099 but failed to secure the Holy Land, and they were driven out by the late thirteenth century. During the Crusades hundreds of thousands of people were killed. Page 9.

crustaceans: chiefly water animals, having no backbone, many jointed legs and a hard external shell, such as a crab or lobster. Page 33.

culvert: a drain or channel crossing under a road, sidewalk, etc.; sewer. Page 99.

cycle: a series of occurrences repeating over and over in the same sequence, running through to completion and then starting once more with the first occurrence. Page 25.

dare(d): to be courageous or bold enough to. Also used in the negative, for example, *"The secrets you dare not tell."* Page 110.

dawdle (around): to waste time being idle or waiting; to move aimlessly. Hence, *"dawdle around for verbal orders"* means to be waiting, without purpose or activity, for a communication or command to take action of some kind. Page 175.

dazzle: impress deeply or surprise with one's skill, brilliance or other qualities. Page 131.

dean: a senior member of the academic staff of a university or college who manages the whole institution or a department. Page 99.

Death (grim gentleman): a reference to the *Grim Reaper,* a representation of Death, often portrayed as a man or cloaked skeleton carrying a scythe (an agricultural instrument with a curved cutting blade attached to a handle) in his duty as a "harvester" or "collector" (reaper) of bodies and souls. *Grim* in this sense means shockingly frightful, horrible or threatening evil. Page 130.

death has lost its sting: a reference to lines from the Bible, "Death is swallowed up in victory. O death, where is thy sting? O grave, where is thy victory?" referring to the power of the spirit over the body. *Sting,* used figuratively here, means the capacity to hurt or inflict an acute pain or sharp wound on the mind or feelings. Page 17.

deduced: reasoned or figured out by drawing conclusions from general principles or ideas assumed as true as a basis for further investigation or development of ideas. For example, if one accepts that "all apples are sweet" and one comes across an apple, then one might conclude that this apple is sweet as the basis for further reasoning or confirmation. *See also* **induced**. Page 265.

delusion: a persistent false belief or opinion that is resistant to reason and confrontation with actual fact. Page 39.

delve (into): to examine carefully or thoroughly in order to discover more information about. *Delve* literally means to dig, as with a spade. Page 85.

demise: death; the end of a person's existence. Page 135.

demonstrable: capable of being shown, proven or made evident. Page 10.

denote: signify, mean, refer to or be a mark or sign of; indicate. Page 299.

denoting: serving as an indicator of; showing by signs the presence or existence of. Page 307.

desensitized: made less forceful or capable of impact. Page 209.

devise: form something, as a plan of how to do something, in the mind; formulate by thought. Page 16.

dirty jokes: jokes that are considered morally unclean or impure and offensive to accepted standards of decency. Page 241.

discharge: to pour forth, or allow to be released, an emotion, feeling, etc. Page 175.

discharged: relieved of charge (anger, fear, grief or apathy); unburdened. Page 38.

discount: to disregard something, or to set something aside as inaccurate, unworkable, etc. Page 18.

disparaged: thought, written or spoken of as being of little value or importance. Page 208.

dither: an agitated state of confusion, fear, indecision, etc. Page 151.

docile: easily managed or handled; lacking in independence; giving in or tending to give in to the demands of others. Page 111.

Doppler effect: the apparent change in frequency (how many vibrations per second) of sound, light or radio waves caused by the relative motion between the source of the waves and their observer. For example, the pitch (vibrations per second) of a train whistle seems higher when the train approaches an observer and lower after it passes and begins to move away. In fact, the actual pitch of the whistle does not change. Knowing this principle, scientists can measure such things as the motion between Earth and a star. From Christian Doppler, an Austrian physicist, who described the effect in 1842. Page 131.

doubtful-class: a *class* is a category, division, level or any of several grades set apart from others based on common characteristics, qualities, conditions or rank. *Doubtful-class* refers to a category characterized by uncertainty or hesitancy, or where something is open to question or more data is needed for proof. Page 65.

do very much for: bring about or cause an important or considerable benefit to (someone or something). Page 159.

DRAMATIZING PSYCHOTIC: ONE WHO DRAMATIZES ONE TYPE OF FACSIMILE ONLY. (From *LRH Glossary*.)

drops away: falls away or descends (gradually), as to become progressively lower, one level at a time. Page 20.

dual: composed or consisting of two parts (unlike) together, such as a Life static in a body. Page 134.

dub-in: a term used to characterize vision or recall which is imaginary. The term comes from the motion-picture industry. To "dub," in moviemaking, is to create and add sounds to a picture after filming is complete. This process ("dubbing") results in a fabricated soundtrack that *seems* to the audience like it actually took place when filmed, but much or *all* of it was created in the studio long after filming was finished and then "dubbed in." Hence, "dub-in" is something put there that seems like it happened, but in reality it did not. Page 194.

dwell on: spend (much) time upon or linger over (a thing) in action or thought; remain with the attention fixed on. Page 150.

dynamic: from the Greek *dunamikos,* powerful. Hence, of or pertaining to a motivating or energizing force (of existence or life). Page 267.

DYNAMICS: THE CENTRAL DRIVES OF AN INDIVIDUAL. THEY ARE NUMBERED FROM ONE TO EIGHT AS FOLLOWS: (1) SELF SURVIVAL; (2) SURVIVAL THROUGH CHILDREN (INCLUDES SEXUAL ACT); (3) SURVIVAL BY GROUPS INCLUDING SOCIAL AND POLITICAL AS WELL AS COMMERCIAL; (4) SURVIVAL THROUGH MANKIND AS A WHOLE; (5) SURVIVAL THROUGH LIFE INCLUDING ANY SPECIES, VEGETABLE OR ANIMAL; (6) SURVIVAL THROUGH MEST; (7) SURVIVAL THROUGH THETA OR THE STATIC ITSELF; (8) (WRITTEN AS INFINITY—∞) SURVIVAL THROUGH A SUPREME BEING. EACH INDIVIDUAL IS SURVIVING FOR ALL EIGHT. (From *LRH Glossary.*) Page 26.

earnest, in: in reality; with a purposeful or sincere intent. Page 131.

echelon: a level, as in a step-like arrangement or order. An *echelon* is one of a series in a field of activity. From the French word *eschelon* meaning rung of a ladder. Page 302.

effect: bring about; accomplish; make happen. Page 18.

effected: made the effect of. Page 232.

effort: in physics, *effort* is force (push or pull upon an object) applied to either get something moving or to slow down or stop something already in motion. Page 26.

EFFORT: THE PHYSICAL-FORCE MANIFESTATION OF MOTION. A SHARP EFFORT AGAINST AN INDIVIDUAL PRODUCES PAIN. A STRENUOUS

EFFORT PRODUCES DISCOMFORT. EFFORT CAN BE RECALLED AND RE-EXPERIENCED BY THE PRECLEAR. NO PRECLEAR BELOW 2.0 SHOULD BE CALLED UPON TO USE EFFORT AS SUCH, AS HE IS INCAPABLE OF HANDLING IT AND WILL STICK IN IT. THE ESSENTIAL PART OF A PAINFUL FACSIMILE IS ITS EFFORT, NOT ITS PERCEPTIONS. (From *LRH Glossary.*) Page 34.

Effort: shortened form of *Effort Processing,* processing done by running moments of physical stress. These are run either as simple efforts or counter-efforts or as whole precise incidents. Such incidents as those which contain physical pain or heavy stress of motion, such as injuries, accidents or illnesses, are addressed by effort. Effort Processing is described in the Sixth Act of this book. Page 177.

EFFORT PROCESSING: EFFORT PROCESSING IS DONE BY RUNNING MOMENTS OF PHYSICAL STRESS. THESE ARE RUN EITHER AS SIMPLE EFFORTS OR COUNTER-EFFORTS OR AS WHOLE PRECISE INCIDENTS. SUCH INCIDENTS AS THOSE WHICH CONTAIN PHYSICAL PAIN OR HEAVY STRESS OF MOTION (SUCH AS INJURIES, ACCIDENTS OR ILLNESSES) ARE ADDRESSED BY EFFORT PROCESSING. (From *LRH Glossary.*) Page 2.

ego: in psychoanalysis, that part of the mind which is said to experience the external world through the senses and rationally organize thought processes and govern action. *Ego* is Latin for "I". Page 130.

Einstein: Albert Einstein (1879–1955), German-born American physicist whose theories on the nature of mass and energy led to development of the atomic bomb. Page 131.

electric shock: the firing of 180 to 460 volts of electricity through the brain from temple to temple or from the front to the back of one side of the head. It causes a severe convulsion (uncontrollable shaking of the body) or seizure (unconsciousness and inability to control movements of the body) of long duration. Page 137.

elucidation: the act of explaining or giving a detailed statement of. Page 261.

eludes: escapes, avoids or evades, as if by quickness or deception. Page 150.

embraced: included or contained as part of something broader. Page 26.

embroidering: adding exaggerated or fictitious (made-up) details to an account of something often to make it more interesting. Page 39.

emerge from the sea: a reference to one of the earliest stages in the theory of the evolution of life forms, when animals that had lived in the sea for millions of years, such as fish or shellfish, etc., began to come ashore. Their bodies adapted to living on land, changing gradually over many millions of years and finally becoming human bodies. *Emerge* means to rise from a surrounding fluid. Page 163.

EMOTION: THE CATALYST USED BY THE CONTROL CENTER TO MONITOR PHYSICAL ACTION. THE RELAY SYSTEM, VIA GLANDS, INTERPOSED BETWEEN "I" AND SELF AND, BY THOUGHT, OTHERS. THE MAIN EMOTIONS ARE HAPPINESS IN WHICH ONE HAS CONFIDENCE AND ENJOYMENT IN HIS GOALS AND A BELIEF IN HIS CONTROL OF ENVIRONMENT; BOREDOM IN WHICH ONE HAS LOST CONFIDENCE AND DIRECTION BUT IS NOT DEFEATED; ANTAGONISM WHEREIN ONE FEELS HIS CONTROL THREATENED; ANGER WHEREIN ONE SEEKS TO DESTROY THAT WHICH THREATENS AND SEEKS WITHOUT GOOD DIRECTION BEYOND DESTRUCTION; COVERT HOSTILITY WHEREIN ONE SEEKS TO DESTROY WHILE REASSURING HIS TARGET THAT HE IS NOT SO SEEKING; FEAR WHEREIN ONE IS CATALYZED TO FLEE; GRIEF IN WHICH ONE RECOGNIZES LOSS; APATHY IN WHICH ONE ACCEPTS FAILURE ON ALL DYNAMICS AND PRETENDS DEATH. OTHER EMOTIONS ARE A VOLUME OR LACK OF VOLUME OF THOSE NAMED. SHAME OR EMBARRASSMENT ARE EMOTIONS PECULIAR TO GROUPS OR INTERPERSONAL RELATIONS AND ARE ON A LEVEL WITH GRIEF, DENOTING LOSS OF POSITION IN A GROUP. EMOTION IS THE GLANDULAR SYSTEM PARALLEL OF MOTION AND EACH EMOTION REFLECTS ACTION TO GAIN OR LOSE MOTION. AT A HIGH LEVEL, ONE IS SENDING BACK MOTION; AT A MID LEVEL, ONE IS HOLDING MOTION; AT A LOWER LEVEL, MOTION IS SWEEPING THROUGH AND OVER ONE. (From *LRH Glossary.*) Page 25.

EMOTIONAL CURVE: THE DROP FROM ANY POSITION (ON THE TONE SCALE) ABOVE 2.0 TO A POSITION BELOW 2.0 ON THE REALIZATION OF FAILURE OR INADEQUACY. IT IS EASILY RECOVERED BY PRECLEARS. (From *LRH Glossary.*) Page 198.

employed: put into action for some definite purpose; use as a means of accomplishing something. Page 66.

encoded: a reference to the conversion of information into *code,* a system of writing and symbols in which letters or numbers are given certain meanings and replace concepts and words. Information can then be represented by these letters and numbers, as for example in formulas used in mathematics, chemistry or physics which represent laws of the physical universe. Page 131.

endocrine: having to do with the secretion of chemical substances (hormones) from certain organs and tissues which travel through the blood to all parts of the body. After a hormone arrives at the organ or tissue it affects, it causes certain actions to occur. Hormones regulate such body processes as growth, development, reproduction, response to stress, etc. Page 81.

endocrinologists: medical specialists in *endocrinology,* the study of the glands of the body and their secretions (hormones) and their related disorders. Page 129.

endowed: (of qualities, abilities or characteristics) provided, supplied, given or equipped with. Page 279.

endowment: power, ability, capacity or other advantage which a person naturally has or is given. Page 171.

engaged upon: occupied or involved with; taking part in doing some activity. Page 18.

engaging upon: occupying or involving (itself) with; taking part in doing some activity. Page 18.

engram: recordings of moments of pain and unconsciousness. These recordings can be later brought into play by a similar word or environment and cause the individual to act as though in the presence of danger. They force the individual into patterns of thinking and behavior which are not called for by a reasonable appraisal of the situation. The complete description of engrams is contained in *Dianetics: The Modern Science of Mental Health* and *Science of Survival.* Page 280.

engram, secondary: a period of anguish brought about by a major loss or a threat of loss to the individual. The secondary engram depends for its strength and force upon an engram which underlies it. Hence, the word *secondary,* as it must occur second to an engram. *See also* **engram.** Page 149.

engrossing: that fully occupies or absorbs the attention. Page 9.

enlistment: the act of securing the support and aid of; the action of employing or utilizing in advancing some interest. Page 207.

enrandomed: caused to be in the state or condition of being *random,* without pattern or plan. Page 287.

en route: on or along the way. Page 299.

ensuing: following in time or order; coming after, often as a result or consequence of. Page 266.

entity: something that exists separately from other things and has its own identity. Page 34.

ENVIRONMENT: THE SURROUNDINGS OF THE PRECLEAR FROM MOMENT TO MOMENT, IN PARTICULAR OR IN GENERAL, INCLUDING PEOPLE, PETS, MECHANICAL OBJECTS, WEATHER, CULTURE, CLOTHING OR THE SUPREME BEING. ANYTHING HE PERCEIVES OR BELIEVES HE PERCEIVES. THE OBJECTIVE ENVIRONMENT IS THE ENVIRONMENT EVERYONE AGREES IS THERE. THE SUBJECTIVE ENVIRONMENT IS THE ENVIRONMENT THE INDIVIDUAL HIMSELF BELIEVES IS THERE. THEY MAY NOT AGREE. (From *LRH Glossary.*) Page 9.

environs: environment; surroundings. Page 9.

eons: lengths of time that are too long to measure. From the Greek *aion,* age or lifetime. Page 7.

eradicate: remove or get rid of something completely. Page 60.

eradication: a getting rid of; a complete removal of something. Page 60.

erased: removed or eliminated completely. Page 150.

eroding: wearing away (as land) by the action of water, wind, etc. Page 269.

ethereal: insubstantial, light, airy; intangible (incapable of being perceived by the sense of touch, immaterial). Page 54.

euphoria: a strong feeling of well-being, cheerfulness and optimism. From the Greek *euphoros,* literally bearing well, hence healthy. Page 165.

evaluate: consider or examine something to judge its importance, extent, quality or condition. Page 39.

evaluates: judges or determines (for someone). Page 190.

ever afterwards: throughout all the time after a specified date; from that time onward. Page 34.

evolutionary: having to do with the development of a species or other group through time and the changes that occur within that species or group. Page 9.

excel: to be superior in some respect or area; do extremely well; do better than some given standard. Page 2.

exempt (from): not subject to or bound by a condition, restriction, etc., that applies to others. Page 10.

exert: 1. to put forth or put out (as strength, power or effort). Page 270. **2.** to put (oneself) into action; set in operation; make effective; exercise influence. Page 271.

exhausted: drawn out or drained off so as to empty completely. Page 291.

expense of, to the: without regard for; with no thought for; causing damage to. Page 28.

extensionally: *extend* means to stretch out or reach (to the fullest extent). In regards to theta, it means exerting itself not through physical application of the organism but in a manner that is indirect, through such means as language, ideas, etc. Page 271.

extroverted: having one's interest and attention outward or to things outside the self, as opposed to *introverted,* which is having one's interest and attention inward or to things within oneself. Page 173.

face, present a: put forward or show an appearance, look or character. Page 9.

facetiously: in a manner that is not meant to be taken seriously or literally; humorously. From the French *facétie,* joke. Page 175.

FACSIMILES: A FACSIMILE IS A MEMORY RECORDING FOR A FINITE PERIOD OF TIME. IT IS CONSIDERED THAT MEMORY IS A STATIC WITHOUT WAVELENGTH, WEIGHT, MASS OR POSITION IN SPACE (IN OTHER WORDS, A TRUE STATIC) WHICH YET RECEIVES THE IMPRESSION OF TIME, SPACE, ENERGY AND MATTER. A CAREFUL EXAMINATION OF THE PHENOMENA OF THOUGHT AND THE BEHAVIOR OF THE HUMAN MIND LEADS ONE TO THIS CONCLUSION. THE CONCLUSION IS ITSELF A POSTULATE, USED BECAUSE IT IS EXTREMELY USEFUL AND WORKABLE. THIS IS A POINT OF ECHELON IN RESEARCH THAT A FACSIMILE CAN BE SO DESCRIBED. THE DESCRIPTION IS MATHEMATICAL AND AN ABSTRACT AND MAY OR MAY NOT BE ACTUAL. WHEN A THOUGHT RECORDING IS SO REGARDED, THE PROBLEMS OF THE MIND RAPIDLY RESOLVE. FACSIMILES ARE SAID TO BE "STORED." THEY ACT UPON THE PHYSICAL UNIVERSE SWITCHBOARD, CALLED THE BRAIN AND NERVOUS AND GLANDULAR SYSTEM, TO MONITOR ACTION. THEY APPEAR TO HAVE MOTION AND WEIGHT ONLY BECAUSE MOTION AND WEIGHT ARE RECORDED INTO THEM. THEY ARE NOT STORED IN THE CELLS. THEY IMPINGE UPON THE CELLS. PROOF OF THIS MATTER RESTS IN THE FACT THAT AN ENERGY WHICH BECAME A FACSIMILE A LONG TIME AGO CAN BE RECONTACTED AND IS FOUND TO BE VIOLENT ON THE CONTACT. PAIN IS STORED AS A FACSIMILE. OLD PAIN CAN BE RECONTACTED. OLD PAIN IN FACSIMILE FORM, OLD EMOTION IN FACSIMILE FORM, CAN REIMPOSE ITSELF ON PRESENT TIME IN SUCH A WISE AS TO DEFORM OR OTHERWISE PHYSICALLY EFFECT THE BODY. YOU CAN GO BACK TO THE

LAST TIME YOU HURT YOURSELF AND FIND THERE AND RE-EXPERIENCE THE PAIN OF THAT HURT UNLESS YOU ARE VERY OCCLUDED. YOU CAN RECOVER EFFORTS AND EXERTIONS YOU HAVE MADE OR WHICH HAVE BEEN MADE AGAINST YOU IN THE PAST. YET THE CELLS THEMSELVES, WHICH HAVE FINITE LIFE, ARE LONG SINCE REPLACED ALTHOUGH THE BODY GOES ON. HENCE, THE FACSIMILE THEORY. THE WORD FACSIMILE IS USED, AS BLUNTLY AS ONE USES IT, IN CONNECTION WITH A DRAWING OF A BOX TOP INSTEAD OF THE ACTUAL BOX TOP. IT MEANS A SIMILAR ARTICLE RATHER THAN THE ARTICLE ITSELF. YOU CAN RECALL A MEMORY PICTURE OF AN ELEPHANT OR A PHOTOGRAPH. THE ELEPHANT AND THE PHOTOGRAPH ARE NO LONGER PRESENT. A FACSIMILE OF THEM IS STORED IN YOUR MIND. A FACSIMILE IS COMPLETE WITH EVERY PERCEPTION OF THE ENVIRONMENT PRESENT WHEN THAT FACSIMILE WAS MADE, INCLUDING SIGHT, SOUND, SMELL, TASTE, WEIGHT, JOINT POSITION AND SO ON THROUGH HALF A HUNDRED PERCEPTIONS. JUST BECAUSE YOU CANNOT RECALL MOTION OR THESE PERCEPTIONS DOES NOT MEAN THEY WERE NOT RECORDED FULLY AND IN MOTION WITH EVERY PERCEPTION CHANNEL YOU HAD AT THE TIME. IT DOES MEAN THAT YOU HAVE INTERPOSED A STOP BETWEEN THE FACSIMILE AND THE RECALL MECHANISMS OF YOUR CONTROL CENTERS. THERE ARE FACSIMILES OF EVERYTHING YOU HAVE EXPERIENCED IN YOUR ENTIRE LIFETIME AND EVERYTHING YOU HAVE IMAGINED. (From *LRH Glossary.*) Page 35.

faculty: one of the powers of the mind, as memory, reason or speech. Page 37.

fair game: a legitimate or acceptable object of pursuit, attack, etc. Page 178.

fall prey to: be harmed or affected by; be vulnerable to or overcome by; become a victim of. *Prey* in this sense means one who is defenseless, especially in the face of attack, a victim. Page 60.

faltering, the: those who are failing in strength or collapsing. Page 130.

fare: get along; experience good or bad fortune. Page 15.

favor: to aid or support or tend to aid or support. Page 16.

favor, with: having a particular liking for; showing preference toward. Page 239.

feign: to give a false appearance of; pretend or fake. Page 53.

fend for (oneself): to attempt to manage without assistance; to get along without help. Page 207.

Field, Eugene: (1850–1895) American author who is best known for his sentimental children's poetry. Page 212.

FIFTEEN: (*NOUN*) A DESIGNATION TO DENOTE A FINISHED CASE. SOLELY FOR CASE RECORDING TO DESIGNATE A CASE ADVANCED TO CURRENT COMPLETION. THIS IS A FOUNDATION NUMBER SYSTEM FOR PRECLEARS. A CASE IS NOTED ON RECORD BY THE ACT NUMBER TO WHICH IT HAS BEEN ADVANCED. (From *LRH Glossary.*)

Filipino irregular: a reference to the non-military fighters involved in a Filipino revolt against American rule of the Philippines that occurred between 1898 and 1902. (The people of the Philippines are called *Filipinos.*) The Americans, who had gained possession of the islands from the Spanish in 1898, stopped the rebellion and ruled the Philippines until 1935 when it became self-governing. Page 119.

finite universe: the universe that can be sensed, measured or experienced; the material universe. Page 25.

fire-like swiftness: with the speed and intensity of a spreading fire. Page 8.

fission, atomic: the splitting of the central part of an atom (nucleus) into fragments which is accompanied by a significant release of energy. The pieces of the nucleus then strike other nuclei (centers of atoms) and cause them to fission (split), thus creating a chain reaction. Page 28.

five-alarm fire: a serious fire. In firefighting, when a fire is first reported an alarm sounds in a fire station and firemen rush to the scene. Fires requiring more than one alarm are called *multiple-alarm fires,* and each new alarm brings another fire station with more firefighters and equipment. A *five-alarm fire,* for example, would be five fire stations worth of men and equipment. Page 179.

fix (oneself) up: get oneself into a bad situation. Page 152.

flagrant: shockingly noticeable or evident; obvious. Page 138.

flatten: run until flat, meaning that the incident when "flat" has been discharged of all bad consequences to the preclear. Page 151.

flew into print: rushed to publish opinions in books, magazines and newspapers. *Flew (fly)* means to move with great speed, likened to moving through the air with wings. Page 132.

flick with a feather: a *flick* is a short sudden movement and a *feather* is one of the soft, light structures that makes up the covering of a bird. Thus, a *flick with a feather* would be a very gentle, mild tap. Page 119.

flinch: draw back or shrink, as from what is dangerous, difficult or unpleasant. Page 101.

flinging away: discarding, throwing away. To *fling* means to throw suddenly or with violence. Page 28.

flooded out: poured forth in an abundant or overwhelming flow or outpouring, likened to the great flowing or overflowing of a body of water onto land not usually under water. Page 9.

flounder around: struggle or show confusion in thoughts, words or actions; manage something badly or with difficulty. Page 174.

forebears: persons from whom one is descended; ancestors. Page 163.

foreign matter: something, such as an object, not belonging to the place or body where found and typically introduced from outside. Page 130.

forgetter: literally, something that makes one forget. This alludes to the definition of *forgetter,* an engram command such as "Forget it" or "I don't know" that acts to bar or deny data or information from the person. Page 111.

for the most part: in general; on the whole; to the greater extent; mostly. Page 110.

Foundation: a reference to the Hubbard Dianetics Foundation in Wichita, Kansas, that offered processing and auditor training to public and staff in the early 1950s. From the word *foundation,* as it is the foundation for a new world and a better life. Page 189.

Foundation Auditor's School: the auditor training school of the Hubbard Dianetics Foundation in Wichita, Kansas, where auditor training was conducted in the early 1950s when this book was written. See *Addresses* for current locations. Page 149.

frame of reference: a set of concepts, values, customs, views, etc., by means of which an individual or group perceives or evaluates data, communicates ideas and regulates behavior. Page 152.

framework: the set of ideas, facts or circumstances within which something exists or with which one thinks or acts. Page 19.

Freud: Sigmund Freud (1856–1939), Austrian founder of psychoanalysis who emphasized that unconscious memories of a sexual nature control a person's behavior. Page 29.

friends (win friends and influence people): a reference to self-help works purporting to advise on how to win friends and influence people which advocate agreeing with *anything* anybody says. *Friends* means people whom one knows; acquaintances, particularly with the idea of entering into friendly relations with. Page 176.

fringe: the outside edge of something farthest from the center. Literally, a *fringe* is a decorative edging of short cords or threads. Page 176.

from here on down: from a specific position on a scale descending toward or into successively lower positions. Page 80.

from there on out: from that point or time forward. Page 38.

front end: the very beginning of an incident. Page 203.

game: crippled or injured. Page 153.

garbled: confused, mixed up, jumbled; distorted to such an extent as to make misleading or incomprehensible. Page 208.

gasoline and alcohol: a reference to the mixing of gasoline and alcohol. As alcohol is cheaper than gasoline and can also be burned in a car engine, attempts have been made to mix the two. However, alcohol readily absorbs water directly from the air and when attempting to mix alcohol with gasoline, this alcohol/water combination separates out from the gasoline and can cause damage to the parts of an engine. Thus, gasoline mixed with alcohol is considered harmful. Page 3.

GENETIC: BY LINE OF PROTOPLASM AND BY FACSIMILES AND BY MEST FORMS, THE INDIVIDUAL HAS ARRIVED IN THE PRESENT AGE FROM A PAST BEGINNING. GENETIC APPLIES TO THE PROTOPLASM LINE OF FATHER AND MOTHER TO CHILD, GROWN CHILD TO NEW CHILD AND SO FORTH. (From *LRH Glossary.*) Page 38.

genetic blueprint: the plans of construction of a new body (in the orthodox manner of conception, birth and growth). Page 38.

Genghis Khan: (1162?–1227) Mongol conqueror who founded the largest land empire in history and whose Mongol armies, known for their use of terror, conquered many territories and slaughtered the populations of entire cities. *Genghis Khan* means supreme conqueror. Page 28.

get out of (something): avoid; escape from; be excused from. Page 223.

Gibbon: Edward Gibbon (1737–1794), British scholar and the greatest English historian of his time, famous for his work *The History of the Decline and Fall of the Roman Empire,* published in six volumes. Page 119.

give it up: stop holding on to something (as in the mind). Page 137.

given: stated, fixed or specified. Page 54.

given birth to: brought into existence; originated. Page 8.

given form to: brought into existence or created so as to exist (with shape and structure) in the physical universe. Page 8.

glandular: consisting of, containing or bearing glands (a cell, group of cells or organ producing a secretion for use elsewhere in the body or for elimination from the body). For example, adrenal glands produce *adrenaline,* a hormone that is released into the bloodstream in response to physical or mental stress, as from fear of injury. It initiates many bodily responses, including stimulation of heart action and increase in blood pressure. Page 44.

glue: something that acts to bind or hold things together in a manner suggestive of *glue,* a sticky substance used for joining material objects together. Page 175.

goal continuation: *continuation* means the causing of anything to go on; the continued maintenance of a condition or a repetition of an action. A *goal continuation* for another person or thing would be attempting, oneself, to carry on the goal, the purpose or aim, of others who have failed, departed or are dead. Page 191.

goes without remark: a phrase used to say that something is so clearly true that it does not need to be stated or commented upon; goes without saying. Page 21.

good-fellowship: the spirit or habits of a *good fellow,* one who presents himself to others as a friendly and pleasant person. Page 207.

go wrong: make a mistake or fall into error; err. Also used to mean to fail in an undertaking. Page 179.

grades: marks or ratings on examinations and in school courses, indicating the relative quality of a student's work in school. In US schools, for example, the grade system consists of a scale starting at the bottom with F (failing) and moving up through D (poor or barely passing), C (average or satisfactory), B (good or above average), and A (excellent). Such grades are based on exams, written by teachers, which test whether a student remembers the data he was made to study during the school period. Page 36.

gradient scales: the term *gradient scale* can apply to anything and means a scale of condition graduated from zero to infinity. Absolutes are considered to be unobtainable. Depending on the direction the scale is graduated, there could be an infinity of wrongness and an infinity of rightness. Thus the gradient scale of rightness would run from the theoretical but unobtainable zero of rightness, up to the theoretical infinity of rightness. A gradient scale of wrongness would run from a zero of wrongness to an infinity of wrongness. The word *gradient* is meant to define lessening or increasing degrees of condition. The difference between one point on a gradient scale and another point could be as different or as wide as the entire range of the scale itself, or it could be as tiny as to need the most minute discernment (ability to perceive the difference) for its establishment. Page 19.

grand old man: a highly respected, usually elderly man who has been a major or the most important figure in a specific field for many years. Page 130.

graying the flesh: a reference to the color of the skin when the body is dying (or has died). Page 137.

great-aunt (or uncle): an aunt (or uncle) of one's father or mother, that is, a sister (or brother) of one's grandparent. Page 210.

grim gentleman, Death: a reference to the *Grim Reaper,* a representation of Death, often portrayed as a man or cloaked skeleton carrying a scythe (an agricultural instrument with a curved cutting blade attached to a handle) in his duty as a "harvester" or "collector" (reaper) of bodies and souls. *Grim* in this sense means shockingly frightful, horrible or threatening evil. Page 130.

grinding: laborious, difficult and monotonous. Page 19.

gross: dense, thick, consisting of comparatively large particles. Page 35.

guilt complex: a mental obsession with the idea of having done wrong. Page 215.

habit, break the: manage to get rid of an acquired behavior pattern that has been repeated so often by an individual that it has become automatic with him. Page 46.

hair-trigger: literally, the trigger on a gun that allows it to be fired with very slight pressure. Hence, easily activated or set off; reacting immediately to the slightest provocation or cause. Page 180.

Halley: Edmond Halley (1656-1742), English astronomer who applied Newton's discoveries on the "laws of motion" to accurately predict the orbit of comets. His accurate prediction of the return in 1758 of a comet (now known as Halley's comet) validated his theory that comets rotate around the Sun. Page 131.

halls of learning: large buildings or rooms for instruction, as at a college or university. Also, a corridor or passageway in such a building. *Hall* originally meant a castle, or the large main room of the castle. Page 98.

hallucination: seeing or experiencing imagined realities with which nobody else agrees. From the Latin *hallucinari,* to wander mentally. Page 37.

halt, the: persons who walk with a limp or uneven step, usually due to some defect or injury. Page 2.

hand, in: under control. Page 150.

handbook: a concise manual or reference book, such as may be held in the hand, providing specific information or instruction about a subject for application. Front cover.

handsomely: successfully; in good style; pleasingly. Page 98.

harmonious: having parts, forms, relations or proportions properly in agreement each with the others so that all taken together consist of a pleasing whole. Page 269.

heaven help (someone): a phrase used to express the wish that one does not want (someone) to experience something unpleasant, etc., or to express pity for the person (or people) being spoken to or about. Page 153.

HEAVY FACSIMILE: A HEAVY FACSIMILE USED TO BE KNOWN AS AN "ENGRAM." IN VIEW OF THE FACT THAT IT HAS BEEN FOUND TO BE STORED ELSEWHERE THAN IN THE CELLS, THE TERM "HEAVY FACSIMILE" HAS NOW COME INTO USE. A HEAVY FACSIMILE IS AN EXPERIENCE, COMPLETE WITH ALL PERCEPTIONS AND EMOTIONS AND THOUGHTS AND EFFORTS, OCCUPYING A PRECISE PLACE IN SPACE AND A MOMENT IN TIME. IT CAN BE AN OPERATION, AN INJURY, A TERM OF HEAVY PHYSICAL EXERTION OR EVEN A DEATH. IT IS COMPOSED OF THE PRECLEAR'S OWN EFFORT AND THE EFFORT OF THE ENVIRONMENT (COUNTER-EFFORT). (From *LRH Glossary*.)

heels, cracking (one's): a variation of *clicking one's heels,* meaning to be greatly delighted or happy, so much so, that to express it, one jumps in the air and clicks one's heels together. Page 133.

hence: for this reason; as a result. Page 266.

herd instinct: the natural impulse or tendency (instinct) that people have to belong to or be associated with a group or to act as one of a crowd, likened to animals in herds (groups that feed, live and travel together), who imitate the actions of other group members, for instance following a leader, fleeing as a group, killing prey and eating together. Page 175.

herd reaction: a response (reaction) involving an impulse or tendency that people in groups have toward thinking and acting as one of a crowd, likened to animals in herds (groups that feed, live and travel together), who imitate the actions of other group members, for instance following a leader, fleeing as a group, killing prey and eating together. Page 54.

heroic: having, displaying or characteristic of the qualities appropriate to somebody who commits an act of remarkable bravery or who has shown great courage, strength of character or other admirable qualities (a hero); courageous. Page 95.

heroically: in an extreme or radical manner. Page 165.

high and saintly: characterized by a virtuous way of life, one which is above the common and material concerns of the world, as that befitting a *saint,* a person of great holiness. Page 233.

Hiroshima: a seaport in Japan that was largely destroyed in 1945 during World War II by an American atomic bomb. This was the first atomic bomb used in warfare and killed approximately 75,000 people. Page 131.

hitherto: up to this time; until now. Page 147.

Hitler: Adolf Hitler (1889-1945), German political leader of the twentieth century who dreamed of creating a master race that would rule for a thousand years as the third German empire. Taking over rule of Germany by force in 1933 as a dictator, he began World War II (1939-1945), subjecting much of Europe to his domination and murdering millions of Jews and others considered "inferior." He committed suicide in 1945 when Germany's defeat was imminent. Page 28.

hole: a fault or flaw. Page 176.

honor: adherence to actions or principles considered right, moral and of high standard; integrity; a fine sense of what is right and wrong. Page 16.

hordes: large (moving) numbers or groups of people gathered or crowded together; masses. Page 9.

house-to-house advertising handout: a small printed advertisement designed for distribution by hand and distributed from one dwelling to the next in a given area. Page 110.

hovering like a mother hen: lingering or waiting close by, in an overprotective, insistent, interfering or anxious way. Likened to the actions of a mother hen protecting and looking after her chicks. Page 152.

Hubbard Chart of Human Evaluation: a chart contained in the book *Science of Survival,* which gives a complete description of the Tone Scale. It includes the components and characteristics of the human mind, each one plotted on the Tone Scale, providing a complete prediction of an individual's behavior and an index of their survival potential from lowest to highest. The book *Science of Survival* is written around the Hubbard Chart of Human Evaluation with a chapter devoted to and describing each section of the chart. Page 54.

humbuggery: something made or done to cheat or deceive. Page 187.

hypochondriac: one who suffers with an abnormal anxiety over one's health, often with imaginary illnesses. Also the persistent conviction that one is or is likely to become ill, often involving experiences of real pain when illness is neither present nor likely. Page 159.

id: in psychoanalysis, that part of the mind which is said to be associated with repressed or antisocial desires (usually sexual or aggressive) and dominated by irrational wishing. *Id* is Latin for it. Page 130.

idealism: the cherishing or pursuit of high or noble principles, purposes, goals, etc. Page 16.

idle: being without a basis or foundation in fact; groundless. Page 8.

if only: used to express a reason for something, even if not the only or best of the possible reasons. Page 35.

illusion: a perception that represents what is perceived in a way different from the way it is in reality. Page 39.

imbued: filled with so as to contain or spread throughout, as a particular quality. Page 274.

immunize: to protect from or to make resistant to a disease. Page 2.

imparts: gives a part or share of; makes another a partaker of. Page 264.

impedance: something that prevents or obstructs the progress of (by putting obstacles in the way). Page 29.

impingement: the act of coming into (energetic) contact with; the act of colliding or striking. Page 34.

imposed: forced upon, as something to be endured, subjected or submitted to. Page 10.

impotence: complete absence of sexual power, usually said of the male. Page 233.

impressing (it against reality): literally, applying with pressure; pressing a thing upon something else so as to leave a duplicate mark. Hence, *impressing* as used here means the ability of a facsimile when called into action again, such as during processing, to reimpress itself upon the physical universe (reality) creating the identical circumstances to when the facsimile was first received and recorded. When this is done several times under the precise conditions of processing, the facsimile loses its power, force, effort or thought content. Page 59.

impression(s): literally, a mark produced upon any surface by pressure, especially by the application of some kind of device such as a stamp, seal, etc. Hence, an effect produced by external force or influence on the senses or mind; a sensation or sense perception. Page 35.

in case: if it happens that; if; used to introduce a piece of information and to explain one's reason for giving it. Page 18.

incidental: likely to happen naturally as a result of or along with; occurring or likely to occur as a minor accompaniment. Page 266.

incredulity: the state of being unable or unwilling to believe. Page 17.

incursion: the act of entering in or running against; entrance into or invasion of a place, territory, area, sphere of operation, etc. Page 269.

index: something that serves to act as a reference. Page 288.

individuation: the action or process of becoming more and more individual. Page 274.

induced: reasoned or figured out by starting from particular experiences and facts and proceeding to general laws or principles. For example, if many apples are tasted and all are sweet, one could conclude all apples are sweet as the basis for further reasoning or confirmation. *See also* **deduced.** Page 265.

inertia of populaces: a resistance or reluctance to new action, or change (of ideas) on the part of all the people of a country, region, etc. (In the physical universe, *inertia* is the resistance an object has to a change in its state of motion. That is, an object at rest tends to stay at rest and an object in motion tends to stay in motion unless acted upon by an outside force.) Page 8.

inextricable: incapable of being pulled apart from each other; that cannot be separated out, one from another. Page 292.

infiltrated: passed through and spread out into a substance. Used figuratively. Page 192.

infirmity: disease (producing weakness). Page 135.

inflated: made greater in size, importance, value, etc., than something normally is. Page 172.

in hand: under control. Page 150.

inherent: existing in something as a natural, permanent, essential or characteristic feature or quality. Page 134.

inhibitive: of or pertaining to something that holds back or stops one's actions, desires, thoughts or emotions. Page 287.

innately: in a way that belongs to the essential nature of something; naturally, as if there since birth. From a Latin word meaning to be born in. Page 95.

inner: of the mind or spirit, as opposed to the external or outer world. Page 25.

in order: being suitable to the occasion; fitting; appropriate. Page 174.

in other words: put differently; otherwise stated, often used to introduce an explanation of something and usually in a simpler way. Page 15.

insatiable: impossible to satisfy and always needing more. From the Latin, *satiare*, to fill. Page 234.

insularity: the condition of being cut off or isolated from other people, their ideas, customs, etc., suggestive of the isolated life of an island. Page 9.

interbody: between the parts of the body. *Inter-* means between or among. Page 311.

interpersonal relations: related to or involving personal and social interactions between people. *Interpersonal* means relating to, occurring among or involving several people. Page 54.

interpose: to insert, introduce or place between one thing and another. Page 286.

in valence: being in one's own valence, one's actual personality. Page 159.

invalidate: deprive something of its force, value or effectiveness; make less of or nothing of. Page 164.

inventory: a step taken on a case, where information is gathered, such as name, age, height, weight, as well as information about past treatments, psychosomatic illnesses, operations and early environment. Page 306.

irrefutable: impossible to disprove. Page 135.

is such that: of a degree, quality, condition, etc., as specified by the statement following, as in *"The co-existent relationship between Affinity, Reality and Communication is such that none can be increased without increasing the other two and none can be decreased without decreasing the other two."* Page 292.

jellyfish: any of numerous free-swimming animals of the sea, characteristically having a gelatinous umbrellalike body and long trailing tentacles (long flexible organs used for grasping, feeling or moving). Page 33.

Jung, Adler: psychologists Carl Gustav Jung (1875–1961) and Alfred Adler (1870–1937), who first collaborated with Sigmund Freud but parted company and founded their independent schools of thought as they disagreed with Freud's emphasis on sex as a driving force. Jung theorized that all humans inherit a collective unconscious which contains universal symbols and memories from their ancestral past, while Adler thought people were primarily motivated to overcome inherent feelings of inferiority. Page 130.

keeping (someone) down: causing someone to remain in a state of depression or low spirits. Also, causing or aiding someone to remain in bed due to illness, injury, etc. Page 152.

kicked back: came back or reacted negatively against one, especially with force and energy. Page 138.

kingship: the state, fact or condition of being a *king,* hence having authority or control over a territory, area or sphere of influence. Page 9.

knocked out: made ineffective or inoperative, so as to no longer have any power over one. Page 150.

Krag-Jørgensen: a Norwegian military rifle developed in 1889. Page 119.

lack (for): be wanting or deficient; be without. Page 20.

lags: falls behind; fails to maintain a desired pace or keep up with something. Also, fails or weakens gradually. Page 9.

laid bare: revealed or exposed to view. Page 38.

laid down: put (something) out (toward or on someone); spread. Page 192.

laid down their burdens: escaped something that is emotionally difficult to bear, a source of great worry and stress or responsibilities and duties, by dying; died. Page 123.

laid (something) on: placed (something immaterial such as importance) on something. Page 28.

lame: physically disabled through injury or defect in a limb, as the foot or leg, so as to limp or walk with difficulty. Page 136.

lame, the: persons who are crippled through injury to, or defect in, a limb. Page 2.

latent: coming after the fact of; present or existing but not developed, yet capable of being activated. Page 284.

laws of heat and fission: in physics, a reference to the definite and unvarying laws of the phenomenon of heat and fission cited as representative of scientific facts. For instance, *fission* is a predictable and controllable process which is the splitting of the central part of an atom (nucleus) into fragments which is accompanied by a significant release of energy. The pieces of the nucleus then strike other nuclei (centers of atoms) and cause them to fission (split), thus creating a chain reaction. The resulting energy and heat can be utilized to power machinery. Page 135.

legion: a very large number (as of persons or things). From its original meaning of a large division of the Roman army consisting of from 3,000 to 6,000 men. Page 307.

let: to give opportunity to or fail to prevent or forbid; allow; permit. Page 81.

let out a pint or a quart of blood: a reference to the former medical practice of draining blood from the body (known as *bloodletting*) in the treatment of disease. It was believed that a broad assortment of ailments resulted from the impurity and superabundance of blood in the system and thus could be eliminated by draining blood away in large amounts. Page 129.

let's: a shortening of *let us*, used as a polite way of making a suggestion, giving an instruction or introducing a remark. Page 18.

libido theories: theories originated by the Austrian founder of psychoanalysis, Sigmund Freud (1856-1939), that the urges or driving forces motivating Man's behavior are sexual in origin. *Libido* is Latin for desire or lust. Page 15.

Life: the cause or source of living; the animating principle; soul. Page 27.

life continuum: the phenomenon of an individual's tendency to carry on the fears, goals, habits and manifestations of others who have failed, departed or are dead. Page 234.

life realization: *realization* means the action of making or converting something into reality. A realization of the life of another occurs when a person does a life continuum, carrying on the fears, goals, habits and manifestations of others who have failed, departed or are dead: he makes the life of another person an ongoing reality. Page 123.

Life static: see the Axioms in the chapter *Definitions, Logics and Axioms.* Page 46.

light books: not profound or serious; having little importance. *Light books* refers to self-help works purporting to advise on how to win friends and influence people which advocate agreeing with *anything* anybody says. *Friends* means people whom one knows; acquaintances, particularly with the idea of entering into friendly relations with. Page 176.

light, see the: reach a full understanding or realization; be converted to some idea or belief. Page 130.

limbo: an uncertain, unfavorable place or condition. From *Limbo,* a place where it is believed souls barred from Heaven but not condemned to Hell are sent, such as the souls of children who have died before baptism and those born before the birth of Christ who were moral and good. Page 152.

line of advance: a course or direction of action proceeding forward toward an objective or goal, as in research or thought, etc. Page 66.

line of protoplasm: the evolution of organisms themselves, continuing along a protoplasmic line from generation to generation. *Protoplasm* is the colorless, jellylike liquid that is present in the cells of all living plants, animals and humans and consists of the living matter of plant and animal cells. From German *protoplasma,* literally, first created thing. Page 309.

line signals: signal lights along a railroad track of different sizes and colors which give directions or warnings to trains, such as to stop, slow down, etc. Hence, *"somebody who doesn't get the line signals"* is someone who is not receiving the message or communication being originated. A *line* is a railway track or system of tracks. Page 153.

lint: small cloth fibers or pieces of thread of little strength. Page 105.

lion's share: the largest part or portion. Page 29.

Little Nell: a young girl and heroine of the novel *The Old Curiosity Shop* by English novelist Charles Dickens (1812-1870). The novel tells of the hardships of Nell and her grandfather. Page 212.

Little Orphan Annie: a young orphaned girl in a poem of the 1800s, by American poet James Whitcomb Riley (1849-1916), who is taken in by a family, does daily chores and tells the children frightening stories. Page 212.

live for the present only: give attention to one's immediate needs and concerns only; operate in life for this time right now, such as dealing with each day as it comes, one at a time. Page 111.

loath: unwilling or reluctant (to do something). Page 153.

LOCK SCANNING: A PROCESS WHICH STARTS THE PRECLEAR FROM A POINT IN THE PAST, WITH WHICH HE HAS MADE SOLID CONTACT, UP THROUGH ALL SIMILAR INCIDENTS, WITHOUT VERBALIZATION. THIS IS DONE OVER AND OVER, EACH TIME TRYING TO START AT AN EARLIER INCIDENT OF THE SAME KIND, UNTIL THE PRECLEAR EXTROVERTS ON THE SUBJECT OF THE CHAIN. "BOIL-OFF" OFTEN RESULTS, WHEREIN THE PRECLEAR SEEMS TO GO TO SLEEP. AVOID BOIL-OFF, FOR IT IS NOT THERAPEUTIC AND WILL EVENTUALLY RESULT IN REDUCED TONE. BOIL-OFF IS A LAZY AUDITOR'S EXCUSE TO BE IDLE AND FACSIMILES ARE IN SUCH SEVERE CONFLICT THAT THEY WILL NOT RESOLVE WITHOUT RESOLVING POSTULATES FIRST. LOCK SCANNING IS A STANDARDIZED DRILL, STARTED ON SIGNAL AND ENDED WITH THE PRECLEAR SAYING

HE IS AGAIN IN PRESENT TIME. IT CAN BE DONE ON ANY SUBJECT. *ABOVE* 2.0 ONLY. (From *LRH Glossary.*) Page 171.

lodge: the local branch of a large club, association or organization; the members of such a club, association or organization. Page 27.

long since: in the distant past; long ago. Page 95.

lord of all kingdoms: a reference to Man and his position of being senior to all other forms of life. *Lord* in this sense means one who has mastery or superiority above all others. A *kingdom* is a state or people ruled over by a king or queen, and here specifically refers to any of the three groups (kingdoms)—animal, vegetable and mineral—into which natural organisms and objects are traditionally divided. Page 7.

lose one's nerve: lose one's courage or self-assurance in challenging or exciting circumstances. Page 150.

lost track of: neglected to keep a record of something or some action; failed to pay attention to. Page 48.

lower orders of life: a reference to the kinds or types (orders) of life forms that are relatively simple in structure, which become food for more complex life forms. These simpler life forms are "lower" because they are thought of as earlier on the chain of evolution than later, more advanced, complex and intelligent life forms, which are regarded as "higher." Page 18.

low-scale: pertaining to the condition of being low on the Tone Scale. Page 234.

machine-like scientific consistency: a manner of operation characterized by being systematic and exact, as in the sciences, so as to uniformly produce exact and accurate results, in the unvarying manner of a well-running machine. Page 17.

magic healing crystals: crystals considered to have the power to heal, as those used by certain mystics, medicine men, etc. *Crystal* is a transparent rocklike substance resembling ice. Page 15.

magnitude: relative size, amount, importance, extent or influence. Page 263.

magnitude, comparable: *comparable* means capable of being compared; having features in common with something else to permit or suggest comparison. *Magnitude* means relative size, amount, importance, extent or influence. A datum can be evaluated only by a datum of comparable magnitude. Page 263.

main, in the: in most cases; generally; usually. Page 194.

make one's way: to advance in life or succeed, as by overcoming difficulties by one's own efforts. Page 10.

make out: to write out, complete or fill in necessary details on a form or document with blank spaces for the insertion of answers or information. Page 98.

makes ruin of: destroys; spoils, damages or injures in a complete or destructive manner. Page 234.

maladjusted: badly or unsatisfactorily adjusted, especially in relationship to one's social circumstances, environment, etc.; unable to cope with the stresses of everyday life. *Adjusted* in this sense means to be able to deal with and handle the mental and physical factors in one's life with regard to one's own needs and the needs of others. Page 81.

malformations: faults and departures from the normal shape, form or structure in a part of the body. Page 307.

Man: the human race or species, humankind, Mankind. Page 7.

man: a human being, without regard to sex or age; a person. Page 10.

manifests: displays (a quality, condition, feeling, etc.) by action or behavior; of a thing, reveals (itself) as existing or operating; shows or demonstrates plainly. Page 283.

marauder: one who roves around carrying out violent attacks or looking for items to steal by force. Page 53.

marble bust(s): a piece of sculpture carved out of marble (a type of hard rock that becomes smooth when it is polished), representing the head, shoulders and upper chest of a human body, often of and in honor of a famous person from the past. Page 98.

margin: a spare amount that is over and above what is normally needed or required for a certain purpose and that is available for special (unexpected) situations such as to allow for mistakes, delays or for safety reasons as in *a large margin of safety.* Page 137.

marked: clearly defined and evident; noticeable. Page 18.

markedly: in a manner that is strikingly obvious and clearly defined; to a significant extent; noticeably. Page 9.

mass hysteria: *mass* in this sense is used to mean of, involving or composed of masses of people; done, made, etc., on a large scale. *Hysteria* means excessive or uncontrollable emotion, such as fear or panic. Hence, *mass hysteria* refers to widespread panic, fear, anxiety, etc., shared amongst a population or large group of people. Page 54.

materialistic: of the philosophic doctrine that matter is the only reality and that everything in the world, including thought, will and feeling, can be explained only in terms of matter. Page 34.

materially: to a great extent; substantially; considerably. Page 305.

mathematics: the branch of science concerned with number, quantity and space and applied to physics, engineering and other subjects. Page 132.

maximal: the highest or greatest possible. Page 283.

"maybe," hangs in a: is suspended in indecision. Page 19.

measles: a highly contagious disease, usually occurring in childhood, with symptoms including a high temperature and a bright red rash of small spots that spread to cover the body. Page 153.

measure up to: to be equal (in ability, etc.) to; to match; to have necessary qualifications for. Page 224.

mechanism: 1. a structure or system (of parts, components, etc.) that together perform a particular function as would occur in a machine. Page 18. **2.** the agency or means by which an effect is produced or a purpose is accomplished, likened to the structure or system of parts in a mechanical device for carrying out some function or doing something. Page 46.

medicine: the medical profession. Page 129.

medium: the means through or by which something is carried out or achieved. Page 45.

MEST: A COMPOUND WORD MADE UP OF THE FIRST LETTERS OF MATTER, ENERGY, SPACE AND TIME. A COINED WORD FOR THE PHYSICAL UNIVERSE. THETA IS NOT CONSIDERED AS PART OF THE PHYSICAL UNIVERSE, BUT IS NOT CONSIDERED ABSOLUTELY AS NOT PART OF THE PHYSICAL UNIVERSE. (From *LRH Glossary.*) Page 17.

militate: have a substantial effect, weigh heavily. Page 203.

millennia: the plural form of *millennium,* a period of 1,000 years. From the Latin *mille,* thousand and *annus,* year. Page 15.

millennium: a period of 1,000 years. From the Latin, *mille,* thousand and *annus,* year. As used here, the term is referring to the period of a thousand years from A.D. 1000 to A.D. 2000. Page 9.

mimicry: imitating the actions of another. For example, a person claps their hands, you clap your hands. All of a sudden the fellow recognizes there is something in his vicinity that is similar to him. Page 189.

miracle-class: a *class* is a category, division, level or any of several grades set apart from others based on common characteristics, qualities, conditions or rank. *Miracle-class* refers to a classification of result that is extraordinary or seemingly beyond human power; capable of producing what people generally call a miracle. Page 60.

mires: involves in difficulties (as if stuck in a *mire,* a piece of wet, swampy ground). Page 187.

mirrors: reflects in the manner of a mirror (a polished surface which reflects images of objects). Hence, copies an exact likeness of. Page 35.

misaligns: puts out of proper order, relationship or orientation. Page 281.

mis-emotion: *mis-* abbreviation of *miserable, misery,* hence miserable emotion, such as anger, fear, grief and apathy. *See also* **EMOTION.** Page 149.

molecules: one of the basic units of matter, consisting of one or more atoms held together by chemical forces. They are the smallest particles into which a substance can be divided and still have the chemical identity of the original substance. Page 134.

mollusk: an animal with no backbone and a soft body, often having two shells joined by a hinge, such as an oyster or clam. Page 33.

monitor: regulate or control (some situation, process, operation, etc.); direct. Page 53.

monk in England: a reference to Hugh de Payens, a French nobleman who in 1118 founded in Jerusalem a military, religious group of monks to protect Christian pilgrims in the Holy Land (the Biblical region of Palestine). A decade later de Payens launched a preaching campaign in England, recruiting a massive army of monks who spread across Europe to the Middle East. Page 9.

monocell: an organism composed of a single cell. A *cell* is the smallest structural unit of an organism that is capable of independent functioning. Page 33.

morals: a code of good conduct laid down out of the experience of the race to serve as a uniform yardstick for the conduct of individuals and groups. Page 16.

more or less: to some extent; somewhat. Page 10.

moth-chewed: a variation of *moth-eaten,* old and overused. Page 77.

motivation, backgrounds of: *background* means the part of something toward the back. Specifically it refers here to the past personal circumstances and experiences that have shaped an individual's life. *Motivation* means a force or influence that causes a person to do something or act in a certain way. *Backgrounds of motivation* are forces which are thought to come from an unknown source and cause a person to act in a certain way or want to do particular things. Page 241.

motor: of, pertaining to or involving muscular movement. Page 44.

much less: used to characterize a statement or suggestion as still more unacceptable than one that has been already denied; and certainly not. Page 66.

muck: soft, moist dirt; mud. Page 7.

mumbo jumbo: language or ritualistic activity intended to confuse. Also obscure or meaningless talk or writing; nonsense. Page 3.

myopia: a common condition of the eye in which distant objects cannot be seen sharply. Page 307.

mystic: a person who claims to attain, or believes in the possibility of attaining, insight into mysteries that go beyond ordinary human knowledge, as by direct communication with the spiritual or divine. Page 130.

myth: a widely held but false belief or idea. Page 8.

narrow tolerance: *tolerance* is a scientific technical term for the allowable amount something (such as a machine) can vary from a set standard or limit before normal operation is threatened, breakage follows, etc. A *narrow tolerance* would be one that had a very small amount of freedom from the standard. For example, the human body whose standard operating temperature is 98.6 degrees F has a narrow band above and below that in which it can survive. Page 47.

necessity: an unavoidable need or compulsion to do something. For example, an individual is hit by a car and his neck is hurt. He is invalidated by somebody and told "it wasn't serious" or "it didn't happen." He then "has to" keep putting forward this facsimile and the best way to put it forward is to demonstrate it and try it on his own body. The preclear at this time is not conscious of it; it is manifesting itself as a psychosomatic illness. The facsimile "of necessity" had to be offered because of invalidation and it created a pattern reaction. Page 38.

necessity level: the degree of emergency in present time environment. It would be that amount of commotion necessary to extrovert the individual into action in present time. That would be necessity level. That amount of urgency or commotion necessary in the environment to extrovert the individual and put him into motion in present time. Page 111.

necessity, of: as an inevitable result, consequence; unavoidably. Page 65.

negligible: that can or should be disregarded; not significant enough to be worth considering. Page 279.

nerve channels: a reference to the network of pathways formed by the nerves and along which signals travel. *Nerves* are cells in the body that look like fibers and that transmit information between the brain and the other parts of the body. Page 44.

nerve trunks: multiple nerve fibers formed into thick bundles. Individual nerve fibers branch out from the trunk, somewhat like telephone wires, to carry their messages to parts of the body. Page 35.

nervous system: a network of pathways by which information travels throughout the body. For instance, data is sent to the brain. The brain then sends instructions via other nerve pathways to various parts of the body such as the muscles so that the body can respond to the information. The nervous system also regulates functions such as breathing, digestion and heartbeat. Page 35.

neurosis: an emotional state containing conflicts and emotional data inhibiting the abilities or welfare of the individual. Page 2.

neurotic: a person whose attention is given mainly to the immediate present (as opposed to the past and future). Page 17.

Newton: Sir Isaac Newton (1642–1727), English scientist and mathematician whose discoveries and theories laid the foundation for much of the scientific progress since his time. Newton made major contributions to the understanding of light, motion and gravity. Page 131.

New Year's resolution(s): a positive intention or a making up of one's mind to change something about oneself, such as breaking a bad habit or starting a good one, customarily made at the turning of the New Year. A *resolution* is a settled purpose or fixed determination of the mind, as in a resolution to stop smoking. Page 242.

97 cents worth: a reference to the inexpensive value of the physical substances that make up the human body when vacated by the Life static. Page 134.

Nobel prize: an annual international prize given for distinction in physics, chemistry, economics, medicine, literature, international peace, etc. The Nobel prizes are internationally recognized as the most prestigious awards in each of these fields. Originally established by Swedish inventor Alfred Nobel (1833–1896). Page 98.

noble: of high moral or mental character or excellence. Page 95.

no matter: it is of no consequence or importance; it makes no difference; regardless of. Page 26.

not-beingness: the state of being an effect, being effected by some exterior cause. Page 19.

now and then: occasionally; sometimes; from time to time. Page 60.

nuclear physics: that branch of physics that deals with the behavior, structure and component parts of the center of an atom (called a nucleus), which makes up almost all of the mass of the atom. Page 131.

nullified: reduced to nothing; made of no value or consequence. Page 10.

obituary column: a section of a newspaper that publishes notices of the deaths of people, sometimes with a brief summary of the person's life. Page 110.

obtains: exists; establishes; has a place. Page 282.

occasioned: brought about, caused. Page 167.

occluded: affected by *occlusion,* i.e., having memories shut off from one's awareness; from *occlude,* to close, shut or stop up. Page 17.

offends: acts contrary to or in violation of an agreed-upon code, rule, laws, etc. Page 26.

old-time: old-fashioned; no longer considered suitable or workable; also, relating to or characteristic of a time in the past. Page 3.

olfactory: of or pertaining to the sense of smell. Page 311.

-ology(ies): study or knowledge, usually in reference to any science or branch of knowledge; for example, biology (study of living organisms), geology (study of the physical history of Earth) or ethnology (study of the races of humankind). Page 266.

once upon a time: used, especially at the beginning of a story, to mean a long time in the past. Page 129.

onerous: burdensome or troublesome; causing hardship. Page 47.

on the part of: regarding or with respect to the person or thing that is specified. Page 26.

open arms, with: literally, with arms outspread as if to hug someone. Hence, to receive someone or something with great willingness or eagerness. Page 95.

open the door (to): to furnish opportunity for or allow action to occur. Page 232.

optic nerve(s): the nerve that carries signals from the eye to the brain. *Optic* means of or relating to the eye or vision. Page 311.

optimum: of or pertaining to the point at which the condition, degree or amount of something is the most favorable or advantageous to the attainment of some end. Page 2.

orator: an eloquent and skilled public speaker. From Latin, *orator,* a speaker. Page 175.

order(s): an action, class, group or kind having rank in a scale of quality, excellence or importance, distinguished from others by nature or character. Page 18.

order, in: being suitable to the occasion; fitting; appropriate. Page 174.

organisms: living things, such as plants, animals or bacteria; specifically, any individual animal or plant having various organs and parts that function together as a whole to maintain life and its activities. (An *organ* is a part of an organism, such as an eye, a wing or a leaf, that performs a specific function.) Page 17.

original thought: an idea, concept or imagination that is new and fresh and that comes from the person himself without imitating, depending on or being forced to use what has been done or produced before. Page 109.

orthodox: adhering to what is commonly traditional, accepted or approved of; standard. Page 131.

ostracized: excluded or banished from a group, society, etc. Page 130.

out of sight: out of one's mind or memory. A facsimile that drops "out of sight" is one that goes below the level of the individual's awareness or out of present time. Page 38.

out of valence: the taking on of the physical and/or emotional characteristics or traits of another. Page 159.

oversold: over-emphasized or over-estimated the value, ability, etc., of certain (good) features of something. Page 134.

overwhelmed: overcome or overpowered in mind or feeling, so great as to make opposition (to a force, idea, concept, etc.) useless. Page 26.

overwhelming: present in an excessive amount; so great as to make opposition (to an idea, concept, etc.) useless. Page 34.

packs: groups of animals of the same kind, such as dogs and wolves, that run and hunt together. Page 54.

parching: characterized by excessive or complete dryness, as caused by heat or sun. Page 7.

parlance: a particular manner or way of speaking; speech. Page 307.

particular: separate and distinct characteristics, qualities, etc., from others of the same group, category or nature; of or belonging to a single, definite thing; not general. Page 267.

particularly: 1. to a great degree; especially. Page 1.
2. specifically or individually; more than usual. Page 28.

partner(s): 1. a person who shares or is associated closely with another in some action or sphere of common interest. Hence, something that is commonly found in very close association or relationship with another thing. Page 28.
2. a husband or wife. Page 211.

passersby: people who happen to be walking past a particular place. Page 16.

passes of the hand: a reference to the action of moving one's hands over the surface of or around the vicinity of something or someone in order to cause some effect. Such gestures are commonly seen when someone is attempting to hypnotize a person, in performing magic, performing healing, etc. Page 130.

PAST POSTULATES: DECISIONS OR CONCLUSIONS THE PRECLEAR HAS MADE IN THE PAST AND TO WHICH HE IS STILL SUBJECTED IN THE PRESENT. PAST POSTULATES ARE UNIFORMLY INVALID SINCE THEY CANNOT RESOLVE PRESENT ENVIRONMENT. (From *LRH Glossary.*)

peculiar: 1. different from the usual or normal; uncommon. Page 35.
2. strange; curious; odd. Page 123.
3. distinctive in nature or character from all others; unique or specific to a person or thing or category. Page 267.
4. belonging distinctively or primarily to one person, group or kind; special or unique (usually followed by to). Page 307.

peculiarities: features or traits that are uniquely characteristic of a particular thing. Page 29.

penicillin: a drug that kills bacteria and is used to treat a wide range of infections. Page 130.

perceptics: perceived and recorded sense messages, such as smell, taste, touch, sound, sight, etc. Page 37.

PERCEPTIONS: BY MEANS OF PHYSICAL WAVES, RAYS AND PARTICLES OF THE PHYSICAL UNIVERSE, IMPRESSIONS OF THE ENVIRONMENT ENTER THROUGH THE "SENSE CHANNELS," SUCH AS THE EYES AND OPTIC NERVES, THE NOSE AND OLFACTORY NERVES, THE EARS AND AURAL

NERVES, INTERBODY NERVES FOR INTERBODY PERCEPTIONS, ETC., ETC. THESE ARE ALL "PERCEPTIONS" UP TO THE INSTANT THEY RECORD AS FACSIMILES, AT WHICH MOMENT THEY BECOME "RECORDINGS." WHEN RECALLED THEY ARE PERCEPTIONS AGAIN, BEING AGAIN ENTERED INTO SENSE CHANNELS FROM THE RECALL SIDE. THERE ARE OVER HALF A HUNDRED SEPARATE PERCEPTIONS ALL BEING RECORDED AT ONCE. (From *LRH Glossary.*) Page 35.

persevered: persisted in an undertaking in spite of difficulty, obstacles or discouragement. Page 82.

phenomenon: an occurrence, a circumstance or a fact that is perceptible by the senses, and sometimes viewed as significant or in need of explanation. Page 175.

photon: a unit particle of light. Just as matter is composed of atoms, light is composed of photons. Page 34.

physics: the science that deals with matter, energy, motion and force, including what these things are, why they behave as they do and the relationship between them, as contrasted to the life sciences such as biology, which studies and observes living organisms such as animals and plants. Page 26.

physiological: of the functions and activities of a living, material organism and its parts, including all its physical and chemical processes. Page 300.

pick up: 1. to take hold of and raise something up so as to examine, use, carry, recover, etc. Page 18.
2. to learn something, often in an unsystematic way, for example, by frequently hearing it, seeing it done or trying to do it. Page 98.
3. to find and observe. Page 149.
4. become aware of something; be perceptive about, as in *"you will pick up their fear and try to counteract it with emotion of your own."* Page 176.

piety: enthusiastic devotion to religious duties and worship; reverence and obedience to God. Page 9.

piloting: guiding or conducting through a course or affair; steering or controlling the course of. Page 65.

pinned down: held fast in a spot so that one cannot get away; held down or against something by force. Page 98.

plaint: a complaint. Also an expression of grief or sadness. Page 209.

plastic: easily able to be changed or modified. Page 8.

plastically: in a manner like that of plastic, that is, able to be impressed upon, shaped or molded. Page 287.

platoon pinned down by enemy fire: a reference to a *platoon*, a small body of military personnel functioning as a unit, that is *pinned down*, unable to move or unable to get away, because of heavy gunfire from enemy forces. Used figuratively to refer to being in a restricted condition, with no freedom of choice, because of a force or barrier impossible to move against. Page 98.

play the game: literally, to engage in the activities of a game. Figuratively, the activities of life, with obstacles to overcome and goals to win. Page 135.

plea: an earnest and urgent request. Page 18.

plight: a bad, unfortunate or even dangerous condition, state or situation. Page 95.

plot: to lay out or show the process, condition or course of something, as if with the precision used to chart the course of a ship, draw a map of an area, etc. Page 172.

plus: 1. having a certain quality to an unusual degree, as if being added to what is already being referred to. Page 82.
2. having a certain quantity added to what is already being referred to. Page 278.

polio: short for *poliomyelitis,* a highly infectious disease, widespread in the 1950s, that usually occurred in children and young adults. It affected the brain and spinal cord, sometimes leading to a loss of voluntary movement and muscular wasting (loss of muscular strength or substance). Page 60.

poliomyelitis: a highly infectious disease, widespread in the 1950s, that usually occurred in children and young adults. It affected the brain and spinal cord, sometimes leading to a loss of voluntary movement and muscular wasting (loss of muscular strength or substance). Page 307.

pomposity: an excessive sense of self-importance, usually displayed through exaggerated seriousness in speech and manner or by using long and formal words (to pretend knowledge). Page 187.

ponder: to consider something deeply and thoroughly. Page 8.

populace(s): all the people in a country, region or given area; population. Page 8.

populaces, inertia of: a resistance or reluctance to new action, or change (of ideas) on the part of all the people of a country, region, etc. (In the physical universe, *inertia* is the resistance an object has to a change in its state of motion. That is, an object at rest tends to stay at rest and an object in motion tends to stay in motion unless acted upon by an outside force.) Page 8.

posed: put forward; set forth. Page 10.

POSTULATE: (*VERB*) TO CONCLUDE, DECIDE OR RESOLVE A PROBLEM OR TO SET A PATTERN FOR THE FUTURE OR TO NULLIFY A PATTERN OF THE PAST. (From *LRH Glossary.*) Page 276.

POSTULATE: (*NOUN*) A CONCLUSION, DECISION OR RESOLUTION MADE BY THE INDIVIDUAL HIMSELF ON HIS OWN SELF-DETERMINISM ON DATA OF THE PAST, KNOWN OR UNKNOWN. THE POSTULATE IS ALWAYS KNOWN. IT IS MADE UPON THE EVALUATION OF DATA BY THE INDIVIDUAL OR ON IMPULSE WITHOUT DATA. IT RESOLVES A PROBLEM OF THE PAST, DECIDES ON PROBLEMS OR OBSERVATIONS IN THE PRESENT OR SETS A PATTERN FOR THE FUTURE. (From *LRH Glossary.*) Page 174.

postulate: an assumption, especially as a basis for reasoning. Page 8.

postulated: assumed to be true, real or necessary, especially as a basis for reasoning. Page 27.

PRECLEAR: ONE WHO HAS ENTERED PROCESSING EN ROUTE TO BECOMING A FIFTEEN. (From *LRH Glossary.*) *See* **FIFTEEN.** Page 1.

prefrontal lobotomies: psychiatric operations carried out by boring holes into the skull, entering the brain and severing the nerve pathways in the two frontal lobes, resulting in the patient becoming an emotional vegetable. Page 15.

present a face: put forward or show an appearance, look or character. Page 9.

presume: to do something without adequate qualifications or without having the right to. Page 15.

Prime Thought: the decision moving the original potential being from the state of not-beingness to the state of beingness. Prime Thought can occur at any moment during any lifetime, moving the individual from the state of not-beingness to the state of beingness. A common name for this phenomenon is "necessity level." Page 46.

print, flew into: rushed to publish opinions in books, magazines and newspapers. *Flew (fly)* means to move with great speed, likened to moving through the air with wings. Page 132.

privation: lack of what is needed for existence; hardship. Page 7.

processed out: been removed or made ineffective by the application of auditing techniques. Page 38.

processing: same as *auditing,* the application of a set of exact verbal procedures and exercises which raise tone and increase perception and memory. Page 1.

procession(s): the movement of vehicles in a funeral from the place where the funeral service was conducted to the cemetery. *Procession* may also apply to a church funeral where the mourners follow the casket as it is brought into and taken out of the church. Page 134.

productive of: that causes or brings about; that results in. Page 28.

promiscuity: the state, fact or condition of having sexual relations with many partners on a casual basis. Page 234.

prone: having a natural tendency or inclination to something; likely to (do something). Page 208.

propitiation: a low emotion below anger and close to apathy. *Propitiation* is the act of trying to please or satisfy someone in a way calculated to win their favor in order to defend or protect oneself against their disapproval, attack, etc. Page 80.

pro-survival: from *pro,* in favor of, and *survival.* Hence, *pro-survival* is something in favor of or in support of *survival,* the act of remaining alive, of continuing to exist, of being alive. Page 268.

proteins: natural substances that exist in food such as meat, eggs and beans, which are fundamental components of all living cells, and which are essential for growth and repair of the body. From the Greek *proteios,* primary, from *protos,* first. Page 18.

protoplasm: the colorless, jellylike liquid that is present in the cells of all living plants, animals and humans and consists of the living matter of plant and animal cells. Page 34.

protoplasm line: the evolution of organisms themselves, continuing along a protoplasmic line, from generation to generation; the conception, birth and growth of bodies; the genetic line and evolutionary chain on Earth. Page 134.

protoplasm, unending stream of: a reference to the evolution of organisms themselves, from the very first, continuing along a protoplasmic line, from generation to generation; the conception, birth and growth of bodies; the genetic line and evolutionary chain on Earth. Page 34.

proximity: the fact, condition or position of being near or close by; nearness. Page 81.

pry into view: to bring into one's mind or memory with some effort or difficulty. *Pry* means to open or part, most commonly with a long-handled tool. Page 165.

pseudo-: a word combined with other words to mean "false" or "pretended." Also, apparently similar to (a specified thing). Page 165.

psychosomatic: *see* PSYCHOSOMATIC ILLNESS.

PSYCHOSOMATIC ILLNESS: A TERM USED IN COMMON PARLANCE TO DENOTE A CONDITION "RESULTING FROM A STATE OF MIND." SUCH ILLNESSES ACCOUNT FOR ABOUT 70 PERCENT OF ALL ILLS, BY POPULAR REPORT. TECHNICALLY, IN THIS SCIENCE, "A CHRONIC OR CONTINUING PAINFUL FACSIMILE TO WHICH THE PRECLEAR IS HOLDING TO ACCOUNT FOR FAILURES." ARTHRITIS, BURSITIS, TENDONITIS, MYOPIA, ASTIGMATISM, BIZARRE ACHES AND PAINS, SINUSITIS, COLDS, ULCERS, MIGRAINE HEADACHES, TOOTHACHE, POLIOMYELITIS DEFORMITIES, FATNESS, SKIN MALFORMATIONS, ETC., ETC., ETC., ETC., ARE A FEW OF THESE LEGION OF CHRONIC SOMATICS. THEY ARE TRACEABLE TO SERVICE FACSIMILES. (From *LRH Glossary.*) Page 38.

psychotherapy: the use of psychological procedures in the supposed treatment of disorders of the mind including physical methods such as drugs, medication and surgery. Page 2.

PSYCHOTIC: AN INDIVIDUAL WHO IS OUT OF CONTACT TO A THOROUGH EXTENT WITH HIS PRESENT TIME ENVIRONMENT AND WHO DOES NOT COMPUTE INTO THE FUTURE. HE MAY BE AN ACUTE PSYCHOTIC, WHEREIN HE BECOMES PSYCHOTIC FOR ONLY A FEW MINUTES AT A TIME AND ONLY OCCASIONALLY IN CERTAIN ENVIRONMENTS (AS IN RAGES OR APATHIES), OR HE MAY BE A CHRONIC PSYCHOTIC (OR IN A CONTINUAL DISCONNECT WITH THE FUTURE AND PRESENT). PSYCHOTICS WHO ARE DRAMATICALLY HARMFUL TO OTHERS ARE CONSIDERED DANGEROUS ENOUGH TO BE PUT AWAY. PSYCHOTICS WHO ARE HARMFUL ON A LESS DRAMATIC BASIS ARE NO LESS HARMFUL TO THEIR ENVIRONMENT AND ARE NO LESS PSYCHOTIC. (From *LRH Glossary.*) Page 26.

pummeling: beating or pounding with continuous repeated blows, as with the fists. Used figuratively. Page 135.

pursue: to proceed along, follow or continue with (a specific course, action, plan, etc.). Page 19.

put all the past behind one: to start newly over again by putting all things that happened to one in earlier times behind one so as to no longer be affected by them. Page 223.

put away: place someone into a mental institution. Page 304.

qualms: feelings of uncertainty or unease about the correctness of the course of an action, activity, etc. Page 19.

quarter: a particular but unspecified area or place. Page 232.

queasiness: (of the stomach) the condition of experiencing a feeling of sickness and sometimes desire to vomit. Page 237.

quest: a search or pursuit made in order to find or obtain something. Page 8.

quick study: a rapid observation or examination of some subject or part of some subject, resulting in immediate grasp and understanding of the information. A *quick study* is somebody who is able to learn new things or pick up new skills quickly and easily. Page 98.

quiver: shake with a slight but rapid motion; tremble, as if in fear. Page 20.

ravages: the destructive actions or effects brought about by a disease. Page 133.

razor-edge: literally a very fine, sharp line as is formed by the edge of a razor blade. Hence, a state of affairs consisting of a narrow difference between two different situations or conditions thought of as good or bad; a risky or dangerous condition which could easily result in harm or damage. Page 180.

reaction time: the amount of time it takes someone to react to or do something in the environment (or during a test), such as making a decision, solving a problem, grabbing something dropped, etc. Page 2.

realization, life: *realization* means the action of making or converting something into reality. A realization of the life of another occurs when a person does a life continuum, carrying on the fears, goals, habits and manifestations of others who have failed, departed or are dead: he makes the life of another person an ongoing reality. Page 123.

reason: the capacity for logical, rational and analytical thought; the power of intelligent discrimination in its highest and most enlightened state; the proper exercise of the mind in accordance with right, sane judgment or thinking. Page 26.

recollection: the act of calling back in the mind; a recovering of something known through memory. Page 164.

recourse to: the act or instance of turning to something for aid, use, help or protection as when in a difficult situation. Page 282.

RECOVERY: RECOVERY OF ONE'S OWN ABILITY TO DETERMINE ONE'S EXISTENCE. (From *LRH Glossary*.) Page 199.

reduce: become free of aberrative material as far as possible. Page 54.

refine: to improve with small changes by removing what is considered imperfect while inserting better elements. Page 134.

reimpose: force upon again, as something to be endured, subjected or submitted to. Page 302.

reinflict: to again force something (unwelcome) on someone, usually something that must be endured or suffered. Page 293.

relay system: a functioning related group of elements or parts that pass along (relay) instructions, information, commands, impulses, etc. *Relay* means of or pertaining to a station or unit that receives and passes on information. A *system* is an organized group of elements functioning as one unit. Page 43.

relay unit: a part of the body that passes along (relays) instructions, information, etc., to other parts of the body. *Relay* means of or pertaining to a station or unit that receives and passes on information. A *unit* is an individual, a group, a structure or other distinct entity regarded as functioning on its own usually within a larger group. Page 45.

RELEASE: *(VERB)* THE ACT OF TAKING THE PERCEPTIONS OR EFFORT OR EFFECTIVENESS OUT OF A HEAVY FACSIMILE, OR TAKING AWAY THE PRECLEAR'S HOLD ON THE FACSIMILE. (From *LRH Glossary*.) Page 159.

relics: objects having interest by reason of their age or their association with the past. Also, a piece of the body or a personal item of a spiritual or religious leader kept as an indication of great respect. Page 130.

religionist: one with excessive or exaggerated religious devotion or enthusiasm. Page 28.

reminisce: to spend time thinking or talking about past or remembered events or experiences. Page 301.

remission: in medicine, a temporary or permanent decrease of the symptoms of a disease. Page 129.

repair, in a good state of: in a condition characterized by correct operation, without need of mending or fixing. Page 15.

repercussion: effect or result (often of wide extent or influence) of some event or action. Page 138.

repertoire: the stock of plays, operas, roles, songs, etc., that a company, actor, singer, etc., is familiar with and can perform. Used figuratively. Page 308.

REPETITIVE STRAIGHTWIRE: ATTENTION CALLED TO AN INCIDENT OVER AND OVER, AMONGST OTHER INCIDENTS, UNTIL IT IS DESENSITIZED. USED ON CONCLUSIONS OR INCIDENTS WHICH DO NOT EASILY SURRENDER. (From *LRH Glossary.*)

reprimand: speak to (someone) angrily and severely about having done something wrong; express strong disapproval of someone's behavior, attitude, etc. Page 99.

reserved: opposed to or reluctant to showing closeness with others, or to open expression of thought or feeling; formal or self-restrained in manner and relationship. Page 79.

residual: present or existing, often with the sense of being a quantity left over at the end of a series of actions, conditions, etc. Page 287.

resilience: the ability to recover quickly from illness or a difficult condition. Page 130.

restimulated: having had some past incident reactivated through an approximation of its content perceived in the environment of the individual. Page 46.

reviled: severely criticized or expressed hatred of someone or something. Page 8.

riddle: something that is puzzling; a difficult or unsolvable problem; a mystery. Page 8.

rigorous: marked by difficult circumstances, such as extremes of temperature and other physical barriers; severe and harsh; requiring great effort to overcome. Page 54.

ripe: ready to do, receive or undergo something; fully prepared, likened to fruit which is fully developed and ready to be picked and eaten. Page 174.

road to recovery, well on the: making good progress or moving quickly along a series of actions that will result in an improved condition or state. Page 152.

Roman Circus: popular entertainment for the people of ancient Rome consisting of horse and chariot races, brutal athletic contests, gladiator combat and similar bloody games. The Latin word *circus*, which comes from the Greek word *kirkos* meaning circle, ring, referred to a circular or oval area enclosed by rows of seats for spectators. It was in this circular area (ring) that the events were held. Page 110.

run: audit or process; apply a process or processes to someone. Page 149.

rung: a stage or degree in a scale. Literally, a *rung* is a sturdy stick, bar or rod, often a rounded one, used as one of the steps of a ladder. Page 20.

run out: exhaust the negative influence of something; erase. Page 2.

rut, in a: a *rut* is a deep track that a wheel makes in soft ground. The wheel of a passing vehicle can drop into this rut and get stuck in it. Figuratively, a narrow unaltering course of action. Page 138.

sailing off into, went: moved off of something (one was involved in) with little apparent effort to become energetically involved with something new. Page 130.

Saint Paul: leader of early Christianity and prominent missionary. Saint Paul played an important role in converting Roman slaves to Christianity. He saw in Christianity a spirit of love for Christian slaves as men and brothers (equal to their masters) which had in it the seeds of destruction of human slavery. Page 8.

saline: consisting of or containing salt. Page 36.

salvation: a source or means of being saved, delivered or protected from harm, destruction, difficulty or failure. Page 10.

save: with the exception of; except. Page 119.

saw fit to: regarded as appropriate for the person or circumstance, as in *"he saw fit to dazzle a young mind."* This expression uses *see* in the sense of "view as." Page 131.

say nothing of: without ever needing to speak of. Used to refer in passing to subjects that might be employed to strengthen what a speaker is saying and has the sense that the speaker is holding back from giving the full strength of his case. Page 137.

scale: short for *Tone Scale,* a scale of emotional tones which shows the levels of human behavior. These tones, ranged from the highest to the lowest, are, in part, enthusiasm, boredom, antagonism, anger, covert hostility, fear, grief and apathy. Page 60.

scan (off): the action of Lock Scanning. (*Off* means so as to no longer be attached or connected; eliminate or remove something.) Page 173.

science: knowledge; comprehension or understanding of facts or principles, classified and made available in work, life or the search for truth. A science is a connected body of demonstrated truths or observed facts systematically organized and bound together under general laws. It includes trustworthy methods for the discovery of new truth within its domain and denotes the application of scientific methods in fields of study previously considered open only to theories based on subjective, historical or undemonstrable, abstract criteria. The word *science* is used in this sense—the most fundamental meaning and tradition of the word—and not in the sense of the *physical* or *material* sciences. Page 1.

scores: very many. Literally, a *score* is a group of twenty items (people, things, etc.). Page 133.

scythe, Time's: a reference to lines from a poem by William Shakespeare (1564-1616), as well as a reference to the Grim Reaper. The poem concerns time and the poet's contemplation of the possibility that his son may become a victim of time and die without offspring. The poem contains the line, "And nothing 'gainst Time's scythe can make defense." A *scythe* is an agricultural instrument with a curved cutting blade attached to a handle. The *Grim Reaper,* a representation of Death, is often portrayed as a man or cloaked skeleton carrying a scythe in his duty as a "harvester" or "collector" (reaper) of bodies and souls. Page 130.

secondary engram: a period of anguish brought about by a major loss or a threat of loss to the individual. The secondary engram depends for its strength and force upon an engram which underlies it. Hence, the word *secondary,* as it must occur second to an engram. *See also* **engram**. Page 149.

second-hand: 1. from an intermediate source, only one person away from the original source. Page 131.
2. used or worn, as from previous usage; hence poor condition. Page 137.

see the light: reach a full understanding or realization; be converted to some idea or belief. Page 130.

self-auditing: self-auditing is the action of an individual going around and continually running processes on himself. Page 159.

semicolon(s): the punctuation mark (;) that shows a separation in a sentence not so complete as that shown by a period (.) but more so than that shown by a comma (,). A *semicolon* can be used to join clauses which are too closely related for a period to be used but separate enough to make a comma inadequate. Example: "Joe enjoys reading detective stories; his sister prefers science fiction." Page 99.

send Man to the stars: to advance technology to the extent that Man would be capable of traveling through outer space to distant planets. The stars in this sense refer to objects (as suns, meteors or planets) in the sky resembling a point of light and usually only bright enough to be seen at night. Page 82.

serene: (of a person, his mind, circumstances, etc.) not affected by disturbances; calm, peaceful and untroubled. Page 20.

SERVICE FACSIMILE: A DEFINITELY NON-SURVIVAL SITUATION CONTAINED IN A FACSIMILE WHICH IS CALLED INTO ACTION BY THE INDIVIDUAL TO EXPLAIN HIS FAILURES. A SERVICE FACSIMILE MAY BE ONE OF AN ILLNESS, AN INJURY, AN INABILITY. THE FACSIMILE BEGINS WITH A DOWN EMOTIONAL CURVE AND ENDS WITH AN UPWARD EMOTIONAL CURVE. BETWEEN THESE IT HAS PAIN. A SERVICE FACSIMILE *IS* THE PATTERN WHICH IS THE CHRONIC "PSYCHOSOMATIC ILLNESS." IT MAY CONTAIN COUGHS, FEVER, ACHES, RASHES, ANY MANIFESTATION OF A NON-SURVIVAL CHARACTER, MENTAL OR PHYSICAL. IT MAY EVEN BE A SUICIDE EFFORT. IT IS COMPLETE WITH ALL PERCEPTIONS. IT HAS MANY SIMILAR FACSIMILES. IT HAS MANY LOCKS. THE POSSESSION AND USE OF A SERVICE FACSIMILE DISTINGUISHES A HOMO SAPIENS. A SERVICE FACSIMILE IS THAT FACSIMILE WHICH THE PRECLEAR USES TO APOLOGIZE FOR HIS FAILURES. IN OTHER WORDS, IT IS USED TO MAKE OTHERS WRONG AND PROCURE THEIR COOPERATION IN THE SURVIVAL OF THE PRECLEAR. (From *LRH Glossary.*) Page 2.

SERVICE FACSIMILE CHAIN: THE ENTIRE CHAIN OF SIMILAR INCIDENTS WHICH COMPRISE THE TOTAL REPERTOIRE OF THE INDIVIDUAL WHO IS EXPLAINING HIS FAILURE AND THUS SEEKING SUPPORT. (From *LRH Glossary.*)

servomechanism: a mechanism that serves, services or aids something. Specifically, the human mind is a servomechanism to all mathematics because mathematics is something which Man uses to solve problems: Without the human mind mathematics is of no use. Page 266.

sessions: periods of time given to or set aside for the pursuit of a particular activity. Specifically, it refers to a period of time set aside for processing, the application of a set of exact verbal procedures and exercises which raise tone and increase perception and memory. Page 1.

Shakespeare: William Shakespeare (1564–1616), English poet and author of many plays, including the well-known tragedy *Hamlet*. In this play the main character, Hamlet, prince of Denmark, utters the famous line: "To be or not to be; that is the question" while thinking over whether to live or die. Page 19.

shamans: priests or priestesses who are said to act as intermediaries between natural and supernatural worlds and to use magic to cure ailments, foretell the future and contact and control spiritual forces. Page 8.

shirking: avoiding or neglecting (a duty or responsibility). Page 100.

shortened: reduced in force, power, effectiveness or intensity; restrained. Page 26.

short, in: in few words; in summary; briefly, concisely. Used to introduce or accompany a summary statement of what has been previously stated. Page 27.

shoulder: to take on or assume as a responsibility. Page 92.

shows up: appears or is present (in); becomes visible. Page 54.

sick: suffering from or affected with a physical illness. Page 17.

sight, out of: out of one's mind or memory. A facsimile that drops "out of sight" is one that goes below the level of the individual's awareness or out of present time. Page 38.

signpost: literally, a long piece of wood or other material set upright into the ground bearing a sign that gives information or directions, such as the proper road to a place or the like. Hence, any immediate indication, obvious clue, guide, etc. Page 110.

sinusitis: inflammation of a sinus or the sinuses (the spaces in the bone behind a person's nose which serve to lighten the head and cushion the brain from blows to the front of the skull). Page 60.

size and wear them, let's try these on for: a variation of the phrase *try (something) on for size,* meaning to consider (a principle, theory, etc.) to see if it fits the facts, much like one would put on a glove to see if it fits the hand. Hence, *let's try these on for size and wear them* refers to considering principles, observing how they work and applying them when they do work. Page 18.

slaughter: the killing of a large number of people in a cruel or violent way. Page 7.

slave philosophies: a reference to those theories, opinions or views that say some human beings should be slaves, owned as property and entirely subject to the will of another person, without any freedom and personal rights. Page 10.

sloth: a slow-moving, tree-dwelling mammal with a fur-covered body, a flat, short head, large eyes and a snub nose. It characteristically hangs, back down, from tree branches. Page 33.

slow road: a route or way that heads toward some desired outcome but takes a long time. Page 174.

slump: decline or deteriorate (suddenly) into a poorer state or condition. Page 190.

snapping: quick and sharp. Page 98.

snarled up: thrown into confusion; impeded; messed up, likened to a rope that is twisted and knotted up. Page 135.

snatching at: making a sudden effort to seize something, in order to (eagerly) secure hold or possession of it. Used figuratively. Page 137.

sociology: the study of the origin, development and structure of human societies and the behavior of individuals and groups in them. Page 266.

solid ground: support (ground) for one's position or attitude which is logical, firm and not liable to change. Page 135.

somatic: the word *somatic* is used to denote physical pain or discomfort of any kind. It can mean actual pain, such as that caused by a cut or a blow; or it can mean discomfort, as from heat or cold; it can mean itching—in short, anything physically uncomfortable. It is a non-survival physical state of being. Page 178.

sordid: demonstrating the worst aspects of human nature such as immorality, violence, etc. Page 110.

so to speak: one could say; to use a manner of speaking; figuratively speaking. Page 164.

southpaw: left-handed. The term comes from the fact that in American baseball the playing field is arranged such that the person trying to hit the ball (the batter) is facing east to avoid the sun. The person throwing the ball (pitcher) faces sideways before throwing the ball to the batter. Therefore, the pitcher who throws the ball with his right hand is usually facing north. A pitcher throwing with his left hand is usually facing south, hence *southpaw*. *Paw* is informal for the human hand. Page 163.

span: a period of time. Page 8.

spare: to save or protect from damage, cruelty, suffering or the like, or from a particular cause of it. Page 95.

species: a group or class of animals or plants having certain common and permanent characteristics which clearly distinguish it from other groups and which can breed with one another, such as tigers, rabbits and squirrels. Page 27.

species, the: the human race; Mankind. Page 10.

speculations: conclusions, opinions, reasons, etc. Also, contemplation or consideration of a subject as well as the conclusion(s) reached from that. Page 37.

Spencer: Herbert Spencer (1820-1903), English philosopher known for his application of the doctrine of evolution to philosophy and ethics. Page 98.

sphere: a field of knowledge, interest or activity; the place or environment within which a thing exists. Page 26.

sphere of control: the area or region (thought of as moving outward from a person or source), that someone or something directs, manages or influences. Page 46.

sport: an activity in general that provides entertainment, fun or recreation; pleasant pastime. Page 98.

stamina: enduring physical or mental energy and strength. Page 1.

Standard Procedure: the name of the auditing procedure as contained in *Dianetics: The Modern Science of Mental Health*. Page 180.

started on signal: begun upon the receipt of a known sign or event, likened to the use of a gun in the starting of a race, where participants start running as soon as they hear the sound of the gun being fired. *Signal* means anything that serves to indicate, direct or command. Page 308.

state of affairs: the way in which events, conditions or circumstances stand (at a particular time or within a particular sphere). Page 166.

state of mind: the way one is thinking or feeling at a particular time or under particular conditions. Page 15.

static(s): a thing of no motion. It is a causative static. A true static does not have wavelength so it is not in motion. It does not have weight, it does not have mass, it does not have length nor breadth. It is motionlessness. See the Axioms in the chapter *Definitions, Logics and Axioms*. Page 34.

stem: arise or originate from; come forth or come into being. Page 29.

stem the tide: in the original sense, to urge the stem of a boat or ship against the force of the tide so it makes forward progress. The *tide* refers to the rise and fall of the ocean. The *stem* is an upright piece of wood or metal right at the front of a ship and to which the sides of a ship are joined. Hence, to hold back something of great pressure or strength; to resist. Page 130.

sting, death has lost its: a reference to lines from the Bible, "Death is swallowed up in victory. O death, where is thy sting? O grave, where is thy victory?" referring to the power of the spirit over the body. *Sting,* used figuratively here, means the capacity to hurt or inflict an acute pain or sharp wound on the mind or feelings. Page 17.

stone cold: completely indifferent and unfeeling. (*Stone* is used to emphasize the degree of a quality, usually a quality associated with stone, such as coldness, stillness or lifelessness.) Page 153.

straight and narrow road: from the phrase *straight and narrow,* which means the way of virtuous and proper conduct, from the Bible: "Because straight is the gate and narrow is the way which leads unto life, and few be there that find it." Hence, the phrase is used here to define the precise road one must follow to find answers in researching the problems of the human mind. Page 131.

STRAIGHTWIRE: A PROCESS OF RECALLING FROM PRESENT TIME, WITH SOME PERCEPTION OR AT LEAST A CONCEPT, A PAST INCIDENT. THE NAME STRAIGHTWIRE DERIVES FROM THE MEST COMMUNICATIONS PROCESS OF CONNECTING TWO POINTS OF A COMMUNICATIONS SYSTEM. IT IS ESSENTIALLY MEMORY WORK. IT IS APPLIED TO POSTULATES, EVALUATIONS, INCIDENTS, SCENES, EMOTIONS, OR ANY DATA WHICH MAY BE IN THE STORAGE BANKS OF THE MIND WITHOUT "SENDING THE PRECLEAR" INTO THE INCIDENT ITSELF. IT IS DONE WITH THE PRECLEAR SITTING UP, EYES OPEN OR SHUT. THE AUDITOR IS VERY ALERT. STRAIGHTWIRE IS DONE RAPIDLY. THE PRECLEAR IS NOT PERMITTED TO WANDER OR REMINISCE. HE RESPONDS TO QUESTIONS ON THE PART OF THE AUDITOR. *MANY PRECLEARS DISLIKE BEING QUESTIONED. THE AUDITOR MUST THEN FIRST RESOLVE THE POSTULATES AGAINST BEING QUESTIONED.* THIS WOULD BE CALLED "CLEARING FOR BROAD STRAIGHTWIRE." (From *LRH Glossary.*)

strapping: applying a bandage or pieces of adhesive plaster to (an injury, wound, etc.). When a bone is fractured or broken, strapping assists in keeping the bone unmoving and together. Page 130.

strikes: comes across, encounters or discovers (sometimes suddenly). Page 190.

striving(s): exerting much effort or energy; struggling or fighting forcefully; trying hard. Page 7.

stroke(s): brain damage caused by a lack of blood flow to part of the brain such as when a blood vessel becomes blocked. A *stroke* results in permanent damage to the brain tissue and may cause paralysis on one or both sides of the body. Page 164.

structure: how something is built or its physical design; the way in which parts are arranged or put together to form a whole as compared with function, the operation of something; the way something works in fulfilling its purpose. Page 16.

subjected to: caused to undergo the action of something specified; exposed (to). Page 148.

submerged: originally, covered with water. Hence, hidden from view. Page 47.

subservient: under the authority of something else; secondary to. Page 300.

substance: the actual matter of a thing. Page 233.

substantiated: demonstrated or verified by proof or evidence. Page 266.

successive: happening or existing one after another. Page 26.

succumbs: gives way to (something overpowering) or yields. From the Latin *succumbere*, to lie under. Page 16.

such and such: definite or particular, but not named or specified. Page 36.

supplementarily: in a manner of a *supplement*, something added to complete a thing, or strengthen the whole. Page 65.

supposition: something that is assumed to be true (which may be either true or false) as the basis for forming a theory or course of action. Page 29.

surer: more effective; more certain not to miss or fail. Page 17.

sure route: a certain course, direction or means of obtaining or achieving some objective. Page 110.

swamped: covered with or as if with water. Literally, to swamp means to flood or submerge something with or as if with water. Page 193.

sweep: the range or scope as encompassed by a wide curving motion; the range over which something is directed, usually a wide arc (a section of a circle or other curved figure). Page 111.

sweepingly: so as to have a wide-ranging influence or effect; extensively and completely. Page 35.

sweep through: an action of passing over a series of events (with the mind), as if with a rapid, steady, continuous motion. Page 125.

sweep up: to remove, clean or clear away (something), as if with a broom or brushing action. Page 242.

switchboard: having to do with a *switchboard,* a board containing switches and other devices for controlling electric flows and used to connect and disconnect communication lines. Used to describe the brain and nervous and glandular system. Page 35.

symbolization: the act or process of representing a quantity or relation through the use of symbols, letters, figures or other characters or marks, or a combination of letters or the like, as in mathematics. Page 265.

SYMPATHY: THE POSING OF AN EMOTIONAL STATE SIMILAR TO THE EMOTIONAL STATE OF AN INDIVIDUAL IN GRIEF OR APATHY. (From *LRH Glossary.*) Page 54.

synthetic: not real or genuine; artificial. Page 48.

tab: a tag or label that identifies or gives information about something. Page 188.

tactile: touching (things) as with the hand or other body part. Page 189.

taken root: literally (of a plant) began growing by putting out roots in the ground. Hence, become established or widely accepted. Page 132.

take off: depart or leave; go away. Page 135.

take on: to assume or acquire as or as if one's own. Page 123.

take (something) on: to undertake or begin to handle or deal with. Page 95.

taking the stand of: supporting or defending the cause of. Page 187.

talking behind people's backs: speaking about someone in their absence, often negatively, and without their knowledge. Page 219.

talk (one) out of: to prevent someone from doing something by talking to him or her. Page 180.

tangible: literally, capable of being touched or felt. Hence, something that can actually be experienced or felt emotionally or mentally; clear, definite and real. Page 78.

tar-bucketsful: a coined expression meaning large amounts or abundance. A tar bucket was a bucket of tar and other ingredients hung on the back of wagons in the Old West. Used as a wheel lubricant, the tar was an essential part of the wagon's equipment. Page 179.

tarsus: a reference to a *tarsier,* a small nocturnal (active at night) tree-dwelling mammal with long legs, a short fur-covered body, a rounded head and unusually large eyes. Page 33.

teeth of, into the: in direct opposition to, in defiance of, in spite of. Page 242.

TEN: A CASE ADVANCED TO THE POINT OF RELEASED SERVICE FACSIMILE. (From *LRH Glossary.*)

tenacious: holding or tending to hold persistently to something. Page 136.

tendonitis: inflammation of a tendon, an elastic cord or band of tough white tissue that attaches a muscle to a bone or other part of the body. Page 307.

tenets: principles and truths in religion, philosophy, etc., accepted and taught by a group. Page 21.

tenth-hand: very indirectly; in a very indirect manner, as from an intermediate source nine times removed or remote from the original source. Page 131.

thermal: of or pertaining to heat; measured, caused, operated or determined by heat. Page 269.

thesis: a systematic spoken or written treatment of a subject which includes results of original research and establishes by proof or evidence the existence or truth of specific phenomena. Page 132.

THETA: THE MATHEMATICAL SYMBOL—θ—FOR THE STATIC OF THOUGHT. BY THETA IS MEANT THE STATIC ITSELF. BY "FACSIMILE" IS MEANT THETA WHICH CONTAINS IMPRESSIONS BY PERCEPTION. (From *LRH Glossary.*) Page 268.

theta facsimile(s): a picture of the physical universe. It is not the actual thing, it is a memory recording. It is a number of perceptions all packaged up. *Facsimile* means something similar to. Page 271.

THOUGHT: THE FACSIMILES ONE HAS RECORDED OF HIS VARIOUS ENVIRONMENTS AND THE FACSIMILES HE HAS CREATED WITH HIS IMAGININGS, THEIR RECOMBINATION AND EVALUATIONS AND CONCLUSIONS, FOR THE PURPOSE OF DETERMINING ACTION OR NO ACTION OR POTENTIAL ACTION OR NO ACTION. THOUGHT IS USED ALSO TO MEAN A PROCESS TREATING AWARENESS LEVEL RECORDINGS, AS DISTINCT FROM NON-AWARENESS LEVEL RECORDINGS. (From *LRH Glossary.*) Page 34.

thrust: 1. pushed, driven or forced into a specified condition or situation. Page 179.
2. a driving, vital, energetic force thought of as moving forward. Page 275.

thud: the action of a heavy strike, blow or loud sound, as a single sharp clash of thunder or a firing cannon. Page 8.

thundering: a sound that resembles or suggests thunder. Hence, moving or going with a loud noise or violent action; rumbling or roaring by or along. Page 9.

tidal wave: an exceptionally large ocean wave along the seashore, caused by very strong winds, underwater earthquake or volcanic eruption. Page 7.

ties which bound them: literally, ties are cord or rope used to securely fasten something. Hence, situations, conditions, states of mind, etc., that are firmly connected, brought together or restrained, as if tied by a rope. *Bound* means tied or secured, as with a rope or cord. Page 137.

Time's scythe: a reference to lines from a poem by William Shakespeare (1564–1616), as well as a reference to the Grim Reaper. The poem concerns time and the poet's contemplation of the possibility that his son may become a victim of time and die without offspring. The poem contains the line, "And nothing 'gainst Time's scythe can make defense." A *scythe* is an agricultural instrument with a curved cutting blade attached to a handle. The *Grim Reaper,* a representation of Death, is often portrayed as a man or cloaked skeleton carrying a scythe in his duty as a "harvester" or "collector" (reaper) of bodies and souls. Page 130.

Tiny Tim: a young crippled boy in the short story *A Christmas Carol* by English author Charles Dickens (1812–1870). Page 212.

To be or not to be?: a famous line from the well-known tragedy *Hamlet,* a play by English poet and author William Shakespeare (1564–1616). In this play the main character, Hamlet, prince of Denmark, while wavering over whether to live or die, expresses his indecision with the words "To be or not to be; that is the question..." Page 19.

tolerance band: the range or level (as on a scale) in which something has the capacity to survive. Page 271.

tone: the momentary or continuing emotional state of the person. Page 19.

Tone Scale: a scale of emotional tones which shows the levels of human behavior. These tones, ranged from the highest to the lowest, are, in part, enthusiasm, boredom, antagonism, anger, covert hostility, fear, grief and apathy. Page 19.

track: a path along which something evolves or develops. Page 33.

track: the time track, the track of time through which a person has lived. Page 172.

track of, lost: neglected to keep a record of something or some action; failed to pay attention to. Page 48.

transient: lasting only a short time; existing briefly; temporary. Page 25.

transits: instruments with a telescope on top, employed in measuring land and ensuring buildings are constructed level. Page 131.

travail: mental (or bodily) pain or suffering. Page 137.

trial: the action of trying or testing something to determine its quality, performance, usefulness or the like. Page 9.

trial and error: the process of making repeated trials or tests, improving the methods used in the light of errors made, until the right result is found. Page 9.

trick: 1. an underhanded action or plan that is intended to cheat or deceive. Page 10.
2. an act involving or requiring skill and effectiveness. Page 18.

trifle: a small quantity or amount of anything; a little. Page 20.

try these on for size and wear them, let's: a variation of the phrase *try (something) on for size,* meaning to consider (a principle, theory, etc.) to see if it fits the facts, much like one would put on a glove to see if it fits the hand. Hence, *let's try these on for size and wear them* refers to considering principles, observing how they work and applying them when they do work. Page 18.

turned up: was discovered or encountered; presented itself casually or unexpectedly. Page 223.

turn, in: one after the other; in the proper order or sequence. Page 65.

turn, in one's: when one's opportunity comes in appropriate succession. Often used to indicate an act that naturally follows a similar act on the part of another, but without being pre-arranged. Page 18.

turn on: 1. to attack suddenly and violently; to become hostile to without warning. Page 28.
2. start operating as if by means of a switch, button or valve; activate. Page 38.

ulcers: open sores (other than a wound) on the skin or some internal organ, as the lining of the stomach, characterized by the disintegration of the affected tissue. Page 60.

ultimates: greatest or most nearly perfect states or conditions. Page 20.

unconscious: a condition of having an absence of awareness, a period of non-awareness, or a degree of non-awareness. Page 172.

unconsciousness: a condition in which there is an absence of awareness, a period of non-awareness, or a degree of non-awareness. Page 173.

underscores: marks with a score (line drawn or scratched) underneath the printed words on a page, as for emphasis. Page 18.

unending stream of protoplasm: a reference to the evolution of organisms themselves, from the very first, continuing along a protoplasmic line, from generation to generation; the conception, birth and growth of bodies; the genetic line and evolutionary chain on Earth. Page 34.

uniformly: being always the same, as in character or degree; unvarying. Page 301.

unit facsimile: a unit is a single thing. A *unit facsimile* is a *single* facsimile which is a consecutive related experience and is the total of *all* perceptions recorded in that experience; a complete memory package. Page 36.

Unknown: something great and unknown or mysterious; something that is undiscovered or unexplored. Page 20.

unwarranted: not agreed upon; without approval. Page 287.

up and down the line: in several parts of or in different places throughout the procedure or course of action. Page 257.

up and down the track: in several parts of or in different places throughout a person's time track. Page 209.

up point: a particular moment or stage in a process at which a significant development (such as an advance or improvement) occurs. Page 190.

uttered: spoken or pronounced; expressed audibly. Page 96.

vague blur: something that is indistinct or hazy to the mind and so difficult to recall. Page 179.

valence(s): literally, the word means the ability to combine with or take on parts of another. In its specialized meaning, *valence* is an actual or shadow personality. Being *out of valence* is the taking on of the physical and/or emotional characteristics or traits of another. *In valence* means being in one's own valence, one's actual personality. The subject of valences is described in the Processing Section, in the Sixth and Seventh Acts. Page 159.

valence, in: being in one's own valence, one's actual personality. Page 159.

valence, out of: the taking on of the physical and/or emotional characteristics or traits of another. Page 159.

validate: prove or confirm that something is true or correct. Page 18.

Validation MEST Processing: processing whereby the concentration is on the analytical moments of any given incident, as opposed to the painful moments. This processing also orients the individual to the present time and the physical universe—matter, energy, space and time—MEST. See *Self Analysis.* Page 129.

vectors: things which have both direction and quantity. For example, force would be a vector as it has a direction and an amount but mass is not a vector as it has no direction. Page 278.

venereal: related to a disease that is sexually transmitted. From Latin *venus,* desire, love. Page 99.

vibrations: rhythmic, repeating movements back and forth of matter. Matter is actually vibrating. Page 35.

vicinity of, in the: near or close to; in the environment or area of. Page 81.

virus: a minute particle that lives as a parasite in plants, animals and bacteria and can only multiply within living cells and not independently. Page 273.

vocal cords: a pair of bands of elastic connective tissue in the throat that produce sounds (speech) by vibrating. Muscles tighten the cords, narrowing the gap between them, and as air is expelled from the lungs they vibrate, causing the formation of sounds that are amplified in the throat. Page 78.

Voltaire: (1694-1778) French author and philosopher who produced a range of literary works, often attacking injustice and intolerance. Page 98.

volume: 1. a collection of written, typewritten or printed sheets bound together; book. Page 1.
2. the amount of space occupied within or by an object, figured out by measuring its length by its width by its height. Page 34.
3. a quantity or amount (of something). Page 279.

wavelength: a wavelength is the distance from the crest to the crest of a wave. The relative distance from crest to crest in any flow of energy. Page 34.

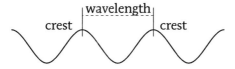

weak-willed: lacking the determination that is needed to continue with a (difficult) course of action; lacking a strong desire or purpose to carry out an action or achieve something. Page 242.

weight: importance or significance. Page 19.

weigh upon (someone's mind): of a thought, feeling or circumstance, lie heavy on; be burdensome, as if from guilt, worry, etc. Page 99.

well on the road to recovery: making good progress or moving quickly along a series of actions that will result in an improved condition or state. Page 152.

which is to say: a phrase used to introduce a clearer, more comprehensible, restatement of what immediately precedes or to limit or modify it. Page 36.

whooping cough: an acute infectious disease, usually affecting children, and characterized by a mucous discharge from the nose and later by repeated attacks of coughing that end in a forced intake of breath (whoop). Page 157.

will, at: just as or when one wishes. Page 37.

win friends and influence people: a reference to self-help works purporting to advise on how to win friends and influence people which advocate agreeing with *anything* anybody says. *Friends* means people whom one knows; acquaintances, particularly with the idea of entering into friendly relations with. Page 176.

wise: way or manner. Page 302.

wishes, against one's: in opposition or contrary to what one desires or believes in. Page 81.

witch doctors: in certain societies, a person supposed to have the power of curing disease, getting rid of evil, etc., through the use of magic means. *"Witch doctors in modern dress"* refers to psychologists, psychiatrists, etc. Page 91.

with favor: having a particular liking for; showing preference toward. Page 239.

with open arms: literally, with arms outspread as if to hug someone. Hence, to receive someone or something with great willingness or eagerness. Page 95.

words, in other: put differently; otherwise stated, often used to introduce an explanation of something and usually in a simpler way. Page 15.

worked: acted upon or influenced; acted on; specifically practiced (one's occupation or profession) on. Page 133.

worked upon: acted or operated on; practiced or performed (one's occupation or profession) on. Page 2.

working (this volume): execute or perform an action with or upon something. Specifically as used here, employing and doing the steps laid out in (this book). Page 67.

works: the collective actions, doings and conduct of men in general. Page 8.

world affairs: matters of public interest or concern; matters concerning men or nations collectively and which extend or are found throughout the world. Page 133.

worst, at: even under the most unfavorable or negative view or circumstances. Page 191.

writhing: a twisting and turning of the body showing great suffering. Page 19.

wrong, go: make a mistake or fall into error; err. Also used to mean to fail in an undertaking. Page 179.

zeal: intense enthusiasm or eagerness in favor of a cause or in the pursuit of some end. Page 9.

Index

A

aberration, 39, 241, 279, 284, 290
  definition, 287
  description, 287
  electing self effect and, 232
  facsimile and, 60
  severe, 109, 111
  severity of, 9
  social, 82
  unable to handle facsimiles, 37
ability
  control over surroundings and, 17
  improvement of, 2
  security and, 105
above the normal, 79
absolutes
  unobtainable, 263
accelerated scanning, 175
accessibility
  definition, 304
Act
  definition, 299
  fifteen Acts, introduction, 65
action, 25, 46
  emotion and, 176
  self-determined, 208
  survival and, 119
  time and, 188
action definition, 263
action phrases, 274
Adler, 130
aesthetic product
  definition, 292
affinity, 77-81, 225
  definition, 283
  description, 77
agreement, 224
  on emotion, 176
alcohol, 111

Alcoholics Anonymous, 111
alignment, 295
amnesia, 165
anger, 20, 78, 149, 175, 226, 306
  catalyst for attack, 53
  emotional curve of sympathy, 214
  seeks to stop, 176
  transfer, 192
anger case, 82
antagonism, 20, 214, 306
  ARC at 2.0, 79
anthropoid, 33
anxiety, 38
apathy, 20, 149, 227, 306
  be dead or feign death, 53
  state of not-beingness and, 111
arbitrary, 264
  introduction of an, 264, 282
ARC, 291
  description, 77
  diagram, 78
  enforced or inhibited, 80
  Life and, 79
  practical use, 82
  Tone Scale levels, 79-82
  with self, 79
ARC triangle, 78
argument, 192
arthritis, 60, 135, 307
artist, 110
assessment
  definition, 306
  Third Act, 91
assists
  definition, 305
associative definition, 263
astigmatism, 307

atmosphere, 179, 194
    around a person or place, 192
    charged, 175
    counter-emotional curve
      and, 199
**atomic and molecular
   phenomena**, 131
atomic fission, 28, 82
Attainment, 25
Attempt, 25
attention, 111
    definition, 272
    fixed and unfixed, 111
    optimum sweep, 111
attitudes
    chart, *see* **Chart of Attitudes**
    past attitudes of others, 95
auditor, 65
    case that badly needs an, 3
    definition, 299
    preclear
        service facsimile and, 203
        Tone Scale and, 60
authoritarian, 29, 187
automatic response, 45
**awareness of awareness
   unit**, 43
Axioms, 261–295
    give definitions, 18
    logical structure, 16

B

Bacon, 98
be, 20, 134, 222
behavior, 283
    aberrated, 287
    Tone Scale and, 54
being(ness)
    healthy state of, 80
    ideal state of, 15–21
    states of, 10
believe
    not necessary, 65
birth, 171
blame, 95, 231
blind man, 136
blueprint, 38, 134, 188
    new body, 47

body, 139
    carbon-oxygen motor, 45, 47
    dual composition, 134
    engine of narrow tolerance, 47
    in construction, 135
    processing, 139, 154
    rehabilitation of, 131
    resilience of, 130
boil-off, 308
    definition, 173
    if boiling-off too much, 174
boredom, 119, 251, 306
brain, 35
broken
    definition, 305
Buck Rogers boys, 131
bursitis, 307
button chart, 66
buttons, 219

C

carbon-oxygen motor, 45, 47,
   134
care of person, 222
catalyst, 306
cause, 20, 135
    blaming yourself or others for
      being, 231
    desiring to be, 231
    effect, 20
    electing someone, 232
    goal of individual and, 28
    ideal state, 20
    Life and, 34
cause and effect, 20, 29, 46–48,
   231, 232, 233
    educational system, 61, 109
    organism, 47
    sex, 232
**Cause and Effect
   Processing**, 235
cell, 273, 275
center of control
    definition, 300
    see also **control center**
change
    capacity for, 8
changing things, 221

charge, 150
Chart of Attitudes
  button chart, 66
  causes and effects, 232
  description, 66
  figures from chart, 109
  lower band, 193
  present-day environment
    and, 91
  processing with, 91
  ranges, 109
  self-evaluation chart, 66
  use in processing, 85, 182
cheerfulness, 20
  ARC at 4.0, 79
chemical heat engine, 270
child, 165
  bad becomes good, 110
  food and, 234
  native center and, 165
  occlusion and, 195
  seeing and hearing in
    memory, 37
  will try to keep a pet or a
    grandfather from dying, 138
childhood
  occlusion of, 165
chronic
  pains, 193
  "psychosomatic illness," 308
  somatics, 307
circuit, 45
  definition, 305
Clear
  definition, 300
clothing, care of, 222
cohesion, 77, 283
colds, 307
collectivism, 9
Come up to present time, 119
Commander Thompson, 131
communication, 78–81, 225
  definition, 283
  description, 78
  interchange of, 283
  mimicry, psychotic and, 189
complexity, 187
compulsions, 60

computing psychotic
  definition, 305
conception, 25, 134, 171
conclusion
  definition, 276
  recoverable, 293
  theta facsimiles of a group of
    combined data, 276
conquest
  of environment, 9
  of MEST, 17
  of physical universe, 25
conservative
  ARC at 3.0, 79
construction
  alignment of data, 295
control
  emotion and, 306
  environment and, 282
  give up sphere of, 46
  low-scale, 233
  mis-emotion and, 193
  of environment, 9, 17
    of oneself and, 21
  of facsimile, 193, 231
  of human being by
    another, 192
control center, 43–47, 166, 251
  cause, 43
  definition, 285
  description, 43
  diagram, 44
  double, 163
  "genetic" boss, 163
  left side versus right side, 163
  rehabilitation, 253
  shift, 164–166
  suppression of, 285
counter-effort, 59, 147–148,
  279–292
  description, 176
  pain and, 291
  survival, 148
counter-emotion, 147, 149,
  192
  "atmosphere" around a person
    or place, 192
  control of facsimile and, 193
  counter-effort and, 176

description, 54
explanation, 175
failure and, 179
handling of, 187
running any and all, 179
scanning, 177
counter-emotional curve
definition, 199
Counter-Emotion
Scanning, 177, 180
counter-thought, 192
description, 193
covert hostility, 306
cowardice, 226
"cracking cases," 147
Creator of All, 27
criminology, 266
crippled or lame to "help"
another, 136
critical people
caution, 151
crustaceans, 33
cycle
action to failure, 25
of an organism, 275
of randomity, 277
of survival, 25

D

datum
alignment of, 295
definition, 262, 276
evaluation of, 112, 263
unknown, 282
daydreams, 147
dead, 20
dead men's goals, 123
death, 19, 25
definition, 273
running of, 149
shift of centers and, 166
Tone Scale and, 79
tried to help and failed, 138
ultimate in being effect, 20
value of, 17
Decay, 25
decision(s), 208, 242
aberration and, 241

"hang up" in Lock Scanning
and, 174
psychotic and, 191
to be or not to be, 19, 134
today's versus tomorrow's, 46
two, 19
definitions
aberration, 287
accessibility, 304
Act, 299
action definition, 263
aesthetic product, 292
affinity, 283
assessment, 306
assists, 305
associative definition, 263
attention, 272
auditor, 299
boil-off, 173
broken, 305
center of control, 300
circuit, 305
Clear, 300
communication, 283
computing psychotic, 305
conclusion, 276
control center, 285
counter-emotional curve, 199
datum, 262, 276
death, 273
delusion, 292
descriptive definition, 262
differentiative definition, 262
dramatizing psychotic, 305
dreams, 292
dynamics, 26, 275, 310
effort, 148, 272, 309
emotion, 306
emotional curve, 198
environment, 304
facsimile, 35, 37, 302
Fifteen, 299
force, 272
genetic, 309
genetic blueprint, 134
hallucination, 77
happiness, 119
heavy facsimile, 303
knowledge, 262

lambda, 270
language, 281
Lock Scanning, 172, 307
Logics, 261
memory, 36
MEST, 17, 310
mind, 48, 271
motion, 188, 272
motor switchboard, 45
neurotic, 291
out of valence, 203
pain, 291, 293
perception, 148, 285, 311
persistence, 270
pleasure, 273
postulate, 174, 241, 301
postulates, past, 301
preclear, 299
pseudo-centers, 165
psychosomatic illness, 307
psychotic, 291, 304
randomity, 277, 278
reality, 283
recall, 285
recovery, 306
release, 309
Repetitive Straightwire, 307
restimulation, 286
rightness, 271
sanity, 291
secondary engram, 149
self-confidence, 241
service facsimile, 153, 208,
    308
service facsimile chain, 308
Straightwire, 300
Ten, 311
theta, 310
thought, 45, 276, 306
unconsciousness, 280
valence, 287
visio, 97
wrongness, 271
**Definitions, Logics and
    Axioms**, 46, 261
delusion, 39
    definition, 292
demanded ARC, 80
descriptive definition, 262

destruction, 295
diagram
    control center, 44
    triangle of ARC, 78
Dianetics, 132
differentiative definition, 262
disk
    employment of, 66
    use of in auditing, 97
Doppler effect, 131
doubts, 65, 223
dramatizing psychotic
    definition, 305
dreams, 119
    daydreams, 147
    definition, 292
    imagination and, 37
drug addict, 111
dub-in, 194
dynamics, 26–29, 275
    ability to translate solutions
        into action, 275
    definition, 26, 275, 310
    eight, 26
    failure and, 29, 138
    goals of survival and, 26
    interactive, 80
    relative emphasis, 28
    resolution of problems
        and, 28, 29
    self-determinism and, 61
        all, 48
    Tone Scale and, 28

E

eating
    effect, 232, 234
economics, 266
education, 61, 98, 109
    thrust out of sight, 179
    valid therapy, 110
effect, 47, 231–235
    blame and, 232
    cause and, 20
    degree of success and, 28
    desire to be, 48, 232
    least desirable state, 20
    must wish to be effect first, 232

permission to be an, 46
physical universe and, 34
Tone Scale and, 232
effort, 147-148, 151, 176, 188, 282
  counter-effort, *see*
    counter-effort
  cover up postulates, 242
  definition, 148, 272, 309
  description, 147
  directed force, 272
  estimation of, 45, 147
  force and direction, 148
  of the environment, 303
  organism, 275
  thought, emotion and, 176
  to survive, 25
  transferred by physical
    contact, 192
Effort Processing, 2, 59, 135, 172, 178
  running of, 148
  "turn on" a facsimile, 38
ego, 130
Eighth Act, 171-183
Eighth Dynamic, 27
Einstein, 131
electric shock, 137
Eleventh Act, 207-215
embarrassment, 226
emotion, 53-55, 149, 176, 188, 192
  between thought and action, 53
    relay, 175
  counter-emotion, *see*
    counter-emotion
  cover up postulates, 242
  definition, 306
    and description, 53
  discharging at people, 175
  facsimiles and, 38, 60
    glue in, 175
  handling of, 187
  inner cycle in a lifetime and, 25
  mass emotion, 175
  subject of, 147
  thought, effort and, 176
  transferred by anger, fear,
    argument, sympathy, 192

two goals, 176
use of disk, 97
without time, 188
emotional curve
  definition, 198
  of sympathy, 214
  running, 198, 203
emotional cycle, 25
emotional system, 45
Emotion Processing, 59
endocrine ills, 81
endowment, 171, 269, 285
  self-determinism and, 279
enduring, 220
enforced, demanded ARC, 80
engineer, 15
engram
  area of plus or minus
    randomity, 280
  counter-effort and, 281
  theta facsimile, 281
  see also **painful incident**
enslavement
  attempts arising primarily from
    fear, 10
enthusiasm, 20
environment
  cause and effect, 61
  conquest of, 9
  control of, 17
  definition, 304
  Man adapts it to him, 9
  preclear and, 61
  valid therapy, 110
epistemology, 261
Eugene Field poem, 212
euphoria, 165
evaluation, 190
  Hubbard Chart of Human
    Evaluation, 66
  law to you, 241
  of data, 112, 242, 263
evolution, 17
exhilaration, 20, 165
experience, 36
  bright mind versus, 98
  value of, 98
extroverted, 173
eye trouble, 60

F

facsimile, 35–39, 310
  ability to handle, 37
  containing a record of
    everything, 60
  counter-efforts and, 188
  definition, 35, 36, 37, 302
  description, 60
  emotional condition, 38
  evaluate experience, 39
  example, 36
  getting rid of, 177
  good memory, 36
  illness, 60
  plus the Prime Thought, to
    be, 46
  process, 178
  recordings of effort, 148
  re-experience, 149
  regaining, 36
  thoughts, 46
  three-dimensional, 37
  time and, 46
  when recording began, 38
failure, 25
  apology for, 39
  counter-emotion and, 179
  dynamics and, 29, 138
  "explanation" of, 208
  help and, 137, 138
  minor reminding of major, 172
  sympathy and, 207
  worry about the past, 119
faith, 226
fatness, 307
fault, 112
fear, 10, 20, 149, 176, 192, 226
  ARC at 1.0, 79
  dynamics and, 80
  of the unknown, 111
  signal to withdraw, 53
Field, Eugene, 212
Fifteen
  definition, 299
Fifteenth Act, 257
Fifth Act, 129–143
Fifth Dynamic, 27
First Act, 71–73

First Dynamic, 27
flatten, 151
food
  cause and effect, 233
force
  definition, 272
forgetter, 111
  alcohol, 111
Foundation, 189
**Foundation Auditor's
  School**, 149
Fourteenth Act, 251–253
Fourth Act, 109–125
Fourth Dynamic, 27
Freud, 130, 131, 132, 133, 189
  sex, 233
front end of incident, 203
full responsibility, 20
future, 224

G

genetic
  definition, 309
genetic blueprint, 38, 188
  definition, 134
"genetic" boss, 163
genetic control center, 300
Genghis Khan, 28
getting
  having versus, 98
**giant tied down with cotton
  lint**, 105
Gibbon, 119
Glandular Switchboard, 44
glandular system
  function, 45
  translation medium for
    thought, 45
goal, 119
  dead men's goals, 123
  effort and, 147
  failure, 119
  individual and, 28
  life and, 25
  Man and, 16, 25, 29
  of processing, 59–60
  rehabilitate, 2
goal continuation, 191

governmental system, 163
gradient scales, 263
    causes and effects, 232
    description, 19
grief, 20, 38, 149, 174–177, 227, 306
    be quiet and initiate nothing, 53
    description, 149
grief charge, 177, 191, 214
group
    Third Dynamic, 27
growth, 25, 134
"guilt complex," 215

H

habits, 46, 222
Halley, 131
hallucination, 37, 194
    definition, 77
    ignoring, 191
Handbook for Preclears
    to whom it is addressed, 2
    use of, 1–3, 65
happiness, 291, 306
    consists in, 295
    definition, 119
    emotional cycle and, 25
happy man
    what is a, 15
having
    getting versus, 98
headaches, 307
health
    perfect, 20
heart, very weak, 180
heavy facsimile
    definition, 303
    see also **engram**
help
    crippled or lame to "help" another, 136
    illness and, 135
    psychotic and, 191
    tried to and failed, 137, 138
herd instinct, 175
herd reaction, 54
hiding things, 219

high-toned individuals, 82
Hiroshima, 131
Hitler, 28
homosexuality, 234
hopelessness, 224
Hubbard Chart of Human Evaluation, 66
human
    anything wrong with you and effort to be, 105
hypnotism, 282

I

"I", 43–45, 47
    I Am, I Am Not, 19
    I Know, I Know Not, 19
id, 130
ideal state, 15–21
    control of oneself and environment, 21
    fully self-determined emotion, 55
illness, 136
    agreement on emotion, 176
    facsimiles and, 37, 60
    self-determinism, 208
    sick man's environment, 17
    to "help" another, 135
illusion, 39
imaginary incident, 39
imagination, 37
    child and, 135
immortality, 135
incident
    front end of, 203
    imaginary versus actual, 39
individual
    collection of "memories," 188
    goal of, 28
    high-toned, 82
individuality, 225
    facsimiles, 188
individuation, 274
infinity, 27
    zero and, 132
infinity-valued logic, 263
influence
    firmest upon you, 96

inhibited ARC, 80, 81
inner cycle in a lifetime, 25
insane, 17
    cannot reason or control
        himself, 189
intelligence, 282
interpersonal relations, 54
**introduction of an
   arbitrary**, 264
in valence, 159
invalidation, 290

J

jellyfish, 33
Jung, 130

K

keeping things, 220
knowing, 222
knowledge, 79
    definition, 262
    evolution of, 187

L

lambda, 268, 269, 270, 272, 274
    definition, 270
    living organism, 268
    ultimate goal of, 272
language
    definition, 281
leadership, 47, 54
learning, 288
left-hander, 163
"libido" theories, 15
life, 18, 34, 46
    cause, 34
    dynamics and, 26
    goal of, 25, 267
    inner cycle in a lifetime, 25
    is a static, 34
    science of, 34
    three interdependent
        characteristics, 77
life continuation, 123
    valences and, 165
life continuum, 234

life forms
    Fifth Dynamic, 27
life realization, 123
Life source
    Seventh Dynamic, 27
Life static, 46, 77, 134, 267, 270,
   275
    physical universe and, 267
    symbol for, 268
    thought, soul, 134
Little Orphan Annie, 212
liver difficulties, 60
locks, 172-174, 282
Lock Scanning
    counter-emotion, 178
    definition, 172, 307
    "hang up," 174
    practice exercises, 180
    running of, 171, 172, 173-175
    speed of, 174
logic, 16, 79
Logics, The, 261-266
    definition, 261
losing things, 220
loss, 284
love, 80
low-toned people, 82

M

"magic drugs," 130
magic healing crystals, 15
Man, 33
    change, 9
    crippled or lame to "help"
        another, 136
    environment and, 9, 17
    goals of, 15, 16, 25-29
    materialistic, 34
    pack hunter, 47
    second goal, 17
    state of, 7-10
Mankind
    Fourth Dynamic, 27
mass emotion, 175
mass hysteria, 54, 175
masturbation, 235
materialistic man, 34
mathematics, 132, 265

maximum scanning, 174
maybe, 19, 112
measles, 157
medicine, 266
memory
definition, 36
description, 60
facsimile, 36
good, 36
very weak heart and, 180
MEST
definition, 17, 310
Sixth Dynamic, 27
symbol for the physical
universe, 268
MEST body, 134
see also **body**
migraine headaches, 60, 135,
307
mimicry, 189
mind, 33–39, 265, 284
basic purpose, 112
complex combinations of
facsimiles, 39
definition, 48, 271
description, 33, 48
estimation of effort
and, 147-148, 271
Man's best weapon, 7
not a brain, 35
purpose, 274
rationality of, 291
rehabilitation of, 16
solution of the operation and
difficulties of, 187
theta command post, 271
unconscious, 241
minus randomity, 278, 279,
288, 289
mis-emotion, 149, 175-192
person blurs out, 194
valences and, 165
mollusk, 33
monocell, 33, 39, 47
motion, 188, 267-272, 284, 289
definition, 188, 272

emotion monitoring, 53
establishment of
optimum, 270
static and, 34
motor controls, 282, 288
motor switchboard, 44
definition, 45
moving things, 221
myopia, 307

N

necessity level, 111
nerve channels, 44
nervous system, 35
neurosis, 2
neurotic, 17, 111
definition, 291
present time
attention to
immediate, 111
computation only of, 291
neurotic band
Tone Scale, 26
newspapers
tone range, 110
Newton, 131
New Year's resolutions, 242
Ninth Act, 187-199
no responsibility, 20
normal, 109
not-beingness, 19, 111
apathy and, 111
"nothing"
thought and, 45
not knowing, 222
not to be, 134, 222
nuclear physics, 131, 132

O

obedience
apathy and, 110
obsessions, 60
occluded, 193
childhood, 165
exercise to restore recall, 195
how people get, 195
perceptions, 286
old ideas, 18

optimum motion
  establishment of, 270
optimum randomity, 278, 279
optimum solution, 28
organism, 47, 269-273
  common denominator of, 272
  cycle of, 275
  history, 33
  motivated by, 35
  worth of, 295
out of valence, 159, 203
owning things, 221

P

pack hunter, 47
pain, 39, 302
  can't get rid of, 178
  chronic, 179, 193
  counter-effort and, 291
  definition, 291, 293
  loss and, 284
  randomity, 293
  turned on, 194
painful incident, 179
  description, 172
  see also **engram**
past, 223
past postulates
  definition, 301
penicillin, 130
perceptics, 37
perception, 285
  definition, 148, 285, 311
persistence
  definition, 270
personal identity, 134
phi, 268
photon, 34
physical ailments, 129
physical function, 129
physical universe, 34, 267
  higher and stronger control of
    the, 17
  Sixth Dynamic, 27
  symbol, 268
pleasure
  definition, 273

plus randomity, 278, 279, 288,
  289
poliomyelitis, 307
  aftereffects, 60
  case history, 208
politics, 266
postulate
  abstract, 264
  definition, 174, 241, 301
  past, definition, 301
  two parts to every, 242
  workability of, 265
preclear
  definition, 299
  environment and, 61
  goal of processing, 60
prediction, 265
  Tone Scale and, 54
prefrontal lobotomies, 15, 137
present time, 224
  assessment, 96
  Come up to present time, 119
  environment, 91
  psychotic and, 190
Prime Thought, 46
problem, 112, 274
  do not solve for two
    reasons, 112
  optimum solution, 28
  resolved by, 264
processing, 38, 59-61, 65
  at specific times, 159
  Cause and Effect
    Processing, 235
  Effort Processing, 2, 38, 148
  goal, 59, 60
  if strenuous, 129
  self-processing, 1
  Validation MEST
    Processing, 129
  valid therapy, 110
Processing Section, 65
professional auditor, 66
promiscuity, 234
propitiation, 80
protoplasm, 34
pseudo-centers
  definition, 165
psychiatry, 137

psychosis, 2
psychosomatic (illness), 29, 39,
  232
    bid for sympathy, 208
    counter-effort, 148
    definition, 307
    description, 38
    "explanation" of failure, 208
    service facsimile and, 153
    Tone Scale and, 60
psychotherapy, 2
psychotic, 189, 190, 191
    computation only of past
      situations, 291
    definition, 291, 304
    steps to handle, 189
    Tone Scale and, 26

Q
quick study, 98

R
randomity, 277–282, 292–295
    cycle of, 277
    definition, 277, 278
    degree of, 278
    minus, optimum and plus, 278
    misalignment, 277
    plus or minus, 288, 289
reaction time, 2
reader
    old ideas, 18
reality, 77–79
    definition, 283
    description, 77
realization, 123
reason, 26
    basic purpose of, 270
recall
    control of facsimile, 189
    definition, 285
    exercise to restore, 195
    process of regaining
      perceptions, 285
    something real, 190

recordings, 46
    awareness level versus
      non-awareness level, 306
    facsimiles and, 148
recovery
    definition, 306
    level of, 150
re-experience, 149, 151
re-feeling, 150
regret, 95, 99, 231
rehabilitation
    ability to handle facsimiles, 37,
      59
    Freud and, 131
    of a human mind, 16
    of body, 131
    of centers, 164, 165, 253
    of goals, 2
    of homosexual, 234
    of thought, 193
release
    definition, 309
    service facsimile, 159
remembering, 36
    see also **recall**
Repetitive Straightwire
    definition, 307
research
    short history, 131–133
responsibility, 231
    full, 20
restimulation, 282
    definition, 286
results
    predictable, 132
return circuit, 45
review, 257
right, 223
right-hander, 163
rightness
    definition, 271
Rome, 8

S
Saint Paul, 8
sanity
    computation of futures, 291

consists of, 279
definition, 291
handling facsimiles, 192
science, 265
ability, 187
of Life, 34
Science of Survival, 54
Scientology, 132
Second Act, 77-87
secondary (engram), 149, 151
definition, 149
running of, 149, 150
examples of, 151
Second Dynamic, 27, 232
cause and effect, 29
secrets, 99
security, 105
self
First Dynamic, 27
Self Analysis
Validation MEST
Processing, 129
self-auditing, 159
self-confidence, 10
definition, 241
security and, 105
self-determined action, 208
self-determined emotion, 55
self-determinism, 91, 208, 279, 283
components of, 284
consists of, 283
dynamics, 48, 61
human mind, 48
native, 48
optimum randomity, 279
restimulation and, 286
self-evaluation chart, 66
selfishness, 136
self-processing, 1
sensory channels, 46
sentence
longest in English, 99
serene, 20
seriously, taking things, 220
service facsimile, 203
auditor tool to locate, 199
definition, 208
and description, 153, 308

Effort Processing and, 179
everybody having one or
more, 153
run by auditor, 2
running out, 203
service facsimile chain
definition, 308
servomechanism, 266
Seventh Act, 163-167
Seventh Dynamic, 27
sex, 235
effect, 232, 233
Second Dynamic, 27
Shakespeare, 19
shame, 226, 307
shock
assists and, 305
electric, 137
facsimile and, 38
psychotics and, 189
shift of control centers
and, 166
sick, *see* **illness**
simplicity, 187
sinusitis, 60, 307
Sixth Act, 147-159
grief charge and, 214
Sixth Dynamic, 27
skin malformations, 307
slave philosophy, 10
sloth, 33
smoking, to stop, 47
sociology, 266
solution
optimum, 28
somatic, 178
source of Life, 267
southpaw, 163
species, the, 10
Spencer, 98
Standard Procedure, 180
starting things, 221
state of being, 15-21
state of not-beingness
apathy and, 111
static, 45, 132, 134, 270, 277, 310
anatomy of, 77
Life and, 34, 267

memory, 302
motion and, 34
state, 272
theta, 310
true static, 34, 132, 302
static of Life, 34
ARC, 77
"stimulus-response
mechanism," 46
stop things, trying to, 221
Straightwire
definition, 300
Repetitive, definition, 307
sub-centers, 166
sub-control center, 163, 300
take over, 164
Success, 25
succumb, 16
low-toned people, 82
suicide, 99
super-center, 166
Supreme Being, 27
surgery, 129
survival, 266, 289
accomplish action, 119
behavior, 295
conquering physical universe
and, 25
control of physical universe
and, 17
cycle of, 25
eight dynamics, 28
future and, 291
goal of Man and, 16
life, teamwork and, 26
lowest level, 19
switchboard system, 35
sympathy, 152, 153, 192,
207–208, 214
life continuum and, 234
mechanism of, 54
non-survival value of, 207
offended before, 214
social aberration, 82
story characters and, 212
sympathy facsimiles, 208

T

tactile, 234
most direct
communication, 189
talking, 219
tarsus, 33
Ten
definition, 311
tendonitis, 307
Tenth Act, 203
therapies
three valid, 110
theta, 268, 271
brings order, 268
component parts of, 283
definition, 310
theta facsimile, 276, 280, 281,
286
Third Act, 91–105
Third Dynamic, 27
Thirteenth Act, 231–247
Thompson, Commander, 131
thought, 188, 284
accomplished by, 271
cause, 46
concerned with motion, 270
definition, description, 45,
276, 306
emotional impulse and, 53
emotion, effort and, 176
facsimiles and Prime
Thought, 46
filed by concept of when they
happened, 188
image of motion and, 34
impulses, 44
timeless, 188
Thought, Emotion and
Effort, 176
running out service facsimile
and, 203
three levels of operation, 188
Thought Processing, 59
thought "recordings," 46
three valid therapies, 110

time, 111, 188, 223
    facsimiles filed by, 46
    motion and, 188
    single arbitrary, 277
time tab, 188
time track
    picture of, 172
Tiny Tim, 212
Tone Scale
    ARC and, 79
        triangle of, 78
    chart, 78
    descriptive data, 19
    dynamics and, 28
    effect and, 232
    high on, 81
    levels which have not been
        attained, 60
    prediction, 54
    psychotic, neurotic and, 26
    pull everyone else to that
        level, 82
    raising individual on, 59
    reaching toward a lower
        level, 81
toothache, 307
true static, 34, 132, 302
Trust–Distrust, 20
truth, 225, 263
Twelfth Act, 219-227

U

ulcers, 60
unconscious mind, 241
unconsciousness, 285
    boil-off and, 173
    definition, 280

understanding, 79
unit facsimile
    description, 36

V

valence, 165, 285
    definition, 287
    in valence, 159
    out of valence, 159
        definition, 203
**Validation MEST
  Processing**, 129
vectors, 278, 289
verbal scanning, 174
virus, 273, 275
visio
    definition, 97
Voltaire, 98

W

war, 133, 163
well man
    what is a, 15
whole track, 193
whooping cough, 157
**"win friends and influence
  people" (light books)**, 176
World War II, 133
writers, 110
wrong(ness), 223
    definition, 271

Z

zero and infinity, 132